Teilhard de Chardin
The Divine Milieu

Explained

A Spirituality for the 21st Century

LOUIS M. SAVARY

PAULIST PRESS
New York • Mahwah, NJ

Unless otherwise noted, the scripture quotations contained herein are from the New Revised Standard Version Edition © 1989 amd 1993, by the Division of Christian Education of the National Council of Churches of Christ in the United States of America. Used by permission. All rights reserved.

Acknowledgment is gratefully given for permission to quote from *The Divine Milieu* by Pierre Teilhard de Chardin. Copyright © 1957 by Editions du Seuil, Paris. English translation copyright © 1960 by Wm. Collins Sons & Co., London, and Harper & Row, Publishers, Inc., New York. Renewed © 1988 by Harper & Row Publishers, Inc. Reprinted by permission of HarperCollins Publishers.

Cover design by Joy Taylor
Book design by ediType

Library of Congress Cataloging-in-Publication Data

Savary, Louis M.
Teilhard de Chardin – the divine milieu explained : a spirituality for the 21st century / Louis M. Savary.
p. cm.
Includes bibliographical references and index.
ISBN-13: 978-0-8091-4484-6 (alk. paper)
1. Teilhard de Chardin, Pierre. Milieu divin. 2. Christianity – Philosophy. I. Title.
BR100.S295 2007
233 – dc22

2007028632

Published by Paulist Press
997 Macarthur Boulevard
Mahwah, New Jersey 07430

www.paulistpress.com

Printed and bound in the
United States of America

Contents

PART TWO
THE DIVINIZATION OF OUR PASSIVITIES

CONCLUSION TO PARTS ONE AND TWO
SOME GENERAL REMARKS ON CHRISTIAN ASCETICISM

Author's Foreword

A few days ago, some friends of mine visiting Florida took a guided tour through the stunning Salvador Dalí Museum in St. Petersburg. They knew that Dalí was a great and powerful painter, utterly contemporary and revolutionary, different from anyone else, yet clearly an integral part of a great art tradition. My friends had, of course, seen many Dalí paintings before this, but they had never before been coached on how to look at his paintings by a knowledgeable docent.

As the museum's trained guide led them around the gallery and pointed out the meaning of the various symbols, shapes, colors, and juxtapositions of the various images in each Dalí work, my friends made comments like, "I never realized..." or "I never noticed that..." or "I never made that connection with..." or "Why, of course..." or "How appropriate..." or "It makes so much sense now..." and so on. It had made all the difference, they later told me, having someone guide them into Dalí's world. "We got ten times more out of the visit than we would have if we had just walked around the museum by ourselves."

I am hoping that with a little guidance from these pages, you will be able to make comments about Teilhard's radically powerful spirituality similar to those my friends made when they were guided through the Dalí Museum.

At about the same time as Salvador Dalí was becoming well known as a Surrealist painter in Europe during the 1920s, a young Jesuit priest-scientist, Pierre Teilhard de Chardin, in quasi-exile from Europe, was working in China as a geologist and paleontologist. In his spare time, he began putting together his ideas about a spirituality that would bring together all the discoveries being made in science and integrate them with what he knew about God, especially what God was trying to accomplish in the world. He called his manuscript *The Divine Milieu.*

The Divine Milieu is a revolutionary book of Christian spirituality. So revolutionary, in fact, that his religious superiors refused to let him have it published. Though Teilhard, as everyone called him, finished writing it around 1929, it was never brought to light until after his death — it was published in French in 1957 and in English trans- lation in 1960. Even today, half a century later, few understand it and many are suspicious of it, because it appears to fly in the face of traditional Christian piety. But, while it is still utterly contempo- rary and revolutionary — different from any other spiritual book you ever read — it is Christian in its roots and to its core. It is joyful, hopeful, and full of enthusiasm, as any Christian spirituality should be. It expresses a love for nature, a delight in scientific discoveries, a rejoicing in human progress, and an underlying almost childlike trust in a benevolent universe evolving in the unconditional love of a benevolent and all-forgiving God. In fact, this book offers to us perhaps the only integrative spirituality that can truly satisfy our twenty-first-century experience.

Just as the docent at the Dalí Museum explained and interpreted the artist's paintings to my friends as they encountered each one while walking through the gallery rooms, I am hoping to take you in a similar way through the paragraphs and sections of *The Divine Milieu,* following exactly its original outline and structure, and helping to reveal some of the riches hidden there. After almost every section, I suggest a simple spiritual reflection that should help personalize and concretize the ideas and insights Teilhard has presented.

Almost four hundred years before Teilhard wrote *The Divine Milieu,* St. Ignatius Loyola, the founder of the Jesuit order, the Society of Jesus, designed a powerfully transformative system of spiritual practices called the Spiritual Exercises. Ever since then, people seeking spiritual growth have been, as the Jesuits say, "making the Exercises." Everyone agrees it can be a life-changing event.

If you were to "make" the Exercises, your culminating experience would be the "Contemplation for Attaining the Love of God" (*Contemplatio ad Amorem*). In this almost mystical exercise, Ignatius hopes you will be graced with the "eyes to see" that it is *within* God, whose name is Love, that we live and move and have our existence. Living in God is like living in the air we breathe. God is the atmosphere, the environment, the divine milieu in which we spend our lives.

The Spiritual Exercises were a transforming experience for Teilhard, too. His purpose in writing *The Divine Milieu* was to share with us how he, as a Jesuit and as a dedicated scientist, learned to use the new eyes that Ignatius gave him in order to see spiritual reality today — in the world contemporary men and women live in, thoroughly informed and transformed by science and technology.

A Transformed World

As the Franciscan Richard Rohr has observed, during the past one hundred years our human race has undergone many radical paradigm shifts in our understanding of ourselves and the world we live in, paradigm shifts demanded by medicine, astronomy, paleontology, anthropology, economics, psychology, and other fields of science. These shifts require much more than people no longer picturing the world as flat or seeing the earth as the center of creation, though many people today still hold these beliefs or act as if they were true, just as almost everyone did in Jesus' time — and in St. Ignatius's time.

First of all, we need to recognize and acknowledge that most of our traditional spiritualities are based on this image of a flat earth, the center of God's creation, covered by a dome-shaped sky, above which is heaven, where God lives.

In contrast, here are some of the facts we have learned about ourselves and our world during the past century and the paradigm shifts of thought they have demanded:

- We now know that our earth didn't begin to be formed until our created, ever-expanding universe was already at least ten billion years old.

- We also learned that our home planet is about four billion years old.

- We also learned that human life appeared only in the last few moments, as it were, of our planet's four billion years.

- We also learned that new stars are being born daily — some say every few minutes — throughout the universe, which means that God's creative word has never stopped calling new things into being that were never in existence before.

- We also learned that humans — with their complex brains capable of language, abstract thought, art, music, literature, mathematics, technology, etc. — are probably evolutionary developments from simian ancestry.

- We also learned, genetically, that a very high percentage of the human genome is shared by all mammals and some of the reptiles. The chimpanzee's genome, for example, is estimated to be 99 percent identical to that of humans. The Neanderthal's genome is estimated to be 99.96 percent identical.

- We also learned that the "atom," which we had believed was the absolutely smallest part of creation, could be broken down into smaller parts, and that these smaller parts could be even further and further broken down into ever-smaller parts.

- We eventually discovered that there was something like a universe of subatomic particles in every living cell — of every living thing.

- We discovered that a human body is made up of some 70 billion cells, and that each cell contains millions of these subatomic particles.

- We also learned that each of us produces a completely new body — not a single cell of the previous body remains — after five years, every five years.

- We learned that every human life is totally connected to the life of all the rest of the planet, that a human being can remain alive only if its life is shared, moment by moment, not only with all other humans, but also with the plants, trees, animals, rivers, and lakes, and with the atmosphere.

- We also learned, in fact, that our planet is really one great big interdependent organism.

Teilhard was a part of some of these scientific discoveries, but not all of them. He realized that humans would continue, as we have done, to make more and more discoveries like these about our world. And these discoveries I mentioned don't even include those that have been made, and are being made daily, in the fields of physics, chemistry, psychology, anthropology, neurobiology, genetics, and brain research, to name just a few.

Teilhard realized we needed a radically new kind of spirituality — an understanding of God and creation and our part in it — that could welcome and easily integrate all these important scientific facts of our existence into itself.

Most contemporary spiritualities, following tradition, usually put these scientific facts aside, assuming they have little to do with our spiritual lives. But in fact they permeate our very existence. They are part of the way we think today. We cannot put them aside. And Teilhard doesn't, because, for him, everything we learn about creation is something we are learning about the Body of Christ — the Christ that lives today, the Christ who is as big as the cosmos.

The Cosmic Christ

In the Spiritual Exercises, St. Ignatius taught Teilhard how to dig deeply into the mind and heart of Jesus of Nazareth and how to be transformed by his suffering, death, and resurrection. In the sixteenth century, when Ignatius lived, he knew few of the many scientific facts that are simply part of our daily assumptions about reality. For him, the earth was the center of God's creation, and God lived up in the sky. And his traditional spirituality reflects those beliefs.

In *The Divine Milieu*, Teilhard the scientist takes us many centuries further in the life of Christ. He invites us to learn to see, as he does, not only the Christ of two thousand years ago, but also the magnificent Being that the Risen Christ with his Total Body has developed into during two millennia. He also invites us to glimpse into Christ's future, to identify the goal toward which that Total Body of Christ has been constantly evolving.

For Teilhard, Christ today is not just Jesus of Nazareth risen from the dead, but rather a huge, continually evolving Being as big as the universe. In this colossal, almost unimaginable Being each of us lives and develops in consciousness, like living cells in a huge organism. At various times, theologians have described this great Being as the Total Christ, the Cosmic Christ, the Whole Christ, the Universal Christ, or the Mystical Body of Christ.

With the help of all the human sciences as well as the scriptures, Teilhard shows how we — the cells and members of the Body of Christ — can participate in and nurture the life of the Total Christ. He also shows, thanks to the continuing discoveries of science, how we can begin to glimpse where that great Being is headed and how we can help promote its fulfillment.

Teilhard's spirituality explains the many ways we can help accomplish the Total Christ's divine destiny. It is Christ's divine task as well as ours to turn this fragmented world, through love of it in all of its visible and invisible dimensions, into one immense shining Being, the Body of Christ, glowing with divine energy. Christ the Lord, the head of this Body, has promised to be with us and guide us, from start to finish. He said, "And remember, I am with you always, to the end of the age" (Matt. 28:20).

At present, many of the cells of this Christ Body are unaware of their divine calling, unaware of how special they are in the eyes of God, and unconscious of the fact that they are already living their lives as part of this Cosmic Body. For Teilhard, this Cosmic Body is meant to become fully conscious of itself in every cell of its being in such a way that every cell is also conscious of the whole Body's magnificent destiny. When this Christ Body realizes itself as the divine reality it has always been meant to be, that moment will be what Teilhard calls the Omega Point (see Rev. 1:8).

It sounds like very heady stuff. That's because it is.

Making Difficult Reading Clear and Practical

When I think of people reading Teilhard de Chardin's *Divine Milieu* for the first time, I am reminded of the story about Philip, a deacon in the early Christian community, that Luke tells in the Acts of the Apostles. It seems there was a wealthy and powerful foreigner, a court official of the Ethiopian queen, who had come to Jerusalem on a spiritual pilgrimage. While there, he purchased or was given a copy of the book of Isaiah the prophet. On his way home in his carriage, departing the Holy City, he opened the scroll and began reading the prophecies of Isaiah, but could not make any sense of them.

At that same moment Philip happened to be nearby, saw the foreigner looking puzzled at the scroll, and, inspired by the Holy Spirit, asked the man, "Do you understand what you are reading?"

He replied, "How can I, unless someone guides me?" (Acts 8: 30–31).

The Ethiopian then invited Philip to get into his carriage and sit beside him. The traveler then read aloud a sentence of Isaiah's prophecy that he couldn't comprehend and asked Philip what the prophet was trying to say. Philip began to explain the passage and how it all tied together with the good news of Jesus of Nazareth. With this help, the foreigner came to appreciate the greater message. He even wished to become a member of the Christian community.

When encountering people reading Teilhard's prophetic *Divine Milieu*, I have often felt like Philip. When I ask them if they understand what they are reading, they often reply to me in similar words. "How can I, unless someone guides me?"

Many people desiring to delve into the thought of Teilhard have told me that they are unable to understand his writings. They may begin reading one of his books, such as *The Divine Milieu,* with great interest and enthusiasm, only to be overwhelmed, bogged down, and discouraged within a few pages.

I have always felt attuned to Teilhard's mind. So at the urging of friends eager to explore — and even practice — Teilhard's spirituality, I have tried in these pages to simplify without distorting *The Divine Milieu* for the Teilhardian beginner and to turn it into a spirituality that any person can actually practice.

For Jesus, it was not enough for his audiences simply to listen to his wonderful ideas about God. People needed to live them out. After hearing Jesus' ideas, they needed to do something that turned these ideas into daily behavior. Once, when Jesus was told that members of his family were outside and wanted to see him, he replied, "My mother and my brothers are those who hear the word of God and do it" (Luke 8:21). In other words, *they put it into practice.* Jesus made practicing his ideas easy because in his sermons he told stories and gave many examples of how to do it. Teilhard, however, seldom gave examples of how to practice his spirituality.

People who feel an affinity with Teilhard's thought don't want to stop at hearing about his revolutionary ideas. They want to know how to live them out. However, few writers have actually tried to translate his ideas into spiritual practices. In Teilhardian studies up till now, except perhaps for the ecological applications of Teilhard's ideas initiated by Rev. Thomas Berry, the missing link has been how to turn Teilhard's spirituality into everyday action.

Teilhard offers an optimistic and future-focused spirituality that, when translated into daily attitudes and behavior, shows you how to live consciously and constantly in the divine atmosphere that he calls the divine milieu. He teaches you, first, how to see with new eyes not only the visible dimensions of God's love, which anyone can see, but the *invisible* dimensions as well; then, second, to see not only what is present but also *what is to come* (see Eph. 1:15–23). In Teilhard's language, he says you will learn to love the "within" of things as well as their "not-yet." In other words, Teilhard will guide you, first, to see "within," that is, to see how each little thing in the world "is charged with the grandeur of God," and, second, to realize that the most exciting thing about the Body of Christ is its "not-yet," that is, its future, what is yet to be revealed.

What is paradoxical about Teilhard's approach and turns traditional Christian spirituality topsy-turvy is that he believes that the best way to open your new eyes to this divine milieu is to put all your effort and strength into loving and serving *this evolving world*. In fact, if you were to ask Teilhard what is the first principle of his spirituality, he would probably give the startling response, "To love the *world* with all your mind, heart, soul, and strength."

Traditionally, spiritual writers saw a conflict between loving and serving God and loving and serving the world. We were told to love God and hate the world. So was Teilhard. But when he looked at this conflict more deeply, he began to realize there only appeared to be a conflict. Rather, the two apparently contrary loves were more like two sides of the *same* love. He experienced an integration of the two loves — of God and the world — in his own heart. Teilhard loved God passionately, but he also loved creation passionately and found no contradiction between these two passionate loves. In *The Divine Milieu*, he invites you to explore the same process he went through, and he gives you the reasons for doing so. He invites you to love the world totally, with your heart and soul and mind and strength, because it is a world that God has created and loved so much that he sent his only-begotten Son to it to transform it (see John 3:16). Most people who quote that scripture passage emphasize the last half of the sentence. Teilhard wants to emphasize also the first half: "God *so* loved the world...." The Greek word for world is *cosmos*, which means all of creation, the whole universe.

If God loved *so much* what he created, this cosmic reality, how can we do anything else but *love* it — if only because God loves it. God apparently loves creation as much as he loves his divine Son.

For Teilhard, we are to love our world *that* much — as much as God the Creator loves it. Teilhard invites us to continue to do all we can to make our world a better place, because every atom and molecule of it, even in its currently still-fragmented state, is saturated with God's divine Spirit at every level, longing for its fulfillment (see Rom. 8:20–23).

In *The Divine Milieu*, Teilhard shows how you can spend your life living consciously, prophetically, and with passionate enthusiasm both as a citizen of the universe and as a citizen of the Kingdom of God. He says you can do this by integrating everything you do or endure in the all-encompassing and ever-evolving Total Christ (see Eph. 4:15–16).

Although Teilhard described *The Divine Milieu* to a friend as a book of "simple piety," and perhaps for him it was just that, it is nevertheless quite radical. Certainly the conservative and cautious Roman Catholic Church censors of his day, if they understood his book at all, found it unacceptable, not to say heretical.

Some people, even today, insist that Teilhard's teachings are unacceptable. But in his spirituality, he merely recaptures for people today what the church has always taught and what St. Ignatius taught him: learning how to see God's benevolent imprint and loving presence everywhere, in all that is visible and invisible, in all that is present as well as all that is to come, and to cooperate with all our ingenuity and creativity with what God is trying to accomplish in creation.

I am reminded of a story told about Mother Therese Couderc, founder of the Sisters of the Cenacle. As an older woman, she had been praying one day, and as she gazed around her room she saw, stamped on everything she looked at, the word *Bonté*, a French word that can mean "blessing" or "gift" or "grace." She had never noticed it before, she explained, but there it was. Wherever she looked — on her priedieu, on her nightstand, on her bed — she found *Bonté* stamped there. When she walked out into the garden, she saw the same *Bonté* label on each tree, each flower, and even on the pebbles of the path. Just as today's clothing manufacturers proudly sew their labels on every product they make, so God was proudly putting his special mark on every created thing, so that Mother Couderc could see it and would be reassured of Christ's loving presence everywhere in her life.

During the past few years, we have been witnessing a highly charged debate about creation between those who believe our world is a product of evolution and those who believe it is a product of intelligent design. If Teilhard were still alive today, he would tell us that our world is not a product of either one or the other, but of both. He would say we are products of *designed evolution*, and the One who created our evolving cosmos and set it in motion is not merely an Intelligent Designer but also an Unconditional Lover.

The Divine Milieu is, at its core, an evolving love story told by a recipient of that love. Teilhard's spirituality teaches us how to recognize this loving divine design in evolution and to nurture it.

Since this is my first attempt at developing an integrative Teilhardian spirituality, I welcome any questions, suggestions, corrections, improvements, and enrichments. I would also like to acknowledge the many who have encouraged me to write this book, especially those who read and edited my earliest drafts of the manuscript, my wife, Patricia Berne, as well as Peter Esseff, John Alvarez, and Florence Murphy. I thank all those who, for over thirty years, have attended my classes, workshops, and study groups on Teilhard's spirituality. I thank all the scholars I have personally known who have taught and written about Teilhard: Robert Johann, S.J., Joseph Grau, S.J., Robert Faricy, S.J., Christopher Mooney, S.J., Thomas King, S.J., James Salmon, S.J., and Sister Kathleen Duffy, S.S.J., among many others.

I am hoping that as you read these pages you will discover that in your spirituality you are already, at heart, a Teilhardian, even though you may not use that name to describe yourself. Two of the people who reviewed an early manuscript of this book said that after they finished reading it they realized exactly that. You can be a Teilhardian without reading his books. What I hope is that by reading this and Teilhard's writings, you will become a more focused and more conscious Teilhardian — loving the Unconditional Lover.

Please forgive me if you don't always get "pure Teilhard" in these pages, but since my mind and heart have been churning with his ideas for almost fifty years some of my thinking inevitably gets mixed in. You can offer your comments on my website: *www.teilhardforbeginners.com*.

I strongly encourage you to obtain your own copy of *The Divine Milieu*, so that you can follow along with my comments. My table of contents follows closely that of *The Divine Milieu*.

HarperCollins has published two editions of *The Divine Milieu* in English translation, a Harper Torchbook edition in 1960 and a Harper-Collins Perennial edition in 2001. In this work, I have indicated the corresponding pages of *The Divine Milieu* for the Torchbook edition. Also, references to Teilhard's *The Phenomenon of Man* are from the Harper Torchbook edition, 1959.

I have not bothered to present Teilhard's life story in these pages, since most editions of *The Divine Milieu* begin with an extensive biography of Teilhard written by his Jesuit friend Father Pierre Leroy (see Torchbook, 13–42 or Perennial, xiii–xlvii). Please read all about him there. Teilhard's story is always a good place to begin, and Leroy's biography needs no commentary. See also the excellent volume by Ursula King, *Spirit of Fire: The Life and Vision of Teilhard de Chardin* (Maryknoll, N.Y.: Orbis Books, 1996).

Louis M. Savary
Tampa, Florida

For more on Teilhard and his revolutionary spirituality see
www.teilhardforbeginners.com

Teilhard de Chardin
The Divine Milieu
Explained

Teilhard's Preface to
The Divine Milieu

Summary

In his preface, Teilhard wants to clarify that his book is primarily about his personal experience. What excites him is his belief that he has found a way to show how traditional Christian concepts — such as Incarnation, Passion, and Resurrection — can include all that is best in today's human aspirations and progress.

He wants *The Divine Milieu* to be read more as a book of personal reflections than as a theological treatise. That is why it will contain little development of doctrinal debates, moral concepts, or discussions of evil and sin. He will of course mention many of these issues in his reflections in later parts of the book. But here he wants to assure the reader that he is Christian to the core and that he believes divine grace permeates everyone and everything that exists in the universe.

◆ ◆ ◆

Teilhard's preface to *The Divine Milieu* is scarcely two pages long, yet it contains a number of points central to Teilhard's thought and spirituality that you will want to keep in mind. Here are five of them.

1. *Teilhard is writing his spirituality book primarily for Christians*, especially those who believe in the real presence of Christ in the Eucharist. After all, Teilhard is a Jesuit priest, which means he is a Roman Catholic and is committed to Christ and to being faithful to his church's doctrines and dogmas. So on every page of his text, keep in mind that this is his unspoken perspective and position. However, no matter what your religious preference may be, you will find great wisdom in

3

his ideas and insights. If they don't enrich your personal spirituality, they will at least challenge you to think about it in new ways. For Teilhard, even a little stretching of your mind and horizon would provide one more small step for our planet in its evolutionary growth.

Since the term "spirituality" is used many, many times throughout this book, it may be useful to present at the outset a general yet personalized definition of the term that everyone, even nonbelievers, could find acceptable.

A spirituality is a person's way of being, thinking, choosing, and acting in the world in light of that person's ultimate values.

Thus, spirituality is not merely a matter of holding beliefs or having ultimate values — everyone holds beliefs and values — but of living and acting in line with those values.

Those whose ultimate values include God, faith, and a religious denomination will naturally have a *religious-values-based* spirituality. Similarly, a person whose ultimate values focus on scientific research will have a *research-values-based* spirituality. Some religious people might consider this latter form a very worldly spirituality and would not even want to call it spirituality. Yet Teilhard understood this worldly spirituality very well, for like many of his fellow scientists he passionately loved the world and passionately loved exploring it to more fully understand it. In fact, Teilhard dedicates his book to those who love the world as passionately as God loved the world — which was very passionately!

Because he understood — and lived out — both his religious spirituality and his worldly spirituality, Teilhard wants to create a spirituality for people, like him, who love passionately both God *and* the world.

2. *Teilhard claims to be writing his book primarily for "wavering" Christians, whom today we might call seekers or searchers.* These waverers tend to find the currently available forms of traditional Christian spirituality less than satisfying or inspiring. They want more, each of them for perhaps different reasons. Some may tend to label the currently

available approaches to spiritual practice dry, boring, restrictive, out-of-date, too separated from the concerns of contemporary life. Others may feel that to be spiritual today they are forced to compartmentalize their lives into "sacred" and "secular."

However, these seekers are united in that they want to make a difference in their world and in their professional fields and are hoping their trust in God will help them find the way. Teilhard believes he has found a way that may satisfy them. That's why he is writing for them.

He also makes it clear that he is *not* writing for those who wish merely to live a quiet, unassuming life and not rock any boats or break out of any boxes. (I like to think, however, that someone of this sort who reads Teilhard with an open mind might find some enlightenment there.) Teilhard prefers to address the active seekers. For them, he hopes to show that religion, in the way he sees it, can excite them — the thinking, innovative, pioneering, creative seekers who enjoy being on the forefront of progress and development in all areas of human endeavor: science and the arts, law and medicine, education and politics, and all the rest. Nothing that is truly human is left outside Teilhard's spirituality.

Nor are any individuals, no matter how quiet and unassuming they may be, left outside the divine milieu. No matter what our faith or lack of it, we are all in this enterprise together because we are all interconnected with each other in countless ways. So although Teilhard feels his book is not for the quiet and unassuming folks, I beg to differ. I believe that anyone, no matter that person's religious depth or lack of it, can grasp the essential wisdom and magnificent vision of Teilhard and grow from it. I will try to make that "grasp" as easy as I can for you.

3. *These waverers or seekers are most likely people aware of the vast changes that have happened over the past century:* changes in technology, medicine, law, communication, theology, biblical scholarship, psychology, sociology, anthropology, physics, biology, etc. — changes in our understanding of ourselves and our world. And they want to keep pushing forward in their fields into new advances. *But their desire for*

earthly progress seems to conflict with the "Christian religious ideal" they have been taught in traditional spiritualities.

Since Teilhard first wrote his book — and certainly since his death in 1955 — tremendous strides have been made in understanding life on our planet, advances that he could never have imagined. Consider, for example, in *astronomy*, the Hubble telescope sending us stunning photos of parts of our own solar system as well as the expanding universe we never saw before, showing how immense creation really is; in *astrophysics*, the Big Bang theory and the discovery of dozens of sub-atomic elementary particles like quarks and muons; in *paleontology*, calculating the age of our four-billion-year-old planet and sketching an understanding of the formation of our seven Earth continents from many smaller pieces during the pre-Cambrian period; in *space travel*, an orbiting space station for conducting scientific experiments, a man on the moon, and the robotic exploration of the surface of Mars; in *physics*, the proliferation of nuclear — beyond atomic — energy, quantum mechanics, the search for a unified field theory; in *medicine*, strides in organ transplants, cosmetic surgery, cloning, wonder drugs, and brain surgery; in *biology*, exploration of the life of the cell, the discovery of scores of different enzymes and their functions, tracing evolutionary patterns; in *psychology*, a more fully developed grasp of mental illness, new awareness of the pervasiveness of traumatic experience, new understanding of human development, the exploration of human consciousness; in *anthropology*, discoveries of the commonalities in various cultures, the power of *mimesis* (learning by imitation) in the development of human desire, competition, resentment, and violence; in *neurology and genetics*, including the double helix structure of genes, breaking the genetic codes, mapping the genome, sonograms, MRI and fMRI imaging to watch the brain at work; in *communications*, personal computers, iPods, satellite radio and television, the Internet, global positioning systems, and those person-less telephone answering systems that we so often find frustrating; in *the economy*, the rise of multinational corporations, the global economy, the European Union;

in *manufacturing*, the shift to quality management and systems thinking; in *social justice*, the rise of women's rights, the racial equality movements; in *religion*, the penetration of the Eastern religions into the West, ecumenical and interfaith movements, popes who travel the world. These are some of the advances that Teilhard never lived to see, which we live with every day. Fortunately, his spirituality is open to them all.

All this new understanding is present in the minds of today's believers as they look to find a spirituality that can accept and integrate this spiraling increase in knowledge and technology. Do not all these discoveries and advancements have something to tell us about God and our relationship to God? Teilhard shouts a resounding "Yes." Is God utterly unconcerned about human development? Is human progress insignificant in terms of God's divine plan of salvation, as we Christians have been taught about the meaning of human life? Teilhard says, "No. Not at all."

Until now, most forms of spirituality proposed by traditional religions have simply bypassed or ignored these new scientific and technical complexities of life and new levels of human awareness. For them, spirituality remains an issue between the individual and God. For them, what's been happening on the earth and to the earth for the past few thousand years — and even during the fantastic evolution of the universe since the moment of the Big Bang — is of little concern. This life is short, they say, and the next life lasts forever, so why bother about the changes and vicissitudes of the world?

Most spiritual approaches, at least Christian ones, were formulated when the average lifespan of humans was about twenty-nine years. Today, our expected lifespan is three times longer, enough time to have two or even three careers. And some scientists are saying that a child born today is likely to live to celebrate a two-hundred-year birthday. What does that mean about the purpose of human life? What does that mean in our way of relating to God and to the earth?

For this reason, the basic spirituality question Teilhard poses to himself in his preface is even more pointed today: We each need to ask it of ourselves. *How can I live intellectually consistent and true to myself in both the church and the world? Is there a way to do it?* Teilhard says yes.

4. *These waverers and seekers that Teilhard is writing for have become even more confused because their human efforts and careers today call for their total commitment.* They wonder, if they commit themselves as deeply as they are expected to do to their human pursuits — as professionals in science, technology, research, scholarship, education, medicine, law, government, diplomacy, military, entertainment, sports, finance, industry, agriculture, art, politics, the media, and all the rest — how can they remain true to the gospel path? That path, as it has been presented until now, has taught them that the "things of this world" are only temporary and that the only real pursuit open to them as believers is to turn away from the world and put their focus wholly upon God. "Live not for this world, but for the next." They have been taught that it is impossible to live a life that is both sacred *and* secular. Already, says Teilhard, many of these seekers, committed to noble worldly pursuits, desire to serve both the City of God and the City of Man, but find what they have been taught by their religious teachers to be deeply internally conflicting.

5. Teilhard's point is that this emotionally confusing dichotomy — this fear that if you truly love your human work and enjoy the world, you will lose your place in the Kingdom of God — is unfounded.

Traditional spirituality, he says, has falsely forced us into an either/or choice. "It's either Christ or the world! Take your pick!"

Teilhard wants to show that a true Christian spirituality can be *both/and*. He says that you can love both Christ and the world with all your heart. There is no real confusion or contradiction. For Teilhard, Christ is not only "first" in heaven, but also the "first" within humanity.

A Few Important Observations

Before you begin to read Teilhard's preface, here are three things he wants you to be aware of:

First, Teilhard does not claim to be writing a comprehensive book on the spiritual life. He is not composing a treatise on ascetical theology. Nor is he telling you how to live your personal spiritual life. In these pages, he says, he is just describing what has happened to him; he is merely sharing some of his insights about *his* spiritual path. He calls *The Divine Milieu* an "essay on life or on inward vision." In other words, it's his essay on his inner life and his Christic vision.

However, the book you are holding in your hand is trying to do something more. I am attempting to glean from Teilhard's personal experience reported in his books *a consistent way of being a Christian today* that satisfies the intellect as well as the spirit. Teilhard is the first in our time to attempt such a synthesis for himself.

In this, he is like Ignatius Loyola, the synthesizer and revolutionary founder of the Jesuits, a religious society of which Teilhard was a member and remained so until his death. In the sixteenth century, St. Ignatius formulated his Spiritual Exercises for the seekers of his day, based on his own personal religious experience — with some additional input from others. Why can't we create something like the Exercises for the seekers of our own day basing it on Teilhard's experiences and writings? This is my first attempt at such a venture.

In the interest of continual improvement and developing a more complete Teilhardian spirituality, I bring ideas into these pages from many of Teilhard's other writings, since up to his death in 1955 he produced a quarter century more of speeches, essays, and books, all intended to develop and enrich his earlier insights into humanity's relationship to God.

Second, Teilhard says *The Divine Milieu* paints mostly a *psychological* picture of his spiritual life, not primarily a theological or religious one. So, he cautions readers, in the following chapters they will find only a passing discussion of many traditional religious topics that a comprehensive book on spirituality would contain. Thus, topics like sin, evil, grace, nature, prayer, and worship are not treated in any detail in *The Divine Milieu*.

In the book you are now reading, however, we can begin to summarize what Teilhard says about these topics, from his other writings as well as from *The Divine Milieu*, into the beginnings of a new integrated approach to the Christian life.

Third, in his preface's final paragraph, which reads like the thought-stream of a mystic, Teilhard is simply saying that, whether we know it or not, we live every moment immersed in a sea of divine grace and favor. His paragraph will make much more sense to you when you have absorbed more of Teilhard's thought.

I suggest you now enjoy reading Teilhard's preface in *The Divine Milieu*.

Teilhard's Introduction: "In Eo Vivimus"

Summary

Most people today are familiar with and fascinated by the continuing advances in science and technology. For example, science has made us aware that, despite our sense of being independent individuals walking on the earth's surface, we are all interconnected — not only with each other but also with the earth itself and everything on it and in it. Most traditional spiritualities seem to remain unaffected by this fact or the evolutionary march happening daily all around us.

Teilhard says we could build a new spirituality that finds God's imprint and spirit in everything happening today if only we had the ability to "see him" — to see Christ at the heart of the world and to see God's pervasive and perceptible presence all around us, as easily as we can sense the atmosphere we breathe.

In all our human experiences, what we do and what we undergo, God is waiting for us in everything we touch or that touches us. Everything in the whole world is swimming in a sea of God. In him we live and move and have our being.

◆ ◆ ◆

Teilhard's three-page introduction to *The Divine Milieu* makes a number of points, some obvious, others implied. Let's examine them one by one, the obvious ones first.

Ferment of Religious Thought

Teilhard opens his introduction by discussing the "ferment of religious thought in our time." Even in Teilhard's day scientific discoveries had provided a totally new picture of creation: on a grand scale, of the size and density of the universe and our understanding of time and space and, on a microscopic scale, of the dazzling complexity of each of the billions of tiny cells in each living organism. Three-quarters of a century later, we are still being awed, almost daily, by stunning scientific discoveries and technical advances, and these new discoveries are causing even more ferment about religion and spirituality than they did in Teilhard's day.

In our day, too, the steady rise of fundamentalism in all major religions creates more challenges to any attempt to reconcile scientific knowledge with religious belief. Some Christian fundamentalists, knowing of the centrality of evolution in Teilhard's spirituality, have labeled his thought heretical, and some have relegated him to a place in hell.

On the other hand, some scientists faced with the mysteries of deep space or the mysteries of the submicroscopic world have felt a reverential awe looking into their telescopes or microscopes and have turned to religion in search of the meaning of it all.

Christ of the Gospels

Teilhard would ask himself — and us — a question that might sound like this: Is the Jesus of the Gospels who excited the people living around the Mediterranean Sea two thousand years ago still capable of exciting people today who live in a "prodigiously expanded universe"? Can the Christ whose message touched the minds and hearts of people who saw a flat earth as the totality of the cosmos and Yahweh living in a canopy above it as its overseer — can this Christ still capture and fascinate us, who know that the universe contains billions of galaxies, a thousand billion stars, and probably ten thousand billion planets like Earth?

For many today, God — whether thinking about God or praying to God — seems less and less important, except perhaps at times to comfort a fearful or grieving heart. On the other hand, some strongly religious people cling desperately to their age-old religious devotions and beliefs. Many of these people have been forced to create a kind of mental wall or curtain between the two major domains of their lives, between their spiritual practices and the tasks of their professional careers. They are condemned to live in two different worlds.

Science's Effect on Religious People

Aware of advances in scientific knowledge about the world we live in, some realize the oneness of our planet and see themselves as an atom of this single organism called Earth. Others who begin to comprehend the vastness of space might picture themselves as citizens not merely of Earth but of the entire universe. When you awaken to the awareness of the vastness and complexity of time and space, says Teilhard, it must produce a profound effect on your religious life and beliefs. It may discourage some while it excites others. It may make some anxious while others grow fascinated by it. Teilhard is interested in addressing both the fearful and the fascinated.

However, many religious people never awaken to an awareness of all that science has brought into contemporary religious conscious-ness, and they simply never attempt to integrate facts about science or our universe into their religious mentality. For example, they believe that at Christ's Ascension he was lifting off to some physical heaven above the clouds. We now know that, even if Christ were traveling at the speed of light to some physical location called heaven, he still, to this day, would not have passed beyond the borders of our own Milky Way galaxy. These simple believers have no feelings of anxiety or fascination regarding the grandeur of the universe or its magnifi-cent complexity. Such people, Teilhard says, will not find *The Divine Milieu* useful, inviting or challenging. To them, it would make little sense to explore ideas about the evolving cosmic Body of Christ.

Religion's Consistent Teaching

Teilhard confidently reminds us that religion has always taught us to see God's presence everywhere. That belief is key to growth in the spiritual life. The problem is most don't know how to "see" in this way. We are blocked from this kind of spiritual growth by our inability to see the divine in the earth and in other created things. Since faith-filled eyes are essential to grasping the divine milieu, Teilhard proposes a practical way for us to learn how to see. Teaching us to "see" the way he does is, basically, the main purpose of his book.

Teilhard apparently had developed, through a combination of scientific inquiry and St. Ignatius's Spiritual Exercises, this ability to see God in all things. This Ignatian vision enabled generations of Jesuits, like Teilhard, to become "contemplatives in action."

If you look at the editor's footnote at the bottom of the second or third page of Teilhard's introduction to *The Divine Milieu,* you will read a quote from another of Teilhard's writings: "Throughout my life, by means of my life, the world has little by little caught fire in my sight until, aflame all around me, it has become almost completely luminous from within." It's as though Teilhard has learned to see not only the outer but also the inner life of things, as if every least thing in front of him has a divine light inside it that makes it glow from within.

Teilhard seems to like using the image of fire for God. It seems Teilhard has discovered a new kind of "fire" inside things and wants us all to be able to see this light as he sees it, as a divine fire that penetrates and burns without consuming or destroying. It is reminiscent of Moses and the burning bush that was not consumed, or the opening lines of Gerard Manley Hopkins's poem "God's Grandeur":

> The world is charged with the grandeur of God.
> It will flame out, like shining from shook foil. . . .

Teilhard encourages us to learn this new way of seeing and promises that as we deeply explore our world with it, we will begin to see how

God has "invaded" and "ignited" the universe with a consuming, loving fire. He wants us to be able to see, ultimately, the entire universe as the shining Body of Christ.

God is waiting for you, Teilhard says, to discover the diaphanous divine beauty, not only in the spectacular loveliness of creation on earth or in its ever-expanding vastness in outer space, but also in your daily personal and interpersonal experience.

We learn to develop these new eyes, the same way we learn any art, by ongoing practice. Here is a basic spiritual practice of Teilhardian spirituality. It may remind you of Mother Couderc finding *Bonté* marked on everything she saw. May you find delight in using this practice every day for the rest of your life.

Spiritual Practice: The Luminous World _____

Ω In order to discover and frequently exercise your new eyes to discern the fire or luminosity within things, start small. Chose one living thing, such as a flower, a bug, a pet, or a baby, and with your imagination picture a kind of glow or luminousness surrounding and penetrating the object of your contemplation. Stay with it for a few minutes, focusing not on the external beauty or complexity of the object but upon the glow surrounding and penetrating it, as if that were its source of life and existence.

Once you learn to do this, the glow or luminosity will develop a life of its own. Then you can move on to another object of contemplation to witness its glowing luminosity.

From time to time, say a word of thanks to this benevolent God who is constantly revealing God's self to you everywhere in creation.

_____

The Noninterfering Milieu

Teilhard points out that, just as the water in the fish tank never disturbs the fish's movements, and just as the atmosphere surrounding humans never disturbs their activity, so the presence of the divine milieu — the permeating luminosity — in no way disturbs what we do or what happens to us. It goes unseen and unsuspected.

You can go through life never noticing this divine milieu. But once you have learned to see its luminosity, your life is enriched and your faith enters a new domain. As you recognize and cooperate with this divine presence, it can transform your earthly pursuits and burdens into efforts that further the growth of the Body of Christ and propel forward the evolving design God has built into creation.

The points described above are the more obvious ones Teilhard wants you to note in his introduction. But there are other points, very important ones for understanding Teilhard. These are not explicit but only implied in his text. Here are some of those.

"In Eo Vivimus"

First, the title of the introduction, "In eo vivimus," is easily overlooked. It is a Latin phrase that means "In him we live." It is a quote from St. Paul talking to the Greek people who have not yet heard of Christ (see Acts 17:22–31). In order to make a connection to Christ for them, Paul reminds them that one of their famous poets had described God as one in whom "we live and move and have our being." Paul tells them that Christ is the very one their poets wrote about.

But this phrase, "in eo vivimus," also offers a core insight into Teilhard's spirituality. As a Teilhardian beginner, unless you read each page of *The Divine Milieu* from this "in eo vivimus" perspective, you may miss its richness.

To see how important this perspective is, first notice how different it is from the two major traditional views about relating to God and Christ that have been offered to us for centuries by spiritual books and the liturgy. The two traditional perspectives see God as *transcendent* and God as *immanent*.

The *transcendent* perspective tells us that God is separate from us — above and beyond us — and dwells far away in heaven. From this perspective we raise our voices in prayer to God who is "out there"

In Love with Everyone

A contemporary physician was graced with this ability to "see" as Teilhard describes it. This is his description of how things looked through his new eyes. "Everything and everyone in the world was luminous and exquisitely beautiful. All living things became radiant, and expressed this radiance in stillness and splendor. It was apparent that all of mankind is actually motivated by inner love, but has simply become unaware; most people live their lives as though they're sleepers unawakened to the perception of who they really are. Everyone looked as if they were asleep, but they were incredibly beautiful—I was in love with everyone."

—David R. Hawkins, MD, PhD, *Power vs. Force*

---

or "up there." Most liturgical prayers take this form, addressing an almighty God who lives in faraway heaven. The Gloria prayer begins, "Glory to God in the highest, and peace to his people on earth." God sits high up there, while we are down here. The Lord's Prayer also emphasizes God in a heavenly dwelling: "Our Father who art in heaven...."

The *immanent* perspective, in contrast, stresses that God lives privately within each one of us and is someone we can talk to intimately as one might talk to a beloved spouse or close friend. This is the usual perspective in private prayer, especially after receiving Holy Communion.

Both these traditional perspectives are valid, and certainly they are ways Teilhard was taught to pray by his parents, his church, and his Jesuit spiritual directors. From time to time, Teilhard also uses these perspectives in his prayer. Nevertheless, his main way of visualizing

God's presence is as the *milieu* — that luminosity — in which we all live and move and have our being.

The Word Milieu

The French word *milieu* has no exact English equivalent, so the translators have simply kept the French word in the text wherever it occurs. *Milieu* encompasses both our English words "atmosphere" and "environment," yet for Teilhard it connotes still something more that he tries to capture in images of light, inner luminosity, or fire.

A milieu is as penetrating and omnipresent as the air we breathe; yet we mostly take it for granted. We simply forget about the atmosphere even though we are dependent upon it at every moment. As soon as we are deprived of oxygen to breathe, we quickly become aware of our need for it. Fish live in a milieu of water yet are unaware of its importance until they are taken out of it.

For Teilhard, the most important spiritual fact of our existence is that at every moment you and I are swimming in a divine sea. Fortunately, we can't be taken out of it. At every moment we are inhaling and exhaling the divine life. In the divine milieu we live and move and have our being. While it is true that God is always "in heaven" (transcendent) and also always "within us" (immanent), the more important fact is that we are always living and moving *within* the divine milieu.

Because of this description of God, Teilhard has been accused of being a pantheist (one who believes that everything is God). Teilhard is not a pantheist, but a pan*en*theist (one who believes that everything has its own existence but is living *in* God as in a milieu.) That's what the "en" in pan*en*theist means — everything is living and has its being *in* the sea of God's grace and love. This is not a hard image to grasp, for, just as you have your own identity and at the same time live in the divine milieu, every cell in your body has its own identity yet lives in you. Every cell in your body, if it had the consciousness to say it, could acknowledge to your body, "I am what I am, yet in you I live and move and have my being."

Who Knew?

Most of the cells in our body aren't even human cells. If you did a count, nonhuman organisms called "microbes" would outnumber your human cells by a factor of ten to one. According to Dr. Jeffrey Gordon, who researches intestinal microbial communities, these microbes live on your eyeballs, in your mouth, nose, and ears, and all over your skin. In your intestines alone, there are up to a hundred trillion active microorganisms. Scientists haven't yet figured out names for all of these microbes, but so far they've counted close to a thousand different species of them.

What is most clear is that these microbes are not invaders, but they co-evolved with us so that our bodies serve as a kind of ecosystem for them as well as our own cells. Each of these little creatures follows its own agenda—help digest food, produce vitamins, ward off disease—but collectively they maintain and advance the life of your whole body.

If these microbes saw our bodies as God, they would insist they are not pantheists but panentheists.

—See Joel Achenbach's "Growing on You,"
National Geographic, November 2005

What Lives in the Divine Milieu?

If we humans are living in the divine milieu, so must everything else be swimming in that same sea of divine love. Every tree, plant, animal, mineral, metal, and rock, as well as every one of those hundred trillion active microorganisms in your body. Every atom and molecule, separately and together, is also held in its individual existence in this same divine atmosphere. The all-pervasiveness of the divine milieu is why Jesus could say that not a single sparrow falls from the sky unnoticed by God. And how else could Jesus claim that the hairs on your head are numbered separately, unless each hair lived individually in God's milieu? (see Matt. 10:29–30).

Unless you grasp this idea of living and moving about *in* God, you cannot begin to understand Teilhard's book or his spirituality. The more you can sense this divine bath or ocean in which everything exists — in and through and around it — the more you can grasp the power of Teilhard's words in *The Divine Milieu*. I might go so far as to say, don't even begin reading his book before you begin to feel very familiar with this luminous presence.

Spiritual Practice: Shifting Perspective _____

Ω I suggest you practice this shift in perspective frequently until it becomes habitual. Perhaps, using your imagination, you can begin to see each thing you encounter during your day — your toothbrush, your towel, your frying pan, your coffee cup, your shoes, your pets, your phone, your computer, your car, the sidewalk, the road, the traffic lights — all of them living and moving in the sea or milieu of God, each one being held in existence lovingly by God at every moment. Nothing is outside this milieu.

You may address this benevolent God at any moment with an expression of gratitude.

_____

Practice this exercise, which can quickly become a prayer of praise and thanksgiving, whenever you get a chance — at the dinner table, in traffic, at work, at school, in church, watching television.

Spiritual Practice: The Bubble of Light _____

Ω Another image to use for this practice is "light," which focuses on Teilhard's idea of the luminosity of the divine milieu. Start with something nearby. Anything. Imagine it surrounded and penetrated by a bubble of light. This sphere of light, which represents the divine milieu, holds that object in being. Then let the bubble of light expand until, within its expanding luminosity, it holds the contents of the whole room. Imagine the bubble keeps expanding, without losing any of its intensity, until it engulfs the entire house or building where you are. Let the bubble grow in size until it encompasses the neighborhood, the city, the country, the planet, the solar system, and so on, as far as your imagination can take it. Remember that you are inside that bubble too.

Whenever you feel alone or frightened, you may imagine yourself safely and protectively encased in a bubble of light that is the divine milieu.

Importance of St. Paul's Theology

It is important to recognize that Teilhard builds much of his spirituality on the theological perspectives of St. Paul the Apostle.

For example, you will notice that in their writings Teilhard and Paul seldom focus on Jesus of Nazareth. Rather, they are more interested in the Risen Christ. Seldom do either of them refer to Jesus without adding the title "Christ" or "Lord." Recall that Paul never met the man Jesus of Nazareth, but only the Risen Lord. So Paul rarely talks about Jesus of Nazareth, whom he never knew, but rather about "Christ Jesus" or "Our Lord Jesus Christ," whom he knew very well.

It is also important to notice that, for both Paul and Teilhard, when they say "Christ" they are usually referring to — or picturing — the Total Christ, of whose Body we are all members (see, for example Rom. 12:5, 14:7; Col. 2:19, 3:3). For St. Paul, this Total Christ with us as members (or cells, as we might say today) of his body is *the* most important reality.

For both Paul and Teilhard, the historical Jesus of Nazareth had a very important role to play in salvation history (and they certainly see him as divine). But, today, Jesus of Nazareth is no longer walking the earth in a way that we can physically encounter him and speak to him. He rose from the dead and, for St. Paul, has been completely transformed into the Risen Lord, head of the body of all creation that he has redeemed. For Paul, the only Christ that lives today is the Total Christ. *That* is the Christ that St. Paul and Teilhard are talking about in their writings.

What is really happening *today* is that this Total Christ is growing, developing, and maturing in complexity and consciousness. The Risen Christ who is the head and heart of this great Body is today's reality. And at each successive moment, that Christ Body is the culmination and embodiment of what has gone on before and what is happening now — and it's still developing. It is a Body that has a unique history yet continues to evolve (see Col. 2:19b).

This Total Christ is most important in the thought of both Paul and Teilhard. You and I may prefer, in our prayer, to picture Christ as someone who looks like a human being standing nearby, like a friend at our side. And in a very real sense, that is true. But to adopt the spirituality of either Paul or Teilhard, the more primary reality is that each of us is a cell or element of the much larger Christ Body. In other words, the most important part of our life and being is that we are living each moment of our day and life in Christ's Body (see Col. 3:3). Just as your cells live and move and have their being as part of your body, so you and I are a part of Christ's Body.

Spiritual Practice: A Part of the Body

Ω If you want to begin practicing this aspect of Teilhard's spirituality, you might begin by considering the different parts of your body — eyes, ears, tongue, hands, brain, heart, lungs, liver, gall bladder, arteries and veins — as having their fullest reality not as independent organs, limbs, or elements in themselves, but as parts of you, having their life and meaning because they live in you and have life because of you. Although each of the billions of cells in your body could be isolated under a microscope, they really find their life and meaning as part of you, sharing in the life you give them. Your eye would never be able to see and enjoy the beauties of the world unless it lived in you. Your hand and arm could never write a letter if they were cut off from you.

So St. Paul, who lives with this realization of being a cell in the Christ Body, can say, "I am dead to myself, but alive in Christ" (see Rom. 6:8–11) or, "I no longer live (for myself), but for Christ" (see Gal. 2:20).

Once you see yourself as part of this Christ Body, you take on consciousness of a new identity. You will never picture yourself in the same way again. You have become a part of something immensely great, something cosmically dynamic, something that only divine love could have ever dreamed up.

For Paul and for Teilhard, this Christ Body is not something static or fixed or complete, like a statue, but is something alive and growing that has not yet reached its maturity. But note that, for Paul and Teilhard, the Total Christ, head and members, is not simply a spiritual being but also a physical one. It is striving toward its fulfillment and completion *as a body* (see Eph. 1:10, 1:23, 2:21).

Based on advances in scientific knowledge of our planet and our universe, Teilhard is going to describe this fulfillment more scientifically, and thus carry Paul's thought forward in a number of ways. Remember, Teilhard was both a Jesuit theologian and a dedicated scientist, with over a hundred articles published in research journals. He unites many years of training and experience in both Jesuit spirituality and scientific discipline, specifically in the fields of geology, paleontology, archeology, and anthropology.

Enlarging Paul's Understanding of the Total Christ

First, we know historically that Paul continued to evolve his understanding of the Total Body of Christ. For example, in his earlier letters, he pictured each Christian community or congregation as the Body of Christ. The Corinthian Christian community was one Christ Body, the Thessalonian Christians another Christ Body, the Roman Christians another Christ Body. Later, he realized that the Christ Body, if it is to be one body, must simultaneously incorporate in itself all the believers spread across the earth.

Paul also realized that Christ wanted every human being to be part of this body. Before his Ascension, Jesus exhorted his disciples to preach the gospel message to all the ends of the earth. This is what Paul did, encouraging everyone to live as though they were living life in the Body of Christ.

For Paul and for Teilhard, *Christ is the divine milieu.* It is in Christ that we live and move and have our being. Teilhard picks up this theme in greater depth in Part Three of *The Divine Milieu.*

Teilhard the scientist had come to realize that we as humans could not — as much as we might like to believe we could — separate ourselves from our earth, the oceans, the atmosphere, the animals, plants, and other living creatures. Science assures us that everything on this planet contributes to make the earth a single organism. We humans are not independent beings. We are inextricably bound up with each other, and with the metals, minerals, grains, fruits, and animals we eat to survive, and with the trees that give us oxygen to breathe, and with the lakes and seas that give us water to drink, and with the sun that warms us. Since we cannot be separated from any of these and cannot continue to remain alive without them, therefore, at a minimum, our entire planet must be part of the Body of Christ.

While St. Paul assumed the Christ Body would be made up solely of humans — though he had a sense that all creation was groaning for its fulfillment in Christ (see Rom. 8:22–23) — Teilhard realized the Christ Body must be made up of much, much more than just human beings. Our entire planet as a whole and each of its parts, argues Teilhard, lives and moves and has its being in the divine milieu.

We know, theologically, that Christ, the Divine Word, was with God in the beginning and during the entire creation process. "All things came into being through him, and without him not one thing came into being. What has come into being in him was life" (John 1:1–4). Everything that exists is alive in the divine milieu. Everything that exists is imbued with this life and is inescapably part of the cosmos that God loves passionately (see John 3:16). So why should God want to discard any part of it?

We now know, scientifically, that our planet itself cannot be seen as something independent of our neighboring planets and the sun, but in reality Earth is totally dependent on the balance and makeup of our solar system. If the planets Mars and Venus, for example, weren't in precisely their orbits relative to Earth and all the planets relative to the Sun, then our atmosphere would not be able to sustain life as we know it. We are, in fact, one with our solar system. So our entire solar system must also be a part of the great Christ Body.

In fact, Teilhard realized, and discussed it in a different text, that the Big Bang at the first moment of creation took place within the divine milieu. Through the Divine Word at the Big Bang all things came into being. Whatever came to be had its existence founded in him. So for its truest fulfillment, the Total Christ must be at least as large as the entire universe. We cannot eliminate or reject any part of the universe from the divine milieu or place it outside the eternal loving embrace of God.

Paul may have had a cosmic-sized sense of Christ when in the letter to the Colossians he writes, "He is the image of the invisible God, the firstborn of all creation; for in him all things in heaven and on earth were created, things visible and invisible ... all things have been created through him and for him. He himself is before all things, and in him all things hold together" (Col. 1:15–17). In other words, in him everything continues in being.

Teilhard sometimes also calls the Total Christ the Cosmic Christ as well as the Universal Christ. So when Teilhard is talking about Christ, he is envisioning not just a human person like you or me, but a Being with a divine head connected to the body of the entire universe, all of it living in a sea of divine love. Thus, the fulfillment, or *pleroma*, of Christ involves every fragment of creation, from the Big Bang that kicked off the whole process until the final culminating moment at the end of time — nothing left out.

Second, St. Paul had only a vague notion of what the *pleroma,* or fullest completion of the Christ Body, would be or how it would come about, other than through the conversion and baptism of individual human beings being added to it. Teilhard using his scientific knowledge sees that the Christ Body (the entire universe) is evolving toward becoming a Someone — a divine, immense, highly complex, personal, loving Whole that is greater than the sum of its parts. This culminating ultimate moment of evolution Teilhard called the Omega Point.

From his scientific knowledge of the pervasiveness of the evolutionary process happening at every level of being, Teilhard sees that this evolutionary process also applies to the Total Christ, because the Total Christ is not pure spirit but is developing itself in a material universe, so the Total Christ is constantly changing with the universe in its evolutionary process. The radically revolutionary insight that Teilhard realized was that *the true identity of the Total Christ is continually being revealed to us anew through the evolutionary process.*

From the dawn of creation, the universe has been following a certain upward trajectory. The universe's evolutionary direction, Teilhard discovered, is governed by a *law of attraction-connection-complexity-consciousness,* discussed in greater depth in the next section.

Because that same law also governs the development of the Total Christ, this law lies at the heart of Teilhardian spirituality. The task of spirituality for the twenty-first century is to learn how to put that law into practice. We will explore that law and its practice in more detail in a special section to follow.

For now, enjoy reading Teilhard's introduction.

Interlude

Some Premises
of Teilhard's Thought

The material in this interlude is not found in *The Divine Milieu* and is not essential to it. But it is Teilhard's thought. You may skip it if you wish. I have included it because I feel that by becoming familiar with the ideas discussed in this section — developed from other Teilhard writings — you will gain a much fuller and deeper understanding of the divine milieu.

This interlude is not specifically about his spirituality but more about his general thought and how it affects his spirituality. By understanding the following premises you enrich your grasp of his spirituality. I also suggest some other influences on his spirituality that came from his upbringing and Jesuit education.

The First Premise of Teilhard's Thought:
The Universality of Evolution

According to Teilhard the geologist and paleontologist, *evolution is happening continually on every level of being — and has a direction.*

This premise is at the heart of his thought. In *The Phenomenon of Man* he writes:

> Is evolution a theory, a system or a hypothesis? It is much more: it is a general condition to which all theories, all hypotheses, all systems must bow and which they must satisfy henceforward if they are to be thinkable and true. Evolution is a light, illuminating all facts, a curve that all lines must follow. (218)

So evolution — and the recognition that it is happening "continually and on every level of being" — must penetrate and permeate even our spirituality, if it is "to be thinkable and true." So even our spirituality must satisfy this same "general condition" that governs all things. In other words, even in our spiritual practices we must continue to evolve.

Teilhard says that, by divine grace and divine imprint, our consciousness and our hearts are constrained to see all things in light of the evolutionary process. Although few of us can talk about evolution with the familiarity of the geologist or paleontologist, we have all experienced it on much smaller scales. On the personal level, most of us have watched our own development or the development of our children. We recognize evolution in the human species, for example, in the art of communication: from voice to written languages, from the handwritten letter to the e-mail, from the typewriter to the word processor, from the radio to color television, from the rotary dial telephone to the wireless cell phone, from the primitive computer that filled up a room to the compact personal computer that can sit on your lap and be packed in a briefcase.

Biologically, most of us have seen photos of a human fetus developing in the womb. Anthropologists tell us that each infant in its development in the womb recapitulates the phylogeny of the human race from its earliest forms. Like every human being, Jesus of Nazareth began as a fertilized cell. Like all of us he evolved in his mother's womb through other forms of primitive development, even at one point passing through the stages of fish and other lesser life forms. In other words, the human embryo — Jesus' as well as yours — during its early days in the womb, relives much of the entire evolutionary process of the phylum that eventually produced *homo sapiens*.

Spiritual Exercise

Ω I have listed a few areas where Teilhard's first premise of evolution expresses itself. Consider some other areas where evolution has occurred. Let yourself be convinced of the truth of this first premise.

Consider, for example, evolution in education, in business, in commerce, in aviation, in automobiles, in psychology, in biology, in medicine, in physics, in printing, in meteorology, in photography, and so on. Compare, for example, where each science was one hundred years ago and where it is today. You may even want to take notes for each discipline.

The Second Premise of Teilhard's Thought: The Direction of Evolution

In premise 1, Teilhard asserts that all evolutionary processes seem to have a direction, that is to say, the universe in evolution is following a certain trajectory. In premise 2, he spells out the law that gives all evolution its direction and explains its trajectory. We may call it the *law of attraction-connection-complexity-consciousness.*

Parenthetically, it should be noted that, although Teilhard usually referred to this law in a short-hand way, calling it complexity-consciousness, it is clear from his other writings that the first two stages of attraction and connection were really just as integral to it as the last two, for without attraction and connection it would be difficult to fully understand the emergence of complexity and consciousness.

Therefore, Teilhard's law is not four laws, but only one. The four parts, or stages, of the law — attraction, connection, complexity, and consciousness — cannot be separated in the evolutionary process. This law governs and is operating on all levels of being, from the most inert elementary particles to the most sophisticated human social systems. For example, as elemental things are attracted to each other, they combine to form connections. They join together. Their connection or union is always a bit more complex than the separate parts. Atoms of hydrogen and oxygen combine to form molecules of water. The molecule is more complex than the atom. Since things never stop connecting, because of attraction, the complexity of the unions being created keeps growing. Following the law of connection, molecules of water find their way into a living plant, plants find their way into living animals, animals find their way into humans. When animals became complex enough to have a nervous system, following this fundamental law, they developed sensory awareness. In this way, complexity was leading creation into consciousness.

Basically, Teilhard's law means that everything in creation is attracted to other things in creation to form new connections or, from another standpoint, everything in creation is both attractive and attracted. The most fundamental and pervasive power of attraction in the universe is gravity. But there are many more forces of attraction recognized in physics, chemistry, biology, genetics, sociology, and psychology.

Since this attraction never ceases, complexity is bound to result, and since complexity never ceases growing either, consciousness turns out to be the next stage. Teilhard never mentions a stage of evolution beyond consciousness, though we might surmise that some form of collective, unconditional love might be a possible next stage.

Teilhard's law says that everything, beginning with the original exploding fragments of creation at the Big Bang, had this four-stage law built into it. No particle of matter escaped being imprinted with this law. For example, at the Big Bang, the laws of chemistry as we know them today did not exist, since no chemical compounds existed at the time of the Big Bang. Only eons later, following Teilhard's law, would the laws of chemistry come into existence. The same goes for the laws of physics and biology. But the law of attraction-creating-connections was at work from the first moment. By attraction, everything is continually making connections with other things around it, striving toward greater complexity and awareness.

By this law today, human inventors are driven to continually make things like automobiles, computers, and cell phones more and more complex. Think of the first cell phone. How simple and primitive it seems to us today. Our cell phones keep getting smaller and smaller, yet more and more complex. In addition to serving as telephones, they now can take pictures, hold hundreds of songs, connect us to the Internet, and download Hollywood films.

The Three Infinities

Teilhard pointed out that, for centuries, science has been aware of two infinities — space and time — but only recently have we noticed the third.

First, the infinity of *space*. The universe seems to go on and on, ever expanding. There are always farther reaches of space to discover. Astronomers are those primarily involved in the infinity of space. While ordinary men and women measure space in inches and feet and less frequently in miles and even hundreds of miles, astronomers measure space in light-years, the distance light can travel in a year. To calculate the diameter of our Milky Way galaxy in miles would require the number ten with a book full of zeros after it. That is an example of the infinity of space.

Second, the infinity of *time*. While most of us measure time in hours and days, and less frequently in years and decades, geologists and paleontologists measure time in units of tens of thousands of years, or even millions, going back billions of years. They are involved in the infinity of time. However, when we ordinary people look at any extended duration of time, we can observe that things are never static, cyclical, or fixed. Instead, they are always evolving — or *de*volving (breaking down).

Teilhard announced a third infinity, the *infinity of complexity*. From the first moment of the Big Bang, those first simple chemical elements and gasses that were created, such as hydrogen and helium, tended to be attracted to one another and, over time, to connect with each other to form ever more complex molecules, until they were manifested in crystal structures, metals, minerals, liquids, basic life forms, biological organisms, plants, trees, insects, fish, birds, reptiles, and mammals, up to the most complex biological life form we currently know, that is, humans.

Each new stage of evolution seems to be more complex than the stage before it. This insight is what helped Teilhard to develop his law of attraction-connection-complexity-consciousness, since not only were creatures in the evolutionary process growing more and more complex; they were also growing more and more in consciousness. This led Teilhard to establish the idea that, currently, the true criterion to measure growth and development in the divine milieu is complexity and, more accurately, consciousness.

How Does the Law of Attraction-Connection-Complexity-Consciousness Operate?

From the first moment of creation, particles were attracted to one another. They kept joining, combining, and connecting with each other. While some simple atomic particles of helium and hydrogen clustered together and remained what they were, other combinations of these particles formed more complex atoms and became new, more complex chemical elements. And those new elements either clustered and remained the same or combined to form new, more complex elements.

Attraction gave birth, again and again over time, to newer and more complex connections. Elemental atoms grew into molecules, then crystals, then metals, then minerals. Water, for example, is a molecule made up of two inorganic gases, hydrogen and oxygen, yet it can take the form of a liquid, solid, or gas.

When evolution at inorganic levels reached its highest level of complexity, it broke out of its inorganic limitations into organic forms, whose structures were even more complex than inorganic ones.

Immersed in Attractive Forces

At the *physical level*, the law of attraction is continually expressed in the forces of gravity, electromagnetism, the strong and weak nuclear forces, and dark energy.

At the *chemical level*, it is revealed in those attractive forces that bind atoms and nuclei together. These forces hold water molecules together as water, and chlorine molecules as chlorine.

At the *biological level*, attraction is manifested in the forces that keep bringing insects to plants to fertilize them, and bringing animals in heat together to keep their species reproducing.

In its highest manifestation at the *spiritual level*, attraction is expressed as love that brings humans together in friendship, marriage, and family.

Even though complexity and consciousness may be higher expressions of the fundamental law, *attraction remains the starting point and basic force of the evolutionary process.*

Attraction gives birth to connections, and connections to complexity.

How Did Complexity Give Birth to Consciousness?

Attraction, connection, and complexity, following their trajectory, eventually gave birth to movement, sensation, perception, awareness, and finally consciousness. As we know, there are many layers or levels of consciousness. For Teilhard, evolution's trajectory is urging us humans toward higher and higher levels of consciousness.

This law of attraction-connection-complexity-consciousness, for Teilhard, has brought us from the Big Bang to where we are today, at the apex of evolution's arrow. It is up to us in our spirituality to recognize this trajectory and the law that shows us how to keep evolution on its proper path into the future.

You cannot separate your spirituality from the Big Bang, because it was at the Big Bang that the law of attraction-connection-complexity-consciousness began to have its effects, and it is still the fundamental law governing development everywhere today. This law also helps explain the way in which divine grace is meant to work in us.

Spiritual Practice: The Attractions of My Life _____

Ω Take some time to reflect on — and even begin to jot down — those things that attract you. Then go a bit deeper and see if you can identify the factors in each thing that first catch your attention. What is it about this person that attracts me? What is it about this pet that attracts me? What is it about this flower that attracts me? What is it about this automobile that attracts me? And so on. These are the qualities that bring about connections for you. These form the connections that will bring complexity into your life. These qualities are part of the attractiveness of things that guide you to your destiny. They are all graces, or gifts, if you want — a literal translation of the word for "grace."

Next, see if you can use the law of attraction to trace backward from where you are in life now to discern the path of attractions, even from an early age, that brought you to this point. For example, perhaps, while everyone loved to eat, you were attracted to discover how food was prepared and you became a good cook. Perhaps, while everyone enjoyed driving cars, you were attracted to what went on under the hood and how all the different parts of the engine worked, and you became an auto mechanic. Perhaps, while everyone enjoyed reading a good book, you were fascinated by how a book is created, and you became a writer. You will discover that, all your life, you have been graced and guided by attractions. You are a good example of Teilhard's law of attraction-connection-complexity-consciousness.

Praying within Evolution's Current

You might think that in prayer you stand outside of evolution's current or that only your body is immersed in the flow of evolution while your soul hovers above it. According to Teilhard, evolution's flow today is operating predominantly in the realm of consciousness. That is, at the tip of evolution's arrow are the workings of the human mind and spirit.

For example, even in the past hundred years or so, human consciousness has evolved significantly, at least intellectually. Instead of thinking exclusively in Newtonian terms, physicists today think in terms of Einstein's relativity and particle physics. In organizational management, executives have moved from single-event thinking and cause-and-effect problem solving to systems thinking and more sophisticated systems management. Sociologists have evolved from using direct and exhaustive counting of extremely large numbers of people, for instance, in political opinion polls, to applying probability and statistics to small samples of people to predict accurate outcomes.

Because of continual worldwide media coverage, we can be more conscious of what is happening in different parts of the world. We are much more aware of our interconnectedness and interdependence, for example, of how political or financial events in a remote part of the world can affect our taxes or the price we pay for athletic shoes or gasoline. We are also more conscious than ever before of the need for providing international aid in the forms of food, medicines, technology, education, and all the rest. Yes, Teilhard would say, evolution today is operating predominantly in the realm of consciousness. But what of the area of spirituality? Is that evolving as well?

Our deepest intentions and desires today — many of them different from those of people a century ago — reflect the progress we have made in growth of consciousness, not only in our personal development and evolution but also in the evolution of the universe itself.

Your prayer is a manifestation of that evolution. Your prayer is built upon all that has happened on the earth before you — millennia of primitive religions and worship, ages of spiritual searching and prayer, each generation passing on its slowly evolving understanding of God and the workings of God. Wherever you may be in terms of your own spiritual development, you realize there are further levels of union with God to discover and realize. At the same time, your prayer today reaches out, *on behalf of the entire creation.* Before this generation, did you ever hear of people praying for the ecology? Did people ever acknowledge their need to care for nature at the planetary level? As St. Paul says, "Nature itself is groaning for its own fulfillment." We humans can — in fact, we're the only ones who can — further that fulfillment. As Teilhard says in *The Phenomenon of Man,* "Man discovers that he is nothing else than evolution become conscious of itself" (p. 220).

Since the beginning, evolution has been happening by itself, as it were. The law of attraction-connection-complexity-consciousness was always there driving it. And still is. But now that humans are conscious and aware of that law, humans can use their minds and hearts to maximize the effects of that law and further our own and nature's fulfillment. For example, we can increase our personal attractiveness, multiply our connections, push to make life more complex, and in this way reach for higher levels of consciousness. The future of the rest of creation is in our human hands. How humans use, abuse, or disregard this universal law depends on us. We have the choice to use the complexity and consciousness available to us to continue to shape the Body of Christ — or to promote the Seven Deadly Sins.

The Innocent Seeker

While Teilhard was growing up as a child in France, those who lived in his part of the country were fond of telling stories of heroic figures. Among the most popular were tales of the Innocent Seeker. Though these narratives had a variety of settings and characters, the structure of the plot remained much the same. The Innocent Seeker would feel compelled to travel far and wide in search of the "secret at the heart of the world." In a few versions of the legend, the Seeker would spend his entire life searching and die without ever finding the secret.

But, more often, the Seeker would find the secret and want to return to his people to share it with them. Sometimes, when he came back to his people, they were not interested in what he had discovered or they rejected him as if he were crazy.

In order to be accepted by them, the Seeker, in some versions of the story, conveniently "forgot" the secret. He decided it was the price he had to pay to fit in with the community.

Other times, in the story the Seeker kept trying to explain and reveal the secret to his neighbors and friends, but they couldn't understand it, so at the end of his life the Seeker went to his grave without anyone else grasping and passing on the "secret at the heart of the world."

Teilhard's life echoes the story of the Innocent Seeker who has discovered the secret at the heart of the world and who keeps trying to share it with all the beloved people in his life — his Jesuit comrades and his church. Instead of welcoming it, they rejected it, failed to understand it, or refused even to consider it. And this Innocent Seeker died knowing that his writings had been suppressed and buried by the church and the Society of Jesus that he loved and served faithfully all his life.

Luckily, those writings have "resurrected," and we now can share the secret that he discovered at the heart of the world.

But what is this secret?

Seeking the Indestructible

When Teilhard, as a very young child, heard these Innocent Seeker legends, he intuitively realized that, whatever the secret at the heart of the world might turn out to be, it would have to be *indestructible*. It was the indestructible that attracted him. That was the way the law of attraction-connection-complexity-consciousness worked through him.

So the young Teilhard, living out the myth of the Innocent Seeker in his own childlike way, often searched the harsh countryside where he lived, at the foot of extinct volcanoes, in search of things that might be indestructible. However, each hard stone he found turned out to be a poor candidate and easily destroyed, often with only one sharp blow of a hammer.

One day, he found a piece of iron and, in his childish wish, decided that it might be indestructible. But, left out in the rain, his piece of iron soon started to rust. Iron, too, had failed the test.

In a roundabout way, through his childhood desire to find the indestructible secret, he was led into the sciences, especially geology (the study of earth's elements — rocks) and paleontology (the study of evolutionary processes).

In tracing evolution back to its most ultimate creative source, God, Teilhard discovered that "spirit" was the indestructible secret at the heart of the world. From this arose the revolutionary idea that *evolution is based on spirit, not on matter*. Spirit was what finally explained how all of creation and evolution made sense. All his writings were a series of attempts, in one way and another, to explain to us this secret he had discovered. *The Divine Milieu* is his book for helping people translate this secret into spirituality for our age.

Thomas Aquinas and Teilhard de Chardin

During the thirteenth century, the Dominican theologian Thomas Aquinas recognized that science was surpassing theology in attracting university students. For those intellectuals of Europe had rediscovered the Greek language and with it the rational and scientific approach of Aristotle's scientific methods, especially his ideas about deduction and induction as the primary ways to gain knowledge. These ideas were sweeping the academic and scientific world of the time, leaving traditional theological methods behind, labeling them as old-fashioned and out-of-date. Theology was no longer considered queen of the sciences, because Aristotle had become the rage.

To restore theology to her rightful place as queen, Aquinas set himself the task of bringing theology up to date. His challenge was to rewrite all of Christian theology using only the deductive and inductive methods of Aristotle. He would show that one could use these same Aristotelian methods to derive all the truths of theology. His books were called *The Summa Theologica*. "Summa" means both "sum" and "summary." In the many hundreds of pages of his brilliant response, it was all there.

However, when Aquinas first presented his *Summa* to the theological world, many considered it to be outrageous and even heretical. Yet within a hundred years of Aquinas's death, every theological student was required to use the *Summa* as a basic theological textbook, and it remained the core of all theological studies in seminaries, at least in the Catholic Church, until the last half of the twentieth century.

Once again, at least to the scientific world of today, Christian theological studies and spirituality are considered antiquated, since they have not integrated the scientific facts learned from geology, paleontology, astronomy, physics, biology, chemistry, neurology, and psychology. For the most part, contemporary theology and spirituality have chosen the safe path of completely separating spiritual growth from intellectual growth, and theological knowledge from scientific knowledge, thus forcing the dedicated intellectual seeking a sincere life of faith to live in two separate worlds and to have a divided heart, part of it loving scientific research and other intellectual pursuits, the other part loving God.

Teilhard sensed this cleaving in his own heart and, like Aquinas, set himself the task of integrating the methods and knowledge of science and faith into a single spirituality, so that there would be no longer a need to divide one's heart. And like those of Aquinas, Teilhard's ideas have been ridiculed and even thought to be heretical. They were rejected by his church and, for the most part, by members of the religious order to which he belonged and to which he had dedicated his life.

My dream is that, one day, hopefully sooner than a century from now, Teilhard's ideas, recognized for the healthy revolution they can bring, will become foundational in theology and spirituality.

In Part One of *The Divine Milieu*, discussed on the following pages, Teilhard begins his task very simply by finding a way to classify all the events of our lives to see how they all fit into the divine milieu and the life of the Cosmic Christ.

THE DIVINIZATION OF OUR ACTIVITIES

Summary

All human experience can be divided into two groups: activities and passivities. Activities are what we do by our own effort. Passivities are what we undergo or endure.

In Part One, Teilhard wants to show how all of our human activities and efforts toward personal growth and human progress can be used to help the growth and development of the Body of Christ. Not only are our efforts useful in this regard, but they are also somehow necessary.

Even though we perform these actions as ordinary human beings, and they look like ordinary human actions, they are simultaneously being transformed in the divine milieu and become actions done in, with, and through Christ.

At the same time as these efforts of ours develop us as human beings, they are simultaneously helping develop the cosmic Body of Christ. In other words, in the divine milieu the totality of our human actions, even apparently insignificant ones, can be sanctified. By our activities, we are providing nourishment and enrichment for our personal selves and for the Body of Christ all at the same time.

Each of our works helps to bring Christ's Body one small step closer to its fulfillment. In this way, we become the living extensions of God's creative power. God awaits us at "every instant in our action, in the work of the moment."

　　By sanctifying our human effort, God sur-animates it, that is, God gives it a higher kind of life. If you take a living cell and look at it under a microscope, you can see that it has life of itself. It is animated. But when you put that cell in a person's body, it takes on the life of that human person. It has been sur-animated.

　　Teilhard wants to help us become conscious of the connections—even physical and natural ones—that bind our work with the building of the Kingdom of God. Nothing here below is profane for those who know how to see.

◆　◆　◆

You see that a person is justified by works
and not by faith alone.
　　　—James 2:24

Teilhard arranges all the events of our lives into two major categories: *activities* and *passivities*. *Activities* are things we choose to do or try to do; *passivities* are things that happen to us that we must endure.

For example, an activity of mine might be reading a book or frying some eggs on the stove. An *activity* is usually something I intend or have some control over; it is usually something I choose to do.

On the other hand, a *passivity* is something that is done *to* me. For example, someone knocks me over, the electricity goes off and I can't use my computer, or it begins raining and that keeps me from taking a walk. A passivity is something I did not intend to happen and had little or no control over, but it impinges on my life and I have little choice about it. Passivities are things I must endure whether or not I like them. They are called "my" passivities because they happen to *me*; I must bear with them, deal with them, and manage my life with them. For example, the actions of your parents and siblings are passivities you must deal with. You didn't choose them, but you must live with them.

Passivity: A Precise Choice of Word

On first reading, most people are thrown off by the category "passivity," but Teilhard has chosen the word very wisely. Originally, the word comes from the Latin *passio*, which refers to something we undergo, endure, suffer, or desire. Thus, scripture refers to Jesus' crucifixion and death as his *passion*; it is something he suffers and endures at the hands of others.

From this same Latin root we also get the English words "passion" or "passionate," which tend to reflect a more positive or welcome side. We speak of someone's passion for art or music or science, or of someone who is passionately in love.

At first, the two meanings — passion as love and desire vs. passion as suffering and endurance — seem quite opposite. But they are very closely related as *passivities*, since a passion, even if it is for something beautiful and noble, usually possesses us and we cannot seem to escape or avoid it. For example, if a young man falls passionately in love with a certain young woman, he cannot stop thinking about her. He cannot seem to escape or avoid doing so. Dismissing the loving passion is out of his control. He experiences it as something he must undergo or endure — in the same way as a painful passion. Either way, for Teilhard, all of them are *passivities*.

Not Always a Simple Distinction

It would be nice if each of life's events could be neatly separated and categorized as either an activity or a passivity, in the scientific way Teilhard must have categorized geological fossils or bones that he found. The fact is most events are a combination of activities and passivities. For instance, on a certain day Teilhard may have gone on a geological expedition intending to find fossils (activity), but the places where he happened to look contained none, so he was frustrated (passivity).

The same mixture of activities and passivities occurs to all of us. For example, I might be so intent on typing my letter (activity) that

I get a headache (passivity). Or I may be all set to fry eggs for my breakfast (activity) and the telephone rings (passivity).

Or suppose I go out to play a tennis match with a friend. In the first analysis, all of my shots are my activities, and all of my opponent's shots are passivities that I must endure and deal with. But it is not that simple, as we shall see.

Structure of Part One and Part Two

In Part One of *The Divine Milieu*, Teilhard wants to show how our *activities* may be used to help build the Body of Christ. In Part Two, he wants to show how even our *passivities* may be used to help build the Body of Christ.

As a reminder, whenever Teilhard uses the words "Christ" or "Body of Christ" or "Christ's Body," he is not talking about the physical body of Jesus of Nazareth, but a much bigger physical reality that includes, for him, the Risen Christ as head and all the rest of us humans plus all of creation as the Body. In other words, the Body of Christ for Teilhard is everyone and everything on our planet plus all the rest of the universe.

Also as a reminder, in Christian theology, God the Creator is a separate divine person from the Cosmic Christ. You may like to think of God the Creator as unchanging or nonevolving, but the Cosmic Christ, though living in a divine milieu, has much physicality, is subject to the law of attraction-connection-complexity-consciousness, and is continually evolving, developing, being shaped, and growing in consciousness. Our collective human destiny — and challenge — is to keep that evolutionary movement going in a positive direction. For Teilhard and for St. Paul, it involves consciously developing and more clearly revealing the Body of Christ.

How we can use our activities and passivities to build the Body of Christ is far more important than categorizing this or that event as an activity or passivity, but in order to understand Teilhard's thought it will help if we become somewhat adept at categorizing our experiences.

A Summary of Activities and Passivities

To get a summary picture of the different kinds of activities there are and the many kinds of passivities Teilhard defines, see the chart below:

ACTIVITIES AND PASSIVITIES

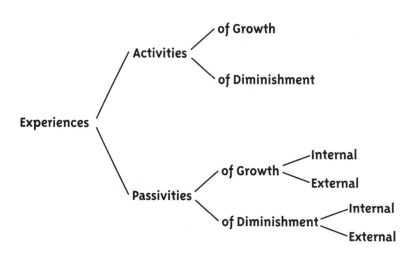

You may make better sense of the chart with the following simple descriptions. Starting on the left, Teilhard says that all of my human *experiences* may be categorized as either *activities* or *passivities*. Following the chart for activities,

- *Activities of Growth* are those efforts we make to promote the development or evolution of the Body of Christ, such as doing scientific research, raising a family, running a business, eating healthily, getting sufficient exercise, taking a shower, sending an e-mail, forming teams for a project, raising awareness of unhealthy conditions in one's neighborhood. And so on. We do thousands of such activities each day.

  It may be important here to clarify what Teilhard means by the word "growth." He means growth in the sense of *development*, that is, growing better, wiser, more complex, more conscious, more effective, and more efficient. He does not simply mean by growth an increase in number or size. For example, one can grow in size without developing, since one can become obese without gaining in intelligence or maturity. Likewise, one can develop without growing in size by maintaining the same weight, yet increasing in wisdom and grace. Although Teilhard certainly wants the Body of Christ to increase consciously in size and numbers, he is much more interested in how that Body increases in love, compassion, consciousness, and inner complexity.

• *Activities of Diminishment* are those efforts we pursue that diminish the development of the Body of Christ, such as the activities we normally label as sins or evil, or whatever harms relationships or jeopardizes whatever constructive things others are trying to accomplish. Such diminishing goals might include the intention to cheat your organization, to cheat your customers, to sabotage some research, to seduce a married person, to use someone merely as a sexual object, to urge a pregnant woman to have an abortion, to manipulate a child or innocent person for unethical ends, to enlist another person in your fraudulent scheme, etc. All of these activities diminish the Body of Christ. Persons can even set up long-range goals that produce diminishment in others as well as themselves, such as plotting revenge or falsely accusing others.

Now follow the chart for the different categories of *passivities:*

• *Passivities of Growth* are things that happen or have happened to us that foster our own progress, so that our activities for the Body of Christ may be more effective because of them. Passivities of growth might include being born into a family that values education and loyalty, going to a school that has inspiring teachers, attending a church that is very involved with social service.

• Some of these passivities of growth are *internal* and unique to each one, such as being born with a creative mind, a healthy body, an aptitude for science, a compassionate nature.

- Other passivities of growth are *external*, that is, they come from outside us but affect our ability to build the Body of Christ, such as being born in a country of opportunity, living in a certain city that offers employment that I like, having neighbors who are very friendly and caring, having parents and grandparents who love me and support what I want to do with my life.

- *Passivities of Diminishment* are things that happen or have happened to us that obstruct our progress and make our activities less effective, such as being born into a family that values greed, laziness, and selfishness.

- Some of these passivities of diminishment are *internal* and unique to each one of us, such as having some congenital disease, susceptibility to illness, weakness of intellect, or other natural failings.

- Other passivities of diminishment are *external*, that is, they come from outside us but affect our ability to make a difference, such as being born into a poverty-stricken family, a minority suffering discrimination, a nation that does not provide education, living in a time of war, bits of ill fortune, auto accidents, family debts that fall upon us, unjust social attitudes, the aging process, etc.

As anyone might observe, there are far more passivities affecting each of us than activities. After all, everyone else in the world and all of nature is always acting upon us and producing experiences that we must endure, whether we like it or not. They generate a lot of passivities for us.

An Example

Suppose you are playing in a football game. There are eleven players on your team, including you, and eleven more on the opposing team. The actions you do by your own effort Teilhard would label as your *activities*. What the other twenty-one players do as their activities produce a variety of effects on your effort, all of which you must deal with. From your perspective, their activities affect you as your *passivities*. They are acting upon you, whether you like it or not. You experience even the activities of your own team members as your passivities; you have little or no control over their actions that affect you. Their behavior, which you must bear with, will influence how well you perform. The same goes for the behavior of the eleven players on the opposing team. Their actions create your passivities, since, by the members of the opposing team, you may be tackled, blocked, pushed aside, guarded, or fouled. You are forced to endure (passivities) whatever they do to you and to your teammates. By the same token, the ways your activities affect the twenty-one other players form their passivities.

When your team coordinates its activities and passivities well and is successful, you might call it a system of activities and passivities of *growth*. When your team loses its effective coordination and loses the ball — or the game — it is experienced as a *diminishment*.

If you begin to get a bit confused by some of these examples, that's because activities and passivities are all intertwined, since we are all connected to each other. But let's start simply.

Spiritual Exercise: My Activities

Ω On a blank piece of paper, make a list of some typical activities you carry out that are *activities of growth*, that is, that help you become a better human being, more aware of the divine milieu, and more involved in shaping the Body of Christ.

Below that, make a list of your activities that are *activities of diminishment*, that is, that make you less a human, that harm your relationships, that diminish the Body of Christ. These might include wasting your talents, preventing others from developing theirs, being cynical about the possibility of improvement or progress.

Life is constantly changing. At any time, you are either evolving or devolving. To not do something constructive you could easily do is tantamount to devolving.

But whatever you do or fail to do, you are still unconditionally loved and held preciously in the divine milieu.

===

Spiritual Exercise: My Passivities _____

Ω Divide a blank piece of paper into four sections. Label them Internal Passivities of Growth, External Passivities of Growth, Internal Passivities of Diminishment, and External Passivities of Diminishment. Fill in each of the sections with a list of things that are your passivities. Find at least five or more items for each section. (A sample of this exercise is given below.)

You may end this exercise with a word of gratitude, knowing that the divine milieu had bestowed on you all your passivities of growth and can transform all your passivities of diminishment.

===

A Sample of the Spiritual Exercise: My Passivities

For example, in the spiritual exercise "My Passivities" under "Internal Passivities of Growth" (the first quadrant), I might list:

- strong body
- good digestion
- optimistic
- patient
- good disposition
- mechanical abilities
- sociable

- musical
- well organized
- lover of nature

Under "External Passivities of Growth" (the second quadrant), I might list:

- born in the United States
- born into a loyal and compassionate family
- born into a family with strong faith in God
- born into a family that loves fun, education, get-togethers,
- live in a community with a great library
- had stimulating teachers in school
- was well liked by schoolmates
- have a job I like and great co-workers
- could afford a college education

Under "Internal Passivities of Diminishment" (the third quadrant), I might list:

- susceptible to headaches
- have allergies
- weak in language skills
- addicted to buying clothes, especially shoes
- am impatient
- tend to be critical
- need to do things perfectly
- have a sharp tongue

Under "External Passivities of Diminishment" (the fourth quadrant), I might list:

- my father is a perfectionist to a fault
- my mother is always concerned about what the neighbors might say
- I am a middle child, often forgotten
- three of us have to share one room
- the room is always cluttered
- our house is always noisy
- we live in a neighborhood full of prejudice
- my job has no great future
- a dozen other people are applying for the job I'd like

Importance of Conscious Recognition

Everyone's life is made up of activities and passivities. Teilhard says there is a way to use any and all activities and passivities to help build the Body of Christ. But we can't use them constructively if we are unaware of them. Thus, the importance of consciously listing as many of them as we can. Whenever you think of another item to add to one of your lists, do so. Each item adds to your awareness of yourself. It raises your consciousness.

A Note

Opening Observations in Note

On the first page of Part One of *The Divine Milieu*, introducing the theme of the divinization or sanctification of our human activities, Teilhard makes a number of observations.

He begins with a note, in which he makes two points:

First, he reminds the reader that *he is using the word "activity" in its normal, everyday sense*, the way a psychologist, not a theologian, might use the word. He is not writing a theological essay about divine grace, nor is he denying the continuous mysterious interaction between inspirations of grace and human will. In these pages, he's just talking about normal human activities and actions as we experience and observe them.

Second, to underline his first point, he wants to affirm that *there is nothing that happens in the divine milieu apart from God,* not even those ordinary activities like brushing teeth, combing hair, and eating breakfast. God's grace fills everything and everyone. By this comment Teilhard wanted to assure the reader (really, the Vatican officials that would read and censor his book) he is not spouting the heresy of Pelagianism.

The Heresy Teilhard Avoids

Pelagianism, which first arose in the fifth century, taught a doctrine of spiritual self-reliance and growth that didn't require God's grace, the sacramental system, or the mutual support of a community of believers. Each person, technically speaking, according to Pelagius, could go it alone, grow spiritually by himself. The theologian Pelagius phrased his doctrine as "Man, created free, is with his whole sphere independent of God and the Church, the Living Body of Christ — though Christ, the Church, and sacraments mightily teach and help." In other words, for Pelagius, a person in and of himself has the capacity to seek God apart from any movement of God's Word or the Holy Spirit. Pelagius taught that *without* God's grace and with the use of his free will alone a person could achieve spiritual advancement. This kind of self-reliance, says Teilhard, would instantly ruin the beauty of the divine milieu and its underlying grace-filled evolutionary thrust. Divine grace is inescapable; the Creator designed creation so that grace would fill every particle of it.

With this apology made, Teilhard jumps into the issue of human activity.

Some Observations about Human Activity

1. First, he notes that *people generally value their activities more than their passivities.* We are willing to put more time, effort, money, enthusiasm, and concentration into developing our activities. This insight,

perhaps, may seem obvious, but Teilhard wants to underline it, since it alludes to a fundamental law of spirit: *Energy follows attention.* In other words, you are most likely to put your effort and enthusiasm into activities that capture your attention and interest. Think about that law for a moment, as it is central to your life and the success of your endeavors.

Spiritual Exercise: Energy Follows Attention _____

Ω   To test the truth of this first observation, make one list of those activities you do that most hold your attention when you are doing them. For each item on your list, consider whether it is an activity in which you are willing to put more time, money, enthusiasm, and concentration.

Then make another list noting your daily activities where you are less attentive or more easily distracted. Consider whether you put into them more or less effort, energy, concentration, and enthusiasm.

2. Second, Teilhard alludes in one sentence to a powerful insight, which seems more paradoxical than obvious. In Teilhard's own words, "When we act, as it seems, with the greatest spontaneity and vigor, we are to some extent led by the things we imagine we are controlling." Teilhard is saying that *what we may think of as an activity, especially in areas of life we enjoy, may well be a passivity at a deeper level.*

Let me give an example. Suppose I desire to earn a graduate degree in science at the university. I make the choice to enroll and begin the process. These actions feel like my activities. I imagine I am in control of this entire process, but in effect once I chose to enroll (activity) I am being led by my choice (passivity). What seem like my activities — I sign up for this course and buy the course textbook — are in effect passivities because they are being driven by the university. The university *requires me* (a passivity, something I must endure) to take this course if I want the science degree, and the professor *requires me* (a passivity, something I must endure) to buy this particular textbook if

I want to succeed in his classroom. Teilhard wants you to realize that often, when we think we are doing an activity, it may also be viewed as a passivity.

More generally, by setting up any desirable goal to pursue, you automatically set up a world full of passivities that you must undergo, bear with, or suffer through. A woman who chooses to have a baby (activity) soon becomes controlled by that choice and must endure restrictions on her diet and her activities, and is likely to have to endure some discomfort throughout her pregnancy and delivery (passivities).

People who chose to be leaders in an organization (activity) must endure learning many skills that are demanded by that position (passivities). For example, they must develop their mind and memory in new ways, they must develop self-discipline, they must develop organizational skills, social skills, tact, time-management skills, etc. They may delight in the learning or find it sheer drudgery; in either case it is something that must be done (passivity).

Jesus chose to be a nonviolent resister to the religious status quo of his day (activity). As a result, he experienced not only the adulation of the crowds, which he may have enjoyed, but also their misunderstanding, which frustrated him. In any case, whether the experience was welcome or unwelcome, he had to experience it (passivities). He had to endure the intellectual debates with the religious leaders, which he may have enjoyed, but he also had to endure their taunts and ultimately his death at their hands, which he certainly did not enjoy. In either case, all of these experiences were passivities.

Spiritual Exercise: Primary and Secondary Choices

Ω Note on paper a few of the major choices you have made in your life. Take each choice one by one. Your primary choice to do each thing, we assume, was an activity. Now, beside each choice, list some of the secondary choices you had to make or things you had to perform or endure (passivities) that were required by your primary choice.

We may be able to separate activities and passivities mentally, but they can't be separated in real life. Nor can passivities be avoided in any ongoing development or pursuit of a goal. We have a constant need to manage our activities but also and more importantly to manage our passivities. Remember, we cannot control our passivities, but we can hope to manage them as we endure them.

This paradox — where certain activities generate many passivities — has a much deeper meaning and leads to Teilhard's next observation.

3. Third, Teilhard believes that when we find ourselves wanting to accomplish something with our lives, to do something significant, to make a difference in the world, *that very desire is written into our being.* It was wired into our psyche by God. It is also the fundamental law driving evolution at every level of being — to continually develop, to improve, and to evolve. It is the law of attraction-connection-complexity-consciousness at work in us. Thus, whenever we work to improve our health, our minds, our choices, our jobs, our training, or our family, we are simply acting in obedience to a higher will implanted in us — and in all of creation — by the Creator.

During his Jesuit training, Teilhard would often have heard quoted the saying of the Jesuit saint Aloysius Gonzaga, *Ad altiora nati sumus,* which means, "We were born for higher things."

Since this inner drive to continue developing and improving, so central to all life, is already inside us, it is an *internal passivity of growth.*

Upon observation, you can see that some people are unaware of this higher will written into our very being, and others deny it. Still others, who may have felt it at one time, have given up on wanting to make a contribution to the world and have settled for having no purpose in life other than to sit on a couch in front of a television set, eat, and be entertained. Still others have redirected — distorted — this drive to develop and improve themselves for the purpose of a selfish and greedy acquisition of wealth and power.

Therefore, for Teilhard's spirituality, it is very important that you become conscious of this hard-wired inner drive, know your capacities, and direct them so that they can become divinized, that is, they can be used to foster the development of the Body of Christ.

Jesuit founder Ignatius Loyola was fond of telling his men always to strive to do something *magis*, a Latin expression meaning "greater" or "better." One might imagine that Ignatius was the originator of "continual quality improvement." "Every process you do," Ignatius might have said to his men, "especially since you're doing it for the greater glory of God, ought to be done each time with improved quality [*magis*], better than the last time."

Spiritual Exercise: Personal Desires

Ω To get in touch with and acknowledge this inner drive for personal development and improvement of things, begin a list of desires you have had that would make a difference in the world and improve your own mind and consciousness. Start with desires to do something with your life that you currently feel (if you are a young person) or may have felt in your youth. These early aspirations you felt may have seemed unrealizable to the adults around you, but to you at the time they seemed something you truly wanted to make happen.

Sample of the Spiritual Exercise: Personal Desires

For example:

When I was a child,

- I wanted to become a policeman or fire fighter to protect people.
- I saw a poor beggar and asked my mother if we could help him.
- I brought home stray animals to care for.
- I wanted to grow up to be like my grandfather, whom everyone loved.

- I wished I could fix Mr. Montgomery's car that was always breaking down.

- I wanted to be an altar server at church.

- I wished I could make my mother's headaches go away because they made her suffer.

- I dreamed of designing and building a house in the country for my mother.

When I was in college,

- I wanted to make a scientific breakthrough in biology.

- I wanted to meet a wonderful girl, get married, and raise a family.

- I wanted to get a job where I could really use my talents.

- I dreamed of providing all sorts of things for my family.

- I joined a political action group in college, wanting to make a difference in politics in our city.

All these positive wants and desires, Teilhard would say, are wired into our hearts and souls by God and nourished by the divine milieu. They wait there for us to make choices and take action based on them. God leaves us free to feel these desires and say yes to them, choose to pursue certain ones from among them, or dismiss them.

Everyone Bound by the Law of Activities and Passivities

The main reason Teilhard wants us to become aware of this dynamic between activities and passivities is that *the entire divine milieu — even God the Creator — is subject to the laws of activities and especially passivities.*

As Teilhard points out later in his book, God has chosen a goal or purpose for his creation, namely, the development of the vast Body of Christ to its fullest level of attraction, connection, complexity, and consciousness. This is God's *desire.* Then by the laws of activity and passivity, all of creation's responses become the Total Christ's passivities of growth and/or diminishment. If God wants his ultimate desire to be realized, God must allow the Body of Christ to endure many things. For the many people who "get" God's message, understand it and put it into practice, there are many more who don't. While many feel these inbuilt desires and set goals for themselves, only some are in a position to achieve those goals. There are many more who, perhaps because of a lack of talent, opportunity, or financial resources, don't succeed.

Then again, suppose there is a position open in an organization and one hundred people applying for it. Only one applicant will get it (a passivity of growth). The others, even though they want the position, don't. The other ninety-nine experience a form of loss, disappointment, or failure (passivities of diminishment). Some may lose self-esteem or self-confidence because they were not chosen. Others may construe the event as a rejection, a setback, a penalty, a punishment, a limitation, or a constriction.

The fact, as Teilhard realizes it, is that there *cannot* be an evolving universe without pain, suffering, loneliness, failure, destruction, and death — internal and external passivities of diminishment. Yet the desire to have meaning and purpose and to make a difference in the world remains wired into the very fiber of our being. This built-in desire to develop ourselves is what urges the person who has been knocked down by life to get up and try again, or try something different.

But what is the Total Christ to do with all the people who have not succeeded, who have not been able to make their mark, the ninety-nine people who did not get the job — all these passivities of diminishment? Christ in his Cosmic Body experiences their passivities, too. In that sense, they are divine passivities as well as human ones.

The Responsibility for Caring

Whenever we bring something into the world — into our own world or the world of others — we assume a certain responsibility for doing so. When you bring a child into the world, you assume a responsibility for caring for it until it can manage on its own; but even after that you still feel responsible for the effects your child is having on others. If you bring a pet home to live with your family, you are assuming responsibility for that animal, its care, health, and welfare. In this same way, God has assumed responsibility for his creation and what it does.

To clarify the word "responsibility," it is important to note that it does not mean that you have complete control over what your child or pet may do. That is impossible. Your child may choose to do something self-destructive or your pet may decide to urinate on your sofa. You have control only over what *you* do or how you respond. To be responsible means that you respond appropriately to any unwelcome passivity. Thus, you may have to help your child manage his or her life better, or you may have to properly train your pet to manage its behavior.

How does God respond to all these passivities of diminishment happening to his creation — failure, rejection, poverty, disease, pollution, natural disasters, racism, unemployment, etc. — in light of God's desire concerning his goal for the divine milieu?

Because God's name is LOVE, says Teilhard, God endures them with compassion, and forgiveness. In an evolving universe, not even God can have full control over the passivities that God and each of us must endure. Like us, God can only *manage*, not control, the losses, failures, rejections, and disappointments; God manages those diminishments by outpourings of grace, compassion and forgiveness.

The suffering produced by all these passivities of diminishment is perhaps one reason why God has such a preferential love for the poor, the sick, the lonely, the victims, the marginalized, and the outcasts — those who must constantly endure internal and external passivities of diminishment. This is the domain of salvation that Christ talked about in the Beatitudes, the "good news" of the gospel. The good news is that all of those who endure internal and external passivities of diminishment can expect to receive salvation. God's infinite love will wipe away every tear. This is the only way God can fully achieve his goal for the Body of Christ — to save everything that was lost. "I have not come to save the righteous but sinners."

How Are Human Actions Divinized?

Before he begins subsection 1, Teilhard invites us to look, with him, at our ordinary activities and try to see how "God presses in upon us and seeks to enter our lives." God enters us through our activities and by developing them to the full. In other words, we want to find out how our human actions can be divinized and sanctified.

1. The Undoubted Existence of the Fact and the Difficulty of Explaining It. The Christian Problem of the Sanctification of Action

Teilhard notes that scripture teaches us of the theological "fact" that human activities can be sanctified, and Christian tradition has always believed that we can do everything we do, as St. Paul says, "in the name of our Lord Jesus Christ" or, simply, "in Christ."

In various places in his letters, Paul uses verbs like "work *with*," "suffer *with*," "die *with*," and "be resurrected *with*" Christ. In their Latin and Greek forms, the preposition "with" is embedded in each of the verb forms, so they might more accurately be translated as we "co-work," "co-suffer," "co-die," and "are co-resurrected" with Christ. Throughout the centuries, Christians have always understood this life in common with Christ as something literal, not just a metaphor. Christ is a real presence who is with us, in us, and in whom we live and act.

Nor is Teilhard talking here simply about religious and devotional activities like prayer, fasting, and almsgiving. He is talking about "the whole of human life, down to its most 'natural' zones." "Whether you eat or drink..." says St. Paul. Every action of your life can be divinized! Every action can be "co-enacted" with Christ.

The Mystery "in Christ"

The Pauline "mystery," a word that occurs again and again in Paul's letters, refers to God's plan to save all humans without distinction of race by identifying them all with his Son in the unity of the Cosmic Body. St. Paul expresses this mystery in various ways, calling the church the "Body of Christ," the faithful the "members of Christ," and Christ himself our "head."

One of his most common expressions of the mystery of divine incorporation is the simple prepositional phrase "in Christ," which occurs 164 times in Paul's canonical epistles.

A Problem Arises for the Seekers

However, Teilhard asks, if we really believed in God's offer of eternal happiness in a life after this short and temporary one, why would we want to carry out our human duties freely, wholeheartedly, and with determination? The material world, we have been taught, is but "vanity and ashes." Spiritual perfection, we were told, consists in detachment from the world around us.

However, says Teilhard, the "problem" or conflict arises when St. Paul encourages Christians to be "an example to the Gentiles" in devotion to duty, in energy, and even in leadership in all the spheres opened up to human activity.

Such energetic people devoted to their worldly jobs are the ones who experience this "spiritual dualism." On the one hand, they feel a love for life, the earth, and the joys of learning and creating in science and art. On the other hand, they want to love God with all their hearts. It seems like an either/or kind of option. Either love God or love the world. The unspoken assumption is that you can't love both.

If those who live life with intensity and passion accept this assumption, says Teilhard, they seem to have only three choices. First, they will either repress their taste for human accomplishments and confine their attention to purely religious activities. Or, second, they will dismiss their religious demands and decide to live a life of completely humanistic values. Third, some will simply give up any attempt to make sense of the two pulls on their love and devotion; they will swing now toward the spiritual life, now toward the secular life.

None of these three solutions is truly satisfying, so Teilhard suggests a fourth way, which reconciles the love of God and a healthy love of the world, that is both "a striving toward detachment and a striving toward the enrichment of our human lives."

There are two stages to this fourth way, an incomplete solution and a more complete one.

2. An Incomplete Solution: Human Action Has No Value Other Than the Intention Which Directs It

Purity of Intention Essential

Teilhard describes the incomplete solution as if it were the advice of a traditional spiritual director talking to you. Basically, the traditional spiritual director tells you that though your human activity has no definite value or direct importance for heaven, you can sanctify your activity by *purity of intention*. You may offer up the works and sufferings of your day in union with Christ. Even though your works and sufferings have no value in themselves in light of eternity, the spiritual director says, you can do them with love "for the opportunity they give you of proving your faithfulness to God."

Teilhard agrees that *having good intentions is a necessary start and an essential foundation of everything we do*. It is the key that unlocks our inner world to God's presence.

However, while the divinization of our activities by good intention puts our *soul* into our actions, Teilhard says, "it does not confer the hope of resurrection upon our bodies." How can our joy at the things we accomplish — our achievements, the beautiful things that are the works of our hands, what we bring into being — be complete unless they are somehow made sacred and saved? Here Teilhard is thinking about the books he has written, the research he has done, the scientific discoveries he has made, but also the beautiful natural world around him — those things that have been for him *external passivities of growth.* Will they not be part of the Cosmic Christ? Teilhard wants to find a way — a spirituality — in which all these earthly things will be divinized in Christ.

Teilhard wants to see if you are feeling this same longing that he feels — the desire that your achievements and the works of your hands be divinized in Christ.

Spiritual Exercise: What to Take with You _____

Ω Begin by making a list of the things you wish could be divinized in Christ. Start with about ten things you would like to take with you to eternal life with Christ. Leave plenty of room to add other items as they occur to you. Hint: begin with some things you loved in childhood. Don't forget to list your accomplishments that you would like to take with you — even the most insignificant of them.

Thank God that you live in a benevolent universe, and that every good moment of your life — even your dreams and desires — is held in the love of the divine milieu and will never be lost.

___

Example of the Spiritual Exercise: What to Take with You

Here are some things a friend listed that he wanted to take with him into eternal life in Christ:

- Whiskers, my childhood dog
- The apple tree in our front yard
- The creek out back
- Some of my favorite doodles
- The ribbon I won in a spelling bee in eighth grade
- My first ice skates
- My wine glasses collected from all over the world
- The sketch of my dream house that I never built
- A box of photos of my children at different ages
- The tools my dad and I used to build a back porch on our home
- All the sand at the beaches where I did sunbathing
- The sun itself
- Those steaks I barbequed to perfection outdoors last summer
- Mom's scalloped potatoes
- The sweater Aunt Mayme knitted for me
- And all kinds of food that brought me joy and comfort

Teilhard wants you to feel your deep love for many physical, material things in your life, including your accomplishments, so you can understand how powerfully lovable creation truly is, and how God would never have created such a fantastic world if he didn't love his creation passionately. God, Teilhard is certain, wouldn't want to leave physical creation out of the salvation process. In fact, Teilhard feels that *as you lose faith in the value of the results of your personal efforts you lose the power to act.*

A Deep Inner Truth

When Teilhard thinks about how doing this spiritual exercise affected him, he discovered a psychological truth reflected in his own deep inner feelings and prayer. "No one lifts his little finger to do the smallest task unless moved, however obscurely, by the conviction that he is contributing infinitesimally (at least indirectly) to the building of something definitive — that is to say, to your work, my God" (Torchbook, 56).

We long for our work — our accomplishments — to follow us into God's Kingdom. If they didn't, we would feel frustrated. Why should we have struggled to accomplish them in the first place? Why would we even feel compelled to struggle to accomplish them, if God had not implanted that drive in us?

3. The Final Solution: All Endeavor Cooperates to Complete the World "In Christo Jesu"

A Classic Argument

Teilhard introduces his more complete solution in the form of a classic syllogism or argument. He presents a "major" theological statement, which appears obviously and undeniably true.

> *At the heart of our universe each soul exists for God in our Lord.*

This is followed by a "minor" statement that he shows to be true.

> *But all reality, even material reality, around each one of us exists for our souls.*

The conclusion is inevitable.

> *Hence, all sensible reality around each one of us exists, through our souls, for God in our Lord.*

Teilhard uses the word "soul" in this argument — I'm not sure why, perhaps because we traditionally speak of "saving our souls" — but in reality by "soul" he means the whole person, body, mind, and spirit. So to restate his syllogism very simply, we might say:

We humans find our fulfillment in God.
Everything else finds its fulfillment in us.
Hence, everything finds its fulfillment, through us, in God.

Teilhard warns us that though this syllogism may seem easily mentally acceptable, our challenge is to truly believe it and put it into practice. Although Teilhard does not spell out how to do this, we can easily design spiritual exercises to help us do it. Each statement in his syllogism becomes a new subhead in his text.

A. At the heart of our universe, each soul exists for God, in our Lord.

Teilhard assures us this statement is basic Catholic dogma, but what is important to clarify is our understanding of it. Some might interpret it as if God is the owner and we are the things he owns, much as the things you and I own — our pets, our cars, our homes, our clothing — belong to us and exist for us. Teilhard says the relationship between God and us is much more physical and deeper than simple ownership. He notes that St. Paul says our relationship to Christ is more like the way members of a physical body relate to its head, or, in Jesus' images, as branches are related to a vine. A body's arms and legs find their fulfillment in serving the wishes of the body's head; they derive their purpose from what the head wants to accomplish. The branches find their fulfillment in serving the vine; the vine is their life source; the branches hold the grapes that the vine wants to produce.

Many Levels of Systems in Christ

Teilhard points out that these images that describe how we are linked to the Incarnate Word share the idea of elements interacting to form a whole or a total system. The many parts of a human body interact to form a *biological system*, each element instinctually carrying out its proper function in interaction with all the other elements.

A group of humans united for a certain purpose, as in an organization, form a *social system*, each element freely carrying out its proper function in interaction with all the others. For example, all the health care workers in a hospital have come together for the shared purpose of patient care. Each department in the hospital — emergency room, x-ray laboratory, pharmacy, intensive care units, surgery, food service, even administration and billing — each in its own way is helping take care of patients in interaction with all the other departments.

Teilhard says that the union we humans have with Christ has often been called a *mystical union*. But mystical doesn't mean something unreal or imaginary, just something less tangible. In fact, for Teilhard, the mystical union of the members or cells Christ's Body is a *system far richer and more real than any biological system or human social system. It is richer because its characteristics include everything a biological system is, and everything a human social system is* — and more. By virtue of the Incarnation, says Teilhard, our persons individually and collectively are wholly dedicated to God, and are living and centered in the Body of Christ.

Systems Thinking

What Teilhard has left unspoken here is that to begin viewing and understanding the Body of Christ and the divine milieu requires a new mind-set called systems thinking. Many are unfamiliar with this new mind-set.

While some people intuitively grasp systems thinking, *most of us have been trained to think linearly. As a rule, we are also single-event thinkers.* Typical of single-event thinkers, we believe that if something happens, we can find a single cause immediately and directly connected to what happened. Usually, we find someone who is to be praised or blamed for it. For example, suppose a patient in a hospital unit gets the wrong medication. Typically, the nurse's aide dispensing medications on that unit gets blamed for it. The error is "her fault."

Systems thinkers look at an event's cause quite differently. *If something goes wrong, they tend to blame the system and the design of its processes, not the person.* Without a doubt, when the error happened some individual may have turned the wrong dial or pushed the wrong button that produced the mistake. But instead of blaming that person, systems thinkers say, "Something is wrong with the procedure, so let's redesign the process or the machinery involved, so that in the future no one can ever mistake a wrong button for the right button again." In other words, instead of focusing on what a person does or does not do, they *focus on how people and machines can be designed to interact to perform any process in better and better ways.*

Looking at the process involved where the nurse's aide administered the wrong medication, a systems thinker might (1) notice that many patient medication labels on the medication cart are jammed together making it easy for someone to mistake one person's medication for another's, (2) observe that the medications on either side of the proper medication for this patient look very similar to each other and a wrong one could easily be mistaken for the right one, (3) notice that some of the overhead lights in this area of the unit are out, thus hampering the nurse's aide's ability to read the small print on the medications, (4) discover that the nurse's aide is doing hospital work as a second job and that she is usually quite tired having already worked an eight-hour day before starting work in the hospital. The systems thinker, instead of blaming the nurse's aide, might suggest that the medication cart arrangement be redesigned, or that different color stickers be used for each medication, or that similar looking medications be placed in separate areas of the cart, and so on.

To a systems thinker, every human action is really an *interaction.* And a truism among systems thinkers is that a system is not primarily the *sum* of the *actions* of its parts, but rather the *product* of their *interactions.* The nurse's aide's error was probably the product of a number of unfortunate interactions. And unless the process is improved, the same mistake is bound to happen again.

Interactivities and Interpassivities

So if we were to challenge Teilhard about dividing human experiences into activities and passivities, he would have to admit that, as a systems thinker, which he was, the division would have to be between *interactivities* and *interpassivities*.

There is no action we can do that is not an *inter*action. You might object and say, "I'm breathing. That's an action that is not an interaction." But think about it for a moment. For certain, within your own organism's system, every act of inhaling or exhaling requires the exquisite interaction of hundreds of parts (organs, cells, muscles, nerves, etc.) of your body. Furthermore, each time you exhale, scientists tell us you exhale as many as 10^{23} particles from your body into the atmosphere, so you are certainly interacting with the atmosphere. By the way, 10^{23} stands for the number 10 with 22 zeros after it. Similarly, every time you inhale you inhale about 10^{23} particles from the atmosphere, which might include particles from other people in the room or from plants that exhale oxygen or from whatever particles (dust, germs, gasses, negative ions, charged particles, etc.) happen to be floating around in the room at the moment. Your action of breathing is really an interaction — a very complex one.

Spiritual Exercise: Interactivities and Interpassivities _____

Ω Imagine you are outdoors in a natural setting. In your imagination, watch yourself exhale and inhale. With what you know about the exchange of particles, picture your exhalation being absorbed by the air and the natural things around you. Then, as you inhale, picture the millions of particles in the air that you take in becoming a part of you.

Consider the air that has been circulating around the globe. Today, for example, you are inhaling something that someone exhaled in China two weeks ago. Think of all the other places where people and nature have exhaled particles that you are now breathing in. Too, all the natural things around you — trees, grass, plants, insects — are giving off particles as part of their own living processes; you are taking these in as well.

During a lifetime, you have taken in, in interpassivities, particles from every imaginable thing on earth through breathing, but also through eating and handling things. Stay with this awareness for a while till you realize how totally connected to the planet your body is, i.e., you are.

Be grateful for the benevolent universe that the divine milieu has provided for you.

B. But all reality, even material reality, around each one of us exists for our souls.

For Teilhard, this statement means that even the most nonphysical part of us — our spiritual being — is continually nourished by the energies and resources of the natural, physical world. Sunlight, water, air, vitamins, minerals, metals — all those elements we take in a daily multivitamin and mineral supplement — allow us to remain healthy and alert and allow our spirit to flourish, for without them we would die. If we wish to fully live our religion and our humanity, we need to explore how closely linked we humans are with the earth and its history. Teilhard asserts that we humans are "incorporated" in every part of our planet and its history.

What We Have Inherited during the Evolutionary Journey

We humans may like to think of ourselves as autonomous beings living only in the here and now, but we are indebted for our very being to an inheritance from all the energies of the earth. As a paleontologist, Teilhard sees our humanness (*Homo sapiens*) evolving by a long journey starting from the first living cells that emerged in an unfathomable past. But even if you only look at your own experience here and now, your spirit is "besieged and penetrated" by influences from outside and within. Consider the more obvious influences: food for your body; sensations for your eyes; sounds and voices for your ears; words to read and truths to discover; people who relate to you. Thousands of stimuli enter our consciousness at every moment. Many millions in a lifetime.

Whatever Affects the Body Affects the Soul

Teilhard wants us to think of the role of these sensory stimuli entering us. Whether we are fully conscious of them or let them enter us passively, "they will merge into the most intimate life of our human spirit and either develop it or poison it." Even the most insignificant food is capable of influencing our most spiritual faculties. A glass of wine may raise our spirits, while a bit too much alcohol can dull our mind and senses. A bite of chocolate can delight the heart, while a teaspoon of some food gone bad can lay the body and mind low for days. Imagine what beautiful music or ideas can do. Imagine what cacophony or malicious ideas can do. In Teilhard's words, "Our bodies do not take nourishment independently of our souls. Everything that the body has admitted and has begun to transform must be transfigured by the soul in its turn."

Not Merely Our Bodies

Teilhard wants us to observe that, just as God cannot separate our souls from our bodies (at least as long as we are alive and breathing), neither can God separate our bodies from the rest of the universe. For Teilhard, that is a scientific fact. It's the way God designed creation. Everything in the universe is inextricably intertwined, constantly interacting, and inescapably interdependent.

We don't like to admit the fact that we are conditioned by our culture to be single-event thinkers instead of systems thinkers. Moreover, we usually prefer to think that we are independent, autonomous beings who just happen to be walking on the surface of the earth. We'd like to think that we are not bound by the laws of gravity, the laws of electricity and magnetism, the laws of atomic attraction, or the makeup of our genes. But we are subject to all of these forces at every second of our lives.

We'd like to believe that we could get along quite well without dirt, water, oxygen, vitamins, metals, and minerals. But we can't. We need them all to survive.

We'd like to believe we could get along quite well without birds, fish, and the other animals. But we can't. We need them all to survive. The fact is we carry around in our bodies all these elements of the universe. Each of us sums up the history of the earth. We, body and soul, are inseparable from it.

The Physical World Influences Our Spiritual Life

This insight — that the physical world influences our spiritual life — is at the heart of Teilhard's spirituality. Almost every other spirituality proposed to the seeker today presents the process of spiritual growth as an internal, subjective process, or as a process of interaction solely between the individual and God, as if other people and all the rest of the planet with its air, water, food, trees, sunlight, plant life, animals, and all the rest were incidental to our spiritual growth.

For Teilhard, spirituality is not just about you and God and saving your soul, but about saving the whole Body of Christ, bringing everything in the divine milieu to its fulfillment. God wants to save the divine milieu as a whole system with all its interacting and interdependent parts.

You are an essential part of that grand salvation. The way Teilhard invites you to "save your soul" is *to commit yourself to working to further God's plan of saving the whole divine milieu.*

Spiritual Exercise: The History of Your Hand _____

Ω Your hand contains the story of our planet's evolution. You may do this exercise as a contemplation or meditation on your hand. In your imagination, recall the evolutionary history of our planet. In its first stages, the planet Earth was a fiery molten ball of metals and gases. Some of those same metals and gases are essential to the bones and blood in your hand today. Your daily vitamin and mineral bottle lists some of those metals essential to your life—iron, copper, zinc, manganese, etc.

When, eons later, Earth cooled and formed its crust, many of the common minerals were formed. They are in your hand too — calcium, magnesium, etc.

Eventually, Earth formed a nourishing layer of water around its surface. Your entire body, including your hand, is at least 80 percent water.

Next, Earth formed its protective atmosphere using various forms of oxygen. The blood in your hand carries oxygen to nourish all the cells in your hand and carries off all the carbon dioxide you do not need, but plants and trees do.

Next, Earth gave birth to microscopic life forms. Your body is filled with independent microscopic life forms such as germs, viruses, microbes, many of which live on your hand's skin and inside it.

And then Earth gave birth to thought; whenever you want to express some thought or feeling you may use your hand, perhaps to type a letter or to cook a meal or to shake someone's hand in greeting.

Finally, Earth gave birth to spirituality. Your hand expresses the feelings of your spirit, as when you bless someone, hold their face so you can kiss them, or grasp the Eucharistic bread.

The entire history of the planet Earth is played out every day in your hand. Teilhard does not want you to take your wonderful hand for granted. Earth has worked its process for almost four billion years of evolution to create that hand of yours. It reveals and retells its whole story in your hand. Treasure that story as you treasure your hand.

═══

It is also true that that same story of earth's creation and evolution was also revealed in the physical hands of Jesus of Nazareth. Earth worked its process for almost four billion years of evolution to create that hand that Jesus used to bless and heal. Thus, the Incarnation means not merely that the Word of God took human flesh, but also that he incarnated into the entire planet — air, water, bacterial and viral life, vitamins, metals, and minerals. By taking food and drink, he assimilated into his sacred body fruits, vegetables, grains, fish, meats, and poultry. He assumed it all, physical and spiritual.

Summary of This Section

In the last few paragraphs, Teilhard summarizes the points he has been making in this second section, subheaded *"But all reality, even material reality, around each one of us exists for our souls."*

First, some masters of the spiritual life claim that God wants only souls. But Teilhard reminds us that *the human soul "is inseparable in its birth and in its growth from the universe in which it is born."* In a philosophical discussion, Teilhard observes, you might be able to mentally or conceptually distinguish the human soul from its body, but in reality you can't separate the physical and spiritual. All of your soul's experience has come to it through your body. All of Jesus' human soul's earthly experience came to it through his body.

Furthermore, we now know, which Teilhard didn't, that your physical body — not only cells in your brain but also cells throughout your body — records and remembers all those experiences that have passed through it. Even those experiences that you might label purely mental, like your wishes, fantasies, imaginings, and inner dialogue, are being processed through your physical brain cells. In other words, you couldn't be you without your body. Furthermore, your body makes you uniquely you. Even Jesus' most spiritual experiences and divine insights had to be processed through his brain cells and would be held in memory in his hypothalamus.

Second, *"In each soul, God loves and partly saves the whole world which that soul sums up in an incommunicable and particular way."* This is a theologically complicated statement. Let me take it apart. Christians agree that God saves the world through the Savior, Christ the Lord. But all persons, Christian or not — each separately and together — are integral parts of the Savior's Total Body. We are all living in the divine milieu, and God wants no part of his creation to be lost or forgotten, for God loves all of it with a passionate love.

So at the end of time, in a very real sense only one Person will be "saved," only one Person is resurrected, only one Person ascends to heaven, and that Person is the Cosmic Christ. Each of us will enjoy that salvation because we are integral parts of the Body of the Cosmic Christ. For Teilhard, that is how God "saves the whole world."

But the choice to be saved — that is, to be an integral part of the Cosmic Christ — happens by "his choice and ours." Christ certainly wants you as part of his Body. He has made his choice clear in that matter. But you, since you have free will, can make your choice to cooperate in that salvation process as well.

God saves the world through Christ — the Cosmic Christ. That means that you and I, since we are integral members of that Cosmic Body, contribute in some small way to that salvation. Each of us in some unique way adds a small but important measure to the completion of the Cosmic Christ. Each of us is called upon to accomplish something that no one else can do, just as each cell, organ, bone, and limb in our physical body contributes something unique to our personal development. In other words, each person sums up and helps account for some small part of that larger salvation process. We contribute by our *activities of growth*.

It is important to remember that we can also hinder that small part of the great salvation process by our *activities of diminishment*. So what we do or don't do is important, since it can affect that special part of creation whose salvation we can uniquely influence during our life. In this way, we each "partly save the whole world."

Third, however, this "summing up" is not given to us ready-made and complete from birth. *Our souls must develop and be shaped over time.* Each of us, through our activities, works to assemble all those elements that enter our soul or influence it. In other words, each one of us *makes* our own soul, and we need each day of our whole lifetime in order to do it. Using all the "widely scattered" experiences and interactions of our years, we weave or build a single soul. This is the area of our responsibility, the area of spirituality and spiritual practice. (Here some readers may spontaneously think of the thousands of children or babies who die without ever growing up. How are their souls shaped over time? That is a mystery Teilhard doesn't mention in this book, perhaps because he is writing for adult seekers. I don't have any easy answers either.)

Fourth, Teilhard's spirituality is not merely one of docile obedience — people doing or avoiding what they are told or commanded to — but also one where *people consciously choose to create and build their own souls using all the elements of the earth available to them.* For Teilhard, life is so much more than keeping the commandments. Life is about "building our souls." This offers us a limitless horizon with limitless opportunities to choose from.

Fifth, at the same time as we are building our individual souls, each of us collaborates in another work, which needs, yet infinitely transcends, our individual achievement: *the completing of the world.* This is the Christ work, bringing the earth and humanity to its fullest maturity, what Teilhard calls the Omega Project. (If Teilhard were to estimate the current maturity of humanity, he might categorize it as in its teen years.) Bringing the earth to its maturity and completing it is the work of the entire Body of Christ, not merely of Christians. This is the great work that is happening in the divine milieu. Most people are unaware of this great work. We are privileged to be aware of it and to realize how each of us can contribute to it.

For Teilhard, this privilege makes life a wonderful adventure, no matter how limited or diminished one might feel in human terms. Even the person who is chronically ill or bedridden has something important to contribute to Christ's fullness. Even persons in prison may use their time for self-development or giving comfort to others or sharing hope in God. Each person can always further the development of the Cosmic Christ, since everyone is in the divine milieu.

Sixth, Teilhard points out that the "completing of the world" happens only over great periods of time. *Successive generations of "souls" are needed to complete this work.* Thus, beneath our individual and collective efforts to give spiritual form into our own lives, and because of these efforts, the larger world is changing and developing its own spiritual form, taking shape, and becoming more and more the Body of Christ.

Some people have a hard time imagining themselves as both individuals and part of the Body of Christ. But anyone who has been part of a large organization is well aware of this twofold experience.

Spiritual Exercise:
Personal Aims, Organizational Aims _____

Ω Imagine you work for a large organization in a service industry. It might be an educational organization, a healthcare organization, or a governmental organization. The organization is made up of many, many people each of whom has his or her own ideals, values, wants, and needs, and is striving to fulfill them.

On the other hand, the organization has its own larger aim or purpose, to which each of the employees is expected to be committed. In a hospital, this aim might be "perfect patient care," or in a school "maximum intellectual development." The organization can fully succeed in its mission only if every employee agrees to pursue that larger aim in his or her department. If there is a right fit between the organization and an individual employee, then pursuing the organizational aim and pursuing one's individual aims should support and reinforce each other. In other words, I can become the best I can be as an individual by being committed to the shared aim of my organization. In contrast, if the organization I work for is a hospital whose aim is "perfect patient care," and my aim in life is to make as much money as possible and have a fun-filled life, my individual aims would not be a good fit with the aim of the hospital.

In this exercise, you are to picture the organization you work for as the Body of Christ. Your task is to examine your personal aims, ideals, dreams, wants, etc., for your life and see how well or poorly they fit with the aim or purpose of the Body of Christ. Do your activities simultaneously promote your growth as well as the growth of the Body of Christ?

We can now bring together the major and minor of Teilhard's syllogism so as to grasp the link between them and the conclusion.

C. Hence, all sensible reality around each one of us exists, through our souls, for God in our Lord.

This is the logical conclusion to Teilhard's syllogism. He argues that if the first two statements are true, this conclusion must also be true. All creation comes to God through us who live in the Cosmic Christ. It is really a stunning conclusion. If we accept that all things in creation exist for us and we for God, then all things in creation exist for God and God's purpose. It follows that all of creation must belong to the Body of Christ. And Christ is all bound up in it.

From the first moment of creation to the last, in the evolutionary process that activates and directs all the elements of the universe, *everything forms a single whole* — a single, immense system. You may picture Christ as its center, its head, its heart — its leader. Choose whatever image you want to use. In the Body of Christ, all of reality finds its ultimate purpose. All of physical creation and all of the phys-ical forces acting around us and upon us are given spiritual meaning, first in our human souls and selves, and again with our souls in the Body of Christ.

This kind of multilevel meaning happens in many spheres, For example, first, all the billions of cells in your body are given func-tional meaning and definition for the kinds of cells they are and for the particular work they do in the muscles, bones, veins, or organs where they operate. Second, they are also given a higher meaning insofar as they are parts of you as a living, thinking, spiritual person.

Collaboration with Christ

Here Teilhard picks up again the theme of collaboration — the shared commitment we have with Christ — that will lead to the fullest maturity and developmental completeness of the Body of Christ.

Teilhard reminds us that we like to think that creation was com-pleted long ago, but it would be quite wrong to think so. For in us and in the Body of Christ creation continues evolving and developing toward its ultimate purpose today "more magnificently than ever." And we serve to complete it and bring it one small step closer to its maturity even by the humblest work of our hands. We do this by bringing back to God that part of the Christ Being, which God desires, in whatever we do. We each bring to Christ some little fulfillment.

Spiritual Exercise: Some Little Part

Ω Just as the individuals in the organization by their personal work bring to the organization some little part of its great fulfillment, so you and I by what we do can bring the Christ Being some little part of its fulfillment. Just as you might come home after work and tell your spouse or your family what you accomplished at work today, in a similar manner you may begin to tell God in prayer what you accomplished today that furthered the work of the Christ Body.

Just as you might be proud of how you contributed to your human organization, you could learn to be proud of how you contributed to the Christ Body. It is important to learn to think of yourself — and picture yourself — as furthering the ongoing creation and maturation of the Christ Body. Thank God for being able to contribute to the building of the Body of Christ.

4. Communion through Action

Teilhard poses the question, How can we see God in all the active parts of our lives? He answers that we could not find a more fitting setting for this "seeing" than in our activities. Here is the way things work in the divine milieu.

Teilhard writes, "In action I adhere to the creative power of God; I coincide with it; I become not only its instrument but its living extension."

In my action, those things I do of my own free will, I merge through my heart and my intention with the very heart and intention of God.

This merging never stops; it is continuous since I am always acting. Teilhard reinforced this insight, saying, "God is inexhaustibly attainable in the *totality* of our action." Not a single activity of mine happens outside the divine milieu, so God's activity and my activity are always merging. I can be taking a shower, reading the morning newspaper, walking the dog, watering the lawn, preparing a meal, making a shopping list, sorting laundry, phoning a friend, putting gas in my car, shopping for groceries, picking up the children from school, helping them with their homework, telling jokes at a party, playing games with my children, planning a picnic, putting out the lights before bed. Whatever I'm doing, I can connect with God in that action.

Once I realize this, I can act in all my human endeavors — in even the simplest and seemingly most inconsequential actions — with fervor and fidelity. I can take my shower with fervor, laughing and singing. I can read the morning paper with fidelity, scanning for signs of goodness and growth in the world and being grateful for them. I can also laugh with gusto at the comics. I can walk the dog talking to him and telling him what a wonderful world God made to have put pets in it. I can water the lawn with a child's delight. And so on.

There is no end or limit to the intensity and depth of my commitment to the work of the Christ Body. It can always be continually improved, continually deepened, continually intensified. I can prepare meals with new touches of flavor and love. I can carry out shopping not simply as something that has to be done, but as a chance to smile at other shoppers, affirm salespersons, and say something nice about the cashier at the checkout. I can show deeper interest in the children when I pick them up. In whatever I do, I can be deepening my commitment to building a better society.

All of this is achieved in the divine milieu — subtly, gently, sweetly — without ever disturbing or deflecting my effort and my aims. No more than the air that surrounds me disturbs or deflects my activity, effort, or aims.

Spiritual Exercise: Merging with God _____

Ω   As you are about to begin some activity—driving your car, preparing a meal, starting your computer, doing homework, turning on the television, going for a walk, eating a snack, whatever—picture your activity immersed in the divine milieu, which is energizing your body as well as nurturing each cell in your body to do precisely what you are about to do. You are acting in the divine milieu, through the divine milieu, and with the divine milieu.

Practice this merging until it becomes habitual.

---

5. The Christian Perfection of Human Endeavor

Notice how the adjectives in this title seem to upset the thinking in traditional spirituality. It would be easier to grasp if the title were "the Christian perfection of Christian endeavor," or "the human perfection of human endeavor." But Teilhard is focused on the *Christian* perfection of *human* endeavor, an apparent paradox in spirituality traditions.

After explaining the significance of this section, Teilhard deals with this paradoxical expression in two stages, showing the essential connections between Christian perfection and human activity. First, he shows how the most mundane human activity can be sanctified. Second, he shows how the most sacred Christian activity can be humanized.

God and the World Are Knit Together through Action

For many centuries, people wishing to be truly Christian were told to leave the world and its pursuits. As a result, religious and monastic orders multiplied. Living life as a priest, monk, or nun was considered a higher form of Christian life than living as a layperson. Human activity was considered a distraction from the Christian life.

In the previous section, Teilhard showed how this cannot be so, since in the domain of action God and the world are knitted together. God presents himself to us as attainable through our every human activity. "The closeness of our union with him is in fact determined by the exact fulfillment of the least of our tasks." God awaits us at every instant in all of our activities, in the work of each moment.

Teilhard says we should become so at one with this basic truth till it becomes as familiar to us as the shape of our room or words on a page. So it calls for a spiritual exercise that we can practice again and again.

Spiritual Exercise: God Awaits You at Every Instant _____

Ω You may be used to picturing God as a person you can see and hear. In this exercise, try to "sense" God as an invisible yet very palpable presence like a gentle breeze. Practice sensing God's presence in this way as coinciding lovingly with your every activity—without interfering in it, just as a breeze would be present to your every activity without interfering with it.

For example, when you pick up your pen to write a note, sense God at the tip of your finger, at the tip of your pen and waiting in the paper. When you sit down at your computer to send an e-mail, practice visualizing God awaiting you in the buttons on the keyboard, in your fingertips as they type, and in every one of the sites listed on your computer address book. When you take a bite of food, practice visualizing God at the tines of your fork as well as waiting on your tongue.

You can practice this exercise all day long. God is waiting on the buttons of your TV remote, on the car keys in your pocket or purse, on your car's steering wheel, on the knob of your front door, on the zippers of your clothing, on each card and piece of money in your wallet, on the touch buttons on your telephone, in the music imprinted on a CD, in the water that flows from your faucet, in the microwaves that heat your supper, in every hair on your head as you run a comb through it, in the wine as you lift the glass to your lips for a sip.

Practice this till you are continually aware of God's loving and life-giving presence.

From time to time, express a word of thanks to the God who created such a benevolent world.

As a child, you may have been told that God is watching you at every moment, ready to catch you if you happen to do something wrong. In contrast, Teilhard would have you delight in the loving God who delights in his creation, ready to welcome your every action and join with it. Rather than worry about avoiding sin, Teilhard's spirituality asks you to focus your attention each day on what you can do for the Body of Christ. At every moment of today, you can choose to promote the development of the Body of Christ as you develop yourself.

Spiritual Exercise: A Fundamental Choice

Ω Instead of focusing on what can go wrong today — for it will — start off your day by making a fundamental choice like:

   • *I choose to be an instrument of God's work in the world today.*

This is an affirmation you can make each day of your life, no matter how talented or untalented you may be, no matter how healthy or handicapped you may be.

Sur-Animation

"Sur-animation" is the word Teilhard coined to explain how, because we are living in the divine milieu, God gives higher life and meaning to all the human actions we perform during our day. In other words, as we struggle to accomplish what we set out to do each day to improve our lives, God is using each of those actions to shape the life of the Body of

Christ. As we are animating our own efforts for our own development, God is sur-animating those same efforts for the development of the Christ Body.

For example, suppose you attend a workshop or take a course to develop your skills for your employment. At the same time as you are applying these new learnings to improve your job skills, God is applying those learnings, through you, so the Body of Christ gains some new capacity.

Whether you develop your skills in communication, time management, stress reduction, playing sports, salesmanship, charm, tact, or persuasiveness, as you animate your personal life with these skills, God is sur-animating the Body of Christ with these skills of yours. In some small way, the Body of Christ learns to communicate a bit better, manage its time better, reduce its stress, and act with more charm, tact, and persuasiveness.

Because you are a cell in the Christ Body, as you begin attending a fitness center or going to a weight-loss clinic to animate your personal life with new energy, vitality, and personal appearance, God is using your effort to sur-animate the Body of Christ by bringing to it more energy, vitality, and attractiveness.

While you are actively trying to stay healthy by keeping your body in shape, developing your mind, and growing ever wiser spiritually, God is actively doing the same for the Cosmic Body of Christ — trying to keep our planet and universe healthy and to develop the mind and spirit of Christ in all living creatures, especially humans, who seem to be the ones that can do the most good — and most harm — to the great Christ Body.

Any activity of growth for you is an activity of growth for the Christ Body. Any activity of diminishment for you is an activity of diminishment for the Christ Body. Whether your action proves to be for growth or diminishment, God is present to it. All of it is happening in the divine milieu. Both you individually and you in the Christ Body are at every moment, inescapably, living in the divine milieu. And because of it God is at work building the Christ Body in and through you, sur-animating your every action.

Sur-animation introduces a higher principle of life and unity into our spiritual life. That higher principle not only makes our human efforts holy (section A below), but also gives our spiritual efforts "the full flavor of humanity" (section B below).

A. The Sanctification of Human Endeavor

Teilhard believes that many deeply serious Christians feel that the time they spend at the office, the factory, the studio, the classroom, or toiling in the fields is time taken away from prayer and adoration. Since, for almost every layperson, it is impossible not to have to work for a living, it also may seem impossible to live a deeply religious life. Holiness, they feel, is reserved for the monks and nuns. All we laypeople have left is a few moments for prayer, and even these are absorbed or at least diluted by family and work responsibilities.

Teilhard says all this is changed when we understand the workings of the divine milieu and how God is present in every least action of my life.

Teilhard does not wish to denigrate or diminish the importance of "those noble and cherished moments of the day" when we formally pray, attend liturgy, or receive the sacraments. We, of course, need to treasure these.

Teilhard, however, wants to emphasize that there is no need to fear that our most trivial or most absorbing occupations should force us to leave the divine milieu or depart from God. Many people who work for the church or as part of a congregation — sacristans, sextons, financial staff, groundskeepers — report that much of their work is tedious and boring. One pastor told me that his most important job every evening is putting the lights out in the church, the hall, and the offices. Hardly an explicitly spiritual task. But Teilhard would say to him that God awaits him at every light switch.

Teilhard's book is written precisely for those who have been falsely led to believe that their "most trivial or most absorbing" daily activities keep them from God.

"*Nothing* here below is *profane* for those who know how to see."

Teilhard's spirituality is all about acquiring those "new eyes" of faith that can sense the divine milieu in which we all live and move. For Teilhard our task, individually and collectively, is to learn to see, with God's help, the connection that unites our personal activity with the building of the Kingdom of God. In his words,

> Try to realize that heaven itself smiles upon you and, through your works, draws you to itself; then as you leave church for the noisy streets, you will remain with only one feeling, that of continuing to immerse yourself in God. (Torchbook, 66)

With these new eyes, perhaps you can begin to see a new and different path to sanctity for the twenty-first century Christian: In short, here is the basic spiritual practice: *before you begin any activity, try to see its potential significance and constructive value in building the Body of Christ, then pursue it "with all your might."*

What does that mean? As you adhere to God with your maximum strength, Teilhard says, you are to find your true meaning and fulfill your life purpose in the role that is destined to be yours alone. You fulfill that role by working with the raw material of your life, which includes both your natural endowments (your special skills and talents) and your supernatural gifts (God's inspiration and grace).

Any new thing that is brought into this world or created by someone usually starts with raw material. The steel mill takes the raw material of iron ore and turns it into bridge girders, I-beams for skyscrapers, automobile bodies, bed frames, bicycles, locomotives, and a million other products. The plastics manufacturers take the raw material of petroleum and turn it into containers, food wrappings, tableware, automobile parts, and so on. Sculptors begin with the raw material of granite or marble. Artists use the raw material of paints and canvas. Composers use the raw materials of sounds and rhythms to create new music.

People use the raw material of their bodies and minds to create their lives, to shape their careers. They use the raw materials of their family backgrounds, their ethnicity, their social status, their financial resources, and their political connections. They use their faith, their know-how, their street smarts, inside information, and everything else they have at their disposal to make a difference. They use the raw materials of failure, setbacks, competitors, emotional depression, physical and mental handicaps as steppingstones to personal development and having a positive impact on others. Not all raw materials are typically considered good, such as having had an abusive childhood or alcoholic parents, being divorced or raped or fired, being diagnosed with breast cancer or diabetes, or having poor eyesight or a speech impediment. However, we all know people who had less than the best raw material to shape their lives with, yet they did well, some very well. I know therapists who are especially gifted in working with abused children or rape victims precisely because abuse or rape has been part of the raw material of their lives. Other therapists are especially compassionate in treating depressed patients because they themselves know, at first hand, the experience of bouts of depression.

No matter what the raw materials of your life might be — or might have been — they may be turned into good.

Spiritual Exercise: The Raw Material of Your Life _____

Ω On a sheet of paper, begin noting the raw material of your life, perhaps by comparing your raw material to that of others. Here are some hints to get started.

+ In what year were you born? What is the significance of that fact now? What if you had been born fifty years earlier or fifty years later? What difference would it make?

- In what country were you born? What if you had been born and raised in some other nation with a very different culture, language, and religion?

- Into what kind of family were you born? What are your family's strengths and weaknesses? What if you had been born into a family with very different values and attitudes? Is your family supportive of you and what you feel called to do? Or in how you are living your life?

- What is your socioeconomic situation? What if it had been radically different?

- What kinds of resources do you have at your disposal? Professional positions? Influential contacts?

- What kinds of intellectual, artistic, interpersonal talents do you enjoy?

- What are the strengths and weaknesses of your personality?

- What are the strengths and weaknesses of your health?

These are just some of the raw materials you have to work with. They make up some of your most important assets and liabilities.

It is your choice, now that you have listed the raw materials of your life, what you want to do with them.

While some persons may, indeed, be called to serve God in vowed religious life, all of us are called to vow ourselves to the task of promoting the overall sanctification of human effort in our "worldly" occupations. These everyday activities, whether ordinary or extraordinary, form the social structure of any society.

In the past, Christians as a whole have left the task of human progress to the "children of the world, that is to say, to agnostics or the irreligious." Teilhard points out that these so-called nonreligious people are also, perhaps unconsciously and involuntarily, collaborating in building the Body of Christ. However incomplete or misdirected their intentions may be, God is organizing and fitting their activity into the great divine work.

Christians who understand what God is about in the world have the opportunity to do their work "in a spirit of *adoration*."

A *Spirit of Adoration*

Teilhard dreams of the day when we will all have the eyes and consciousness to bond with one another throughout the world in carrying out the single, all-embracing work, the continuous Incarnation of the great Christ Body. With such consciousness, people won't be able to give themselves to any task without realizing that, however simple and mundane that task might be, it is being put to good use by Christ, who is the driving force and manager of the universe. When that day comes there will be little separating life in the cloister from life in the world.

Most Christians, Teilhard believes, think that the only times for divine adoration are during communal worship or when kneeling in contemplation before the Blessed Sacrament. Once you understand the divine milieu and realize what God is doing on earth, you realize that every activity of your life can become an act of adoration, insofar as you see it as developing the Body of Christ. During the Middle Ages, in building the great cathedrals in Europe, artisans saw their daily work in shaping stone, marble, and glass as a continuing act of adoration: they saw themselves as building the house of God. How much more is it an act of adoration for us who realize that in our daily efforts we are building, cell by cell, the great Body of Christ?

Spiritual Exercise: Working in a Spirit of Adoration _____

Ω Reflect for a few moments on how God and God's creatures have been working cooperatively so that you may be able to perform your daily activities. The plants and trees are generating oxygen for you to breathe. The skies are bringing sunshine so you can see and rain so you have water. The farm fields, the animals and fish offer themselves to you as food to keep you energized. Workers see that you have electricity, plumbing, and a home to shelter you. Others ensure that you have roads to drive your car to work or to school. Others provide many ways for you to communicate by mail, telephone, fax machine, and e-mail. Others care for your health. Fellow employees help you succeed at your job.

This is the grace and energy of the divine milieu at work in your life, so that you may be free to do your part in building the world, and to adore the Creator as you do it.

B. The Humanization of Christian Endeavor

Many Christians do not believe in the efficacy of human effort. In fact, the more religious they seem to be, the less likely their hearts will be totally committed to their work. Certainly that's the way many nonbelieving scientists saw Teilhard. He was a priest-scientist, a hyphenated person, a priest first, a scientist only second. How could he possibly share "your concern and your hopes and your excitement as you penetrate the mysteries and conquer the forces of nature?"

What Teilhard wanted to tell the "unbelieving scientists" — and us as well — was that, for the true Christian, "it is a matter of life and death that the earth should flourish to the utmost of its natural powers." He explains:

> Far too many Christians are insufficiently conscious of the "divine" responsibilities of their lives, and live like other men, giving only half of themselves, never experiencing the spur or the intoxication of advancing God's Kingdom in every domain of mankind. (Torchbook, 69)

For Teilhard, our faith imposes on us both the right and the duty to commit ourselves to the pursuits of the earth that move things further and deeper into complexity and consciousness.

"The incarnate God did not come to diminish in us the glorious responsibility and splendid ambition that is ours: *of fashioning our own self*." In other words, our human progress is part of the divine work.

Creating our own life and self is precisely part of what the divine milieu is inspiring us to do.

6. Detachment through Action

Attachment and Detachment

To be *attached* (attachment) means your energy and attention — and, perhaps, even your sense of identity — are invested in some specific process or desired predetermined outcome, and you are unwilling to settle for anything else. You are glued to it. You see yourself as inseparable from it. For example, suppose you are a single person. You may be attached to your afternoon nap, or to coming home to a quiet house, or to working only certain hours each day, or to spending every Wednesday night with your friends. No matter what happens, you are unwilling to give up these comforts or pleasures. You are *attached* to them.

To be *detached* (detachment) means you will spend your energy and attention to achieve the outcome you desire, but you are not so glued (attached) to that outcome that you cannot let go of it if things don't turn out the way you wanted. In the example above, suppose you now get married and begin to raise a family. If you are truly dedicated to your family, you may still like to enjoy an afternoon nap, come home to a quiet house, work regular hours, and meet with your friends on Wednesday nights. But if family obligations come up, you are willing to forego these pleasures for the sake of the family.

The same would be true if you were assigned to an important research project that required you to be in the laboratory at all hours of the day or night, seven days a week. You would be willing to forego — renounce — some of your regular pleasures for the sake of the research project.

To devote yourself as a Christian to the pursuit of earthly improvements of itself requires a deep renunciation. You must become a person of great detachment. Why is this so? Teilhard answers that work of its very nature — if you give yourself to it faithfully — is an instrument of detachment. This is true whether your work is to be a parent, a teacher, a businessperson, a salesperson, a scientist, a laborer, a factory worker, an artist, a waiter, a student, a musician, a cartoonist, or a writer.

Teilhard offers six reasons why the effort of our activities requires detachment:

First, it requires a *victory over inertia*, since much work is necessarily boring, whether in the lab, in the nursery, in the studio, at the office, in the classroom, or on the assembly line.

Second, if the work is creative, it generates "the pangs of birth." The act of creating something usually produces *inner tension* and the anxieties of creation. "Will it turn out well?" "It" may be a student paper, a sales effort, a beautiful painting, or a serious talk with an adolescent child.

Third, some attempts end up as *failures and dead ends,* so you must often start over, trying a new approach. Perhaps your usual methods for getting the baby to stop crying don't work. Or the first research design had flaws in it and it had to be jettisoned. The cartoonist must scrap his first five tries. The chef must go back to his spice rack for a better flavor combination.

Fourth, you cannot be attached to *specific outcomes*, since they may not occur as expected. You expected the baby to stay asleep for at least two hours, but she woke up long before you expected. You expected the research project to be over in two weeks; a month has gone by and you are still at it, with no end in sight. You hoped your students would understand long division the first time you explained it, but they didn't. Detachment is required to tear yourself away from your expectations and "cherished beginnings."

Fifth, there is always *something new and better* waiting on the horizon. We must continually keep letting go of the present accomplishments to strive for newer goals. Research work calls for continual improvement. Children turn into teenagers and provide new challenges. Even the laborer and factory worker must learn to use new tools or how to run new computer software.

Sixth, if you remain true to your research and exploration, *you no longer belong to yourself,* but to the divine potential of your work. The work of divinizing the world in the Body of Christ drives your action from ideal to ideal. Just as the salesperson must always strive to satisfy and please the customer, the student to please the teacher, and the writer to please her readership — your work no longer belongs simply to you — so the Christian is always trying to please God in Christ.

Here is the paradox as Teilhard sees it. A person dedicated to human progress must be, at once, the most attached and detached of human beings. Such persons are *attached* to the "unfathomable importance and value concealed beneath their humblest worldly successes." The same is true whether they are working on a cure for cancer, closing a business deal, completing a term paper, attaching a fender to a vehicle along the assembly line, or raising a child. At the same time, such dedicated people are *detached,* for while their interests lie truly *in* things, these things are always in absolute dependence upon God's presence in them.

So even as you are trying to make a difference in the world and pursuing your most personal development, it is not yourself that you are seeking, but that which is greater than you, to which you know that you are destined. The one dedicated to building the Body of Christ forgets and loses himself, says Teilhard, "in the very endeavor which is making him perfect." The divine milieu absorbs our individual powers in the very proportion in which these efforts laboriously rise above our individuality.

As Teilhard well knew, the motto of the Jesuits is "Ad Majorem Dei Gloriam," often simply written as A.M.D.G. It means we do all things, even our personal development, "for the greater glory of God."

Ultimately, your life is not about you.

Part Two

THE DIVINIZATION
OF OUR PASSIVITIES

Summary

In Part Two, Teilhard points out that our passivities (what we suffer, endure, and undergo in life) far outnumber our activities (what we accomplish by our own efforts).

Passivities embrace a much broader range of experience than activities, since passivities can come from *within us* (being born with perfect musical pitch, being born with cerebral palsy) as well as from *outside us* (being born in the United States, being born into a selfish family).

Passivities can come from *the present* (winning the lottery today, being in an auto accident on the way to work today), *the past* (genetic inheritance of a certain body type, susceptibility to allergies) or from *the very deep past* (the evolutionary development of the eye, the ear, the brain, and speech).

Some passivities can foster our growth and *development* (having a family that values education, meeting people that make business connections for me) while others seem only to *diminish us* (living in a dysfunctional family or a community filled with addictions and abuse).

For Teilhard, the most difficult part of this section is to show how our passivities of diminishment — those dark, evil, and useless things that happen to us — can help build the Body of Christ. He has developed a way, a spiritual practice, in which humans afflicted with diminishment can struggle with God against this diminishment. It is a way Teilhard himself learned through his own struggle with failure, rejection, and exclusion. Using this way, within the divine milieu, it is possible to transfigure your own failures and allow them to lead you into the deepest communion with God.

◆ ◆ ◆

Teilhard introduces this section by stating:

> The Christian . . . is more subject than others to this psycholog-ical reversal whereby . . . joy in action imperceptibly melts into desire for submission and the exaltation of becoming one's own self into the zeal to die in another. (Torchbook, 74)

In this quotation, Teilhard is trying to describe two slightly different psychological shifts that typically happen in those who come to realize the significance of participating in the Body of Christ.

1. I take joy in action (that is, delight in my personal accomplish-ments) and that shifts into desire for submission (wanting to do whatever the Cosmic Christ wants or needs from me).

2. I take joy in becoming my own self (creating my own career and life) and that shifts into the readiness to "die" to self and live in another (willing to live primarily in and for the Cosmic Christ).

Both these shifts relate to an awareness of how my activities become Christ's passivities.

At first, I begin to realize how my activities are, in effect, Christ's passivities, that is, Christ must undergo my activities. Christ must deal with whatever I do. Some of my activities produce growth in the Body of Christ, but others — actions of greed or resentment or cruelty, for example — may produce diminishment in the Christ Body.

Now, in this psychological reversal, because I begin to realize how important Christ is, I want to submit or realign my activities so that they will, for certain, promote the activity that Christ is trying to accomplish through me. In other words, I become "submissive" in that I want, not merely to do my will, but, from the start, to align my activities with Christ's will — with what the Cosmic Christ is trying to accomplish in the world. I want, more than anything, to help build the great Body of Christ.

Teilhard is making the same point in a slightly different way when he says my self-development turns into zeal for the development of the Christ Body. This shift of focus is a kind of "dying to self." St. Paul says much the same when he writes, "I live, no longer I, but Christ lives in me." Living is a matter of whose purpose I commit to.

The irony in this "psychological reversal" is that the more deeply you commit to the purpose or aim of the Christ Body, the more you are called upon to develop yourself to the fullest, because you want all of your activities to be passivities of *growth* for Christ, not passivities of *diminishment*. In this sense, Teilhard says, your activities become not so much a matter of developing yourself as developing the Body of Christ. Teilhard calls this shift of perspective "losing yourself in God."

It is really important not to read the expression "losing yourself in God" in a traditional way, as a sort of disappearing from society or spending your life in isolated prayer. That is far from Teilhard's understanding of the phrase. For him, you lose yourself in God by becoming a scientist immersed in research and dedicated to pushing the envelope of evolution. You lose yourself by becoming a businessperson immersed in building complexity and consciousness in yourself and your customers, thereby pushing the envelope of evolution. In whatever field you happen to be engaged in, the way you lose yourself in God is by developing your area of expertise to the fullest, so that you stretch its limits, you break out of the box. Far from asking you to be a wallflower or a nonentity in society, Teilhard is asking you to be the best possible artist or artisan or parent you can possibly be, to develop your skills to the utmost. All because you are caught up in zeal for building the Body of Christ.

Your "self" is a gift from God. At every moment and on all sides, if you have eyes to see, you can "discover possibilities and opportunities for fulfillment in this gift of self." You come to realize that, instead of people seeing themselves as becoming masters of the universe, they become servants of the Christ Body, since Christ is really the true master or Lord of the Universe.

1. The Extent, Depth, and Diverse Forms of Human Passivities

"That which is not done by us is, by definition, undergone." Whatever is not an activity of mine is a passivity of mine. These two parts of our lives are totally intertwined, yet they are extraordinarily unequal. The passive is "immeasurably the wider and the deeper part."

You may recall that at the beginning of Part One, I presented a summary picture of the different kinds of activities there are and the many kinds of passivities Teilhard defines. Here is the same chart:

ACTIVITIES AND PASSIVITIES

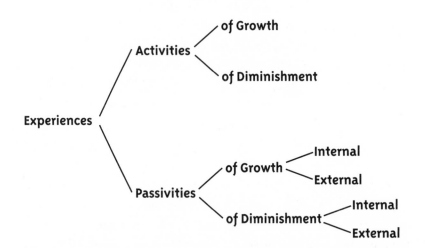

Those passivities external to us — whether of growth or diminishment — are the most obvious. Teilhard notes two general kinds of external passivities.

First, *some external passivities take the form of reactions of others.* Such external passivities ceaselessly accompany every choice, deed, and activity we perform, since our actions usually affect the others around us. Their reactions may direct and sustain our efforts, or oppose them. The effects of their responses may extend far beyond the immediate reaction they produce in us and perhaps even far beyond us. For example, someone may tell me I would make a good teacher. My immediate reaction is to feel complimented, but that comment may also inspire me to enter the teaching profession and in my years of teaching affect hundreds of students. On the other hand, someone may tell me that my singing is terrible. My immediate reaction may be to feel embarrassed, but it may also produce feelings of embarrassment again and again throughout my life every time I wish to join in singing with others at church or a party. We are usually aware of these kinds of passivities. We can see, hear, and feel the reactions of others to the actions we take. They have an impact on us.

Second, *other external passivities are all the rest of the things acting upon us that we are usually unaware of.* We usually see our actions and efforts within a small radius, says Teilhard. But beyond what we can directly see and hear is *a sea of reality all around us that is acting upon us without our awareness and perhaps in spite of it.* Included in this "sea of reality" may be things as basic as today's rainy weather, an unexpected detour on the street where I'm driving, a sick child at home that forces me to rearrange my schedule, an unexpected uplifting phone call from a supportive friend, a generous job offer in today's mail, a neighbor playing loud music near my window, and so on. Each of us may respond to all of this "sea of reality" in different ways, but we *must* all undergo it. We are affected by it, whether we like it or not. We cannot truly escape any of it. These are the other external passivities that surround us.

The proportion of activities to passivities is very unequal. For every single one of my activities, my life is filled with thousands of passivities. Some of these passivities help me to grow; others diminish me and my ability to do my work.

In Teilhard's spirituality, I am challenged to integrate all of these passivities — Teilhard says "illuminate and animate" them — "with the divine presence." Learning how to do this is precisely Teilhard's objective in this second part of *The Divine Milieu*.

Teilhard reminds us, as the chart above shows, that some of these passivities are "friendly and favorable forces, those which uphold our efforts to make a difference and point the way to success — the passivities of growth."

Other passivities have the opposite effect. They "laboriously obstruct our tendencies, hamper or deflect our progress toward heightened being." The child born into a family of physical abusers. The child sexually molested by a trusted family member or a clergyperson. The child born blind. The parents of a child born with cerebral palsy. A young soldier who returns home from the battlefield without arms or legs. These passivities of diminishment thwart our capacities for development.

Teilhard wants us to study both kinds of passivities until in both "we discern the kindling light of the blessed countenance of God."

Learning to do this will prove to be no small matter, especially acknowledging the presence of these diminishing passivities and their integral place in the divine milieu. But we must do it, or reject the divine milieu. In other words, if we don't acknowledge that our unwelcome experiences somehow belong to the divine milieu, we must relegate them to some domain *outside* the divine milieu. If you think about it for a minute, you'll realize that if we all could throw our unwanted experiences outside the divine milieu, the milieu itself would probably empty rather quickly.

The fact we must deal with is that *everything* is in the divine milieu. That includes every action and reaction, productive or unproductive. Nothing can be pushed outside it. Not one single experience. We must undergo life just as much as we must one day undergo death.

Spiritual Exercise: A Learning Experience _____

Ω Rather than ask you to make a list of the unwelcome experiences you would like to throw out of the divine milieu, I take a cue from a therapist friend of mine. Whenever someone comes to her bemoaning an unfortunate event — perhaps failing an exam, being diagnosed with a terminal illness, discovering a newborn child is handicapped in some way, the death of a loved one, and so on — after empathizing with the person, she asks, "What can you learn from this experience?" Her thought is that, despite these sad experiences, people must continue to live. They can live in anger, resentment, bitterness, or feeling victimized, or else they can learn something from the experience, then restructure and reenter life with some wisdom that they didn't have before.

So imagine one of your unwelcome experiences, and imagine this wise therapist sits before you asking you, "What can you learn from this experience?"

With reference to the chart, Teilhard considers the easier group of passivities first; these are the ones that help us grow and develop.

2. The Passivities of Growth and the Two Hands of God

Growth seems so natural to us, Teilhard observes, that we seldom pause to distinguish between our activity and the passivities of growth that foster it, those forces that nourish our activities or the circumstances that promote our success. How many people became good cooks because, as youngsters, they had to spend time helping out in the kitchen? How many became handy with tools like hammers, pliers, and screwdrivers because they were required to help out, as young people, making simple repairs in the home? How many learned to read and appreciate books because they were read to during childhood?

Teilhard asks us to pause and reflect on "the ocean of forces to which we were subjected" that enabled us to grow and develop the skills and capacities we now enjoy.

Spiritual Exercise: Forces of Growth _____

Ω Take some time to consider one or more of your skills and talents — in music, art, sports, business, science, homemaking, etc. Even though you may have spent many hours practicing a certain skill, review the story of your growth in that skill and recall as many forces of growth, small or large, to which you were subjected — happening to be in the right place at the right time — and by whom you were encouraged, guided, pushed, teased, rewarded, or graced.

Also consider the combination of circumstances that conspired to bring you to where you presently are in terms of that skill.

Acknowledge that in all this you are held in the benevolent atmosphere of the divine milieu.

_____

When Teilhard himself did this exercise, the deeper he got in exploring the sources of his talents and skills, the less he recognized who he was. He could, for example, trace his ancestry back for many generations and begin to recognize how, like a twig in a river, he had been borne along by the family current. He explored the geography of the place where he was born and grew up and saw how his surroundings affected him. As a paleontologist familiar with human evolution, he could see the many traits and capacities for thinking that he had inherited from his human ancestors over hundreds of thousands of years. Even all the sensory abilities he possessed — fingers, eyes, ears, nose, tongue, and teeth — were originally developed by countless generations of animals in eons past and bequeathed to him. After exploring these depths and in the hundreds of ways they had affected who he turned out to be, he hesitated to claim his life as his own, so intimately was his life connected to that of the world and its entire history. He concluded, "My self is given to me far more than it is formed by me."

He found this exercise very uncomfortable to pursue, since we all like to believe that we have made ourselves who we are. This exercise proves very devastating to one who considers himself to be a "self-made man." But Teilhard didn't stop there.

He began to explore what he called the "innumerable strands which form the web of chance" surrounding his life. He realized that thousands and millions of these random strands of the world had to come together perfectly to help create and form precisely who he was. It wasn't enough to say that his mother and father fell in love and gave birth to him. There were innumerable strands of the web of chance that brought his parents together. There were innumerable strands of the web of chance that led them to couple in the perfect time and place so he could be born with his particular genetic capabilities to fit into that moment of history, in that community, with that socioeconomic status, within a devout family, amid many loving brothers and sisters, etc., etc. This is where, with little or no active input from him, his ideas and affections as well as his human and spiritual attitudes began to be gradually formed.

On the one hand, realizing this, he sometimes felt conscious of being something totally other than what he normally thought himself to be, perhaps even "something greater than myself." On the other hand, he sometimes felt like an insignificant particle adrift in a vast universe.

He could hardly "complete" himself by himself. In fact, instead of taking the lead in his life, he recognized the millions of passivities that continually pulled his life this way and that, and all he could do was follow — to suffer it to happen.

The Two Hands of God

God, he says, is working with us at two levels of growth. Teilhard describes this work as each one's life being woven by two different threads, the thread of inward development and the thread of outward success — the *Within* and the *Without*. The Within and the Without are what Teilhard calls "the two hands of God."

The one hand, *inward development*, refers to the shaping of ideas, beliefs, emotions, tendencies, and the like. This is the *Within*.

The other hand, *outward successes*, refers to the fact that we always seem to find ourselves "at the exact point where the whole sum of the forces of the universe meet together to work in us the effect that God desires" (Torchbook, 79). This is the *Without*.

Layers Upon Layers

Geologists are taught to look at a hill or mountain in ways different from the rest of us. Using geologist eyes, they see the mountain as a whole series of layers, each layer perhaps representing a geologic period millions of years long. They reflect on the events (passivities) that have happened through the various geological ages, such as the melting of polar ice caps, continental drifts, or the movement of tectonic plates deep below the earth's surface, that brought this mountain to exists as it does in this particular form at this particular time.

Similarly, psychologists may look at a client seated in their office, and with psychologically trained vision see a whole series of psychological layers, fashioned during infancy, childhood, teen years, and adulthood by many physical and emotional events, that brought that client to exist in this particular emotional and mental state at this particular time.

In Teilhardian spirituality, you are invited to learn to see yourself as a product of many layers of events, experiences, decisions, etc. (activities and passivities), that brought you to this point in your process.

Spiritual Practice: The Layers of Your Life _____

Ω Imagine you are a geology student used to sketching the history of a mountain in layers. Instead, take a clean sheet of paper and do a sketch of the many layers of your life, starting at least as far back as your grandparents, perhaps describing their influence at the bottom of the page.

At the grandparents' level, list the many influences they had on your life—your inherited passivities: genetic, racial, environmental, emotional, socioeconomic, religious, educational, inspirational, etc. Note similar factors for your parental layer. Draw it on the same page above the grandparental layer.

Then, above these layers, create a number of other layers that represent the many chronological stages of your life from infancy, to childhood, to school age, to high school, to college or employment, to marriage, to child-rearing, etc. At each stage, list the passivities of growth and the passivities of diminishment that impinged on your life during those years, including people, situations, events, organizations, etc.

Then meditate on the sketch you have made. Acknowledge that God lovingly used these passivities in the divine milieu to bring you to where you are today.

You may also recognize that each person you know has gone through a similar process of growth and diminishment, pushed or carried by the forces that brought them to this place and time. Teilhard would have you picture each person you pray for, like any mountain, as made up of many layers of formation.

Spiritual Practice: Seeing Layers in Others

Ω When you are praying for another person, first use your imagination to picture the many layers—physical, emotional, intellectual, social, and spiritual—that make up who that person is. Think, too, of the events, designed and lovingly arranged by God in the divine milieu, that brought that person to this place and situation in this particular form.

As you ask for God's blessing on them, you might also think of the little ways, either by word or example, that they have added to the complexity and consciousness of your life and of the world. Or how they might contribute to it in the future.

Teilhard's Prayer

Teilhard concludes this section with this prayer:

> *Oh God, that at all times you may find me as you desire me*
> *and where you would have me be,*
> *that you may lay hold on me fully,*
> *both by the Within and the Without of myself,*
> *grant that I may never break this double thread of my life.*
>
> (Torchbook, 80)

3. The Passivities of Diminishment

In this section, you might immediately expect Teilhard to focus on sin. He has the same suspicion, so he adds a footnote explaining that diminishments are far broader than the sinful acts of others that diminish us. Under this heading, he includes physical and emotional evils that we undergo as well as moral evils, conscious gestures that would separate us from God and our fellow humans.

One reason Teilhard doesn't focus on personal sins is because he expects his readers are not people living sinful lives, but are rather seekers who have embarked on a genuine spiritual search. Like everyone else on earth, however, spiritual seekers are subject to passivities of diminishment, both internal and external.

The themes of this section, then, deal with the more general "decidedly negative side of our existences," where it is hard to find any happy or satisfying results. Here, then, Teilhard faces the perplexing challenge to show how God can be grasped in and through every loss and death. These forces of diminishment include *internal* ones like personal sickness, mental illness, physical and emotional handicaps, and chronic pain, as well as *external* ones that create wounds in us, either caused by the behavior of *other people* like lying, cruelty, violence, shaming, and abuse, or those resulting from *natural disasters* such as floods, winds, fires, or epidemics.

An Example

Modeling a spiritual practice that is hopefully clarifying for us, Teilhard summarizes his own list of *external passivities of diminishment* by calling them "all our bits of ill fortune" that spring up on all sides to stop us, detour us, delay us, hinder us, upset us, shock us, separate us, or hem us in. Many of these diminishments begin with an inadvertent gesture: a child with a cold coughs in our face, someone who carries a virus shakes our hand, someone whispers a little criticism about us that infects our mind, someone inadvertently gives us wrong information. Or, perhaps, we are preoccupied and we slip and fall, perhaps breaking a bone, which requires us to limp around for weeks.

While we can eventually recover from these bits of ill fortune, there are many *permanent internal diminishments*, losses that can never be retrieved. These include natural failings like genetic disposition toward heart problems, diabetes, cancer, addictions, and poor vision. They also include physical handicaps, intellectual limitations, family prejudices, irritating habits, limiting cultural beliefs, social biases, faulty ways of thinking, commitments thoughtlessly made, moral weaknesses, the frailty that comes with aging, and the like. We could also add here diminishing things we unconsciously absorbed from our family — prejudices, annoying habits, faulty ways of reasoning, distorted cultural beliefs, socially unjust practices, dysfunctional ways of relating, and so on.

Spiritual Practice: My Diminishments, Internal and External _____

Ω Here the task is to list your internal and external passivities of diminishment. Usually, we are more familiar with those innate things about us that hinder our ability to operate and act at our best. So most people start with those: physical, emotional, intellectual, social, and spiritual are areas to begin getting you started.

Next, begin to track your external passivities of diminishment.

Once you have brought them into awareness and listed them, Teilhard will explain the challenge you face in dealing with them in terms of the divine milieu.

Finding God in Our Diminishments

From a merely human perspective, these internal passivities of diminishment, according to Teilhard, "form the darkest element and the most despairingly useless years of our life." They are sources of disintegration. Death itself is "the sum and consummation of all our diminishments." From a human perspective, even the hero's death and the martyr's death may be viewed as a great diminishment, since the hero and the martyr can no longer physically help promote human progress. They themselves can no longer produce activities on earth.

For most of the diminishments in our lives, there is no simple solution. We are forced to overcome these diminishments, including death, by finding God in them. Once, when a student posed his problem to a wise old man, the old man replied, "There is no solution, but seek it lovingly." Teilhard might have rephrased the old man's response to, "There is no solution, but seek it in the Cosmic Christ."

Teilhard begins with the Christian belief that Christ has conquered death. By virtue of Christ's resurrection, Teilhard asserts, nothing any longer kills inevitably. Nothing is ever a *total* loss. The thrust of growth coming from the divine milieu is continuously revivifying and revitalizing whatever has happened, no matter how bad or seemingly unredeemable events seem to be. God's forgiveness, grace, and healing abound. Every little death can end up in a resurrection. Jesus' resurrection is a promise of that.

Jesus' life and ministry also makes the same promise. No matter what the diminishment was in the people who came to him — paralysis, madness, blindness, demonic possession, poverty, grief, leprosy — Jesus would cure it. In fact, there is not one instance in the New

Testament where Jesus explicitly refused to heal anyone. From this perspective, we can learn to see in every diminishment the blessed touch of God upon us.

Teilhard says that, despite our faults and the circumstances that diminish us, "we can, by a total re-ordering, completely correct the world that surrounds us, and resume our lives in a favorable sense" (Torchbook, 83).

This is one of Teilhard's most puzzling statements. How can we possibly "completely correct the world"? What does a "total re-ordering" mean? To begin an explanation, Teilhard turns to St. Paul's axiom: "To those who love God all things can be transformed into good."

But how can Paul's statement make the difference, we ask? More precisely, how can these apparently useless parts of our lives — all this "waste-matter," Teilhard calls it — find "their necessary place" in the divine milieu and in shaping the total Body of Christ? How do we produce a "total re-ordering" of all these diminishments?

Teilhard says there are three steps or stages to this transformation of our diminishments. The first phase involves our *struggle* against evil, the second the *defeat* of evil, the third its *"transfiguration."* Explaining the phases of this process form the next two sections of Teilhard's text.

Some attempts to explain St. Paul's statement about the transformation of evil and diminishment can lead to dangerous misunderstandings. Most confusion, Teilhard feels, is based on false ideas people may have about the terms "resignation" and "detachment." So he explains what he believes true resignation is.

A. Our Struggle with God against Evil

When a suffering person says, "God has touched me," this simple affirmation of divine connection requires a complex series of inner steps, says Teilhard. We have a right to make this affirmation only when we have completed that series of steps. In this section, he develops the first few of those steps expressed as belief statements.

Spiritual Exercise: A Perspective on Diminishment _____

Ω As you read through each of these inner steps, you may ask yourself
   if you really believe what they say. If you find one you don't — or
can't — believe, you may meditate on that belief. Each one will make more
sense if you can keep the perspective that you and everyone else are really
a cell in the Christ Body. Not only are you struggling for life against the
diminishments that befall you, but so is the Christ Body struggling with
you and through you against the diminishments that befall it.

Thank God for the strength and courage that come to you through the
divine milieu.

---

1. God wants to free me from this diminishment. This belief is an essential first step. If we believe the opposite, namely, that God wants me to
suffer this diminishment or, worse, that it is a punishment from God,
we cannot truly transform any evil that may befall us. We must begin
the process by believing that God hates and rejects this diminishment
as much — and much more — than we do.

People might ask, "Why then did God permit this diminishment
to happen? Why didn't God prevent it?" Teilhard's response might be
that the Kingdom of God on earth — this immense Body of Christ —
is populated by billions of people with free will, each one of us striving
to achieve different and often conflicting personal desires. Thus, the
Christ Body is constantly in turbulent evolution — with many individuals and groups working at cross-purposes — and will remain so
until it reaches its fulfillment. It would have been impossible for God
to create a universe based on evolutionary processes without conflict, confusion, competition, struggle, violence, failure, loss, sadness,
grief, death, and all the rest of the diminishments. That's just the way
evolution works, especially an evolutionary process based on the law
of attraction-connection-complexity-consciousness. The world isn't
perfect yet. It isn't yet complex enough or conscious enough for its

completion. We have a long way to go before every cell of the Christ Body is fully conscious of what it truly is part of.

In the meantime, God tries to heal us with the hands and eyes and mouths that are available to Him in the Body of Christ on earth. Teilhard points out that other human beings in the Christ Body typically serve as the healing hands of God, which is why God inspires people to become physicians, healthcare workers, and benefactors — to find ways to heal the sources of diminishment that surround us.

2. *God wants me to help him remove this diminishment from me.* In this second step, Teilhard contrasts this statement with people who say helplessly, "I am a victim. There is nothing I can do." Instead of making feeble excuses or pleading helpless, Teilhard says we each need to take an active role regarding our diminishments, whether they are personal or social ones. If you are sick or poor or are otherwise burdened, God asks you to struggle against your sickness or your poverty. If you are healthy and well off, then you are called to struggle with those who are sick and poor against whatever is causing that sickness and poverty.

First of all, Teilhard says we must avoid any diminishments we see coming and get out of their way, if at all possible — just as much as you would swerve your car off the road to avoid an accident. So we wholeheartedly repel an oncoming diminishment, if possible. And we loathe it if we are already burdened with it — loathe it in a way that you use every power you have to get rid of the diminishment, because you know God does not directly will you to suffer it.

3. With all your power, *resist the diminishment, but do it without bitterness, without resentment, and without revolt.* At the same time as you resist the diminishment with all your strength, hold an "*anticipatory tendency* to acceptance and final resignation" (Torchbook, 84). That is, be ready to accept the burden of this diminishment. Teilhard notes that physical death is the sum and symbol of all the forces that diminish us. According to Teilhard, we must fight against death, even though we cannot "hope for a personal, direct, and immediate victory."

Spiritual Exercise: Resisting Diminishment _____

Ω Consider times in your life when you have resisted a diminishment with all your strength. Contrast that process with times that
you failed to resist a diminishment and just whined, complained, acted
helpless, or played the victim. Almost everyone has had both experiences.

This exercise is designed to help you recognize the difference, and
to more consciously choose your response the next time you face an
oncoming diminishment.

B. Our Apparent Failure and Its Transfiguration

Although you may believe that, with God's grace, you will save your
soul, there is no guarantee that you will avoid suffering, defeat, and
failure. There are still more steps to the transformation process, to be
able to say, "God touched me in this diminishment."

4. *You must acknowledge that, as a created being, you are incomplete.* In order to move, step-by-step, toward your destined completion
or whatever you desire to accomplish on the way, you inevitably
risk diminishments, if only because every other "incomplete" human,
animal, bird, insect, and plant is simultaneously seeking its own completion. Your blood nourishes the female mosquito that bites you
(diminishment). In this incredibly complex and intertwined process,
there are bound to be conflicts, competition, loss, and failure. In other
words, diminishments are inevitable.

5. *You must acknowledge that the earth itself and everything on it is still
incomplete, still in a state of process.* In the beginning God precisely created a fragmented universe. Even though it is progressing toward its
completion and perfection, it remains partially disorganized. Realize
that any form of disorganization inevitably produces diminishments. If
God had created a world without a spot or likelihood of disorganization, it would be a world already perfect. God could not have created

the real, evolving world without diminishments, so God must deal with these diminishments as they occur, as must we.

However, you may also recognize that the appearance of each diminishment adds new complexity to your life and the lives of many others. Suppose you fall down the stairs and break your arm or leg. Think of how many new people — doctors, nurses, hospital administrators, and medical insurance personnel — must deal with you and complexify your life. Then consider how many of the people you regularly interact with — parents, siblings, friends, teacher, managers, and co-workers — must change, if only slightly, their way of dealing with you because of your broken limb. Your accident has brought more complexity into the world that you and others must bear. To struggle effectively against this diminishment, you must become more conscious of it and all the factors, including people, that surround it or are connected with it. Thus, even diminishments promote the law of attraction-connection-complexity-consciousness.

6. *God is capable of making good out of evil.* God works this miracle, says Teilhard, "by making evil itself serve a higher good of his faithful, the very evil which the present state of creation does not allow God to suppress immediately." The higher good, says Teilhard, will all be accomplished in good time. It isn't necessarily an instant transformation. God is like the sculptor who can make use of a fault or impurity in the stone he is working on, but you may not be able to see how the "evil" has been turned into "good" until the sculpture is finally completed. So we may not be able to perceive how God has turned the "evil" into "good" until the Body of Christ is fully completed.

7. *God transfigures our diminishments, our partial deaths, and even our final death by integrating them into a better plan, provided we lovingly trust him.* This belief covers all our faults and sins, even our most deliberate ones. Not everything is automatically and immediately turned to good for those who seek God. Rather, everything is *capable* of becoming transformed into good.

Although Teilhard is talking here specifically about "personal sins," there are "social sins" that also need to be transfigured, sins like slavery, anti-Semitism, racism, unfair treatment of the handicapped, sexism, religious intolerance, unequal pay for equal work, and so on. Both kinds of sins, personal and social, will be transfigured in the divine milieu. It is perhaps a bit easier to see how, through the evolution of human conscience and consciousness, some of these social sins are slowly being transformed through human laws and more just practices. Slavery was finally outlawed in the United States because enough people became conscious of it as a "social sin." New laws were enacted to protect the rights of the handicapped. For example, fifty years ago handicapped parking spaces, wheelchair access ramps, and handicapped-useable rest rooms were unheard of; today we would be surprised *not* to see these changes. Teilhard's point would be that some of these "social sins" could be reduced and removed simply by the development of consciousness in the divine milieu.

How God Can Turn Evil into Good

Teilhard lists three ways that God in the divine milieu can convert evil, whether personal or social, into good.

First, the diminishment diverts our attention and activity toward a framework that will turn out to be more beneficial than what we were doing before the diminishment. "While I was in the hospital with my broken leg, I met the person I was going to marry." "As women were given higher executive positions in our company, we got an influx of fresh air in our thinking, which has proved profitable for us."

Second, and perhaps more often, our loss or affliction will force us to turn for satisfaction to less material purposes. Lives of many saints experienced this form of transformation. "My child was killed by a drunk driver; now I dedicate my energies to finding ways to prevent inebriated people from driving." "When I was a child, I was taught not to trust Jewish people. Last year, people from our Catholic parish took a trip to the Holy Land with a group of Jewish people from a neighborhood synagogue. Now we have new friends and our neighborhood feels friendlier than ever."

As another example of this second way, people afflicted by chronic sickness and addictions — diminishments that will never really go away — turn to prayer and realize their need for God's help to give them the courage, faith, trust, and strength to carry on the struggle. In some cases, the afflicted person, like a Christopher Reeve, may find ways to provide consolation, courage, or hope to other people with the same affliction, thus helping transform some part of the world.

These first two methods of transformation are quite easy to see and accept. But what about the sufferings that cannot be compensated for, such as premature deaths and stupid accidents, where the person either dies or remains permanently diminished, where the very roots of our lives are ripped out of the earth? How can God turn our very physical "extinction" into an essentially life-giving factor? Here is where Teilhard perceives a third way of transformation for these stupid but radical diminishments, a way he describes as "the most effective way and the way which most surely makes us holy" (Torchbook, 87). It requires a bit of explanation.

Third, the more we deepen our attachment to the fulfillment of the Christ Body, the less we need to set limits to the "tearing up of our roots." This describes a shift of primary attachment from self to the Christ Body, where to serve God is all we wish to do. This shift requires a detachment from seeing the center of your existence in yourself and recentering yourself in the Body of Christ. In making this step, according to Teilhard, we appear to "lose all foothold within ourselves." But it is only an "appearance." Instead of losing ourselves in this shift of centers, we find our true selves, the selves we were destined to be in the Body of Christ. We enjoy the strongest foothold of all.

In a real sense, we must all eventually come to this point of detachment and recentering. In Teilhard's words, "God must, in some way or other, make room for himself, hollowing us out and emptying us, if he is finally to penetrate into us" (Torchbook, 89).

Even though we are expected to fight death to the death, the function of death — even little deaths — "is to provide the necessary entrance [of God *and* ourselves] into our inmost lives." What becomes humanly empty can become fullness and unity in God. It may be summed up:

> God has touched me.
> God has taken away from me.
> His will be done.

Spiritual Practice: Converting Evil into Good _____

Ω Review the three ways, described above, that God in the divine milieu can use to convert evil into good. Find examples of how God has used all three ways in your life or in the lives of people close to you.

C. *Communion through Diminishment*

In this concluding section, showing how the diminishments and waste matter of our lives can become transformed into the Body of Christ, Teilhard presents his ideas in the form of a prayer to God. If you have a copy of *The Divine Milieu* handy, you might read these two pages in a prayerful manner, making Teilhard's sentiments your own (see Torchbook, 89–90).

During his prayer, Teilhard rejoices in knowing that the passivities of *growth* he has experienced have let God grow in him, and he asks that he be able to freely consent to communion through his passivities of *diminishment*, especially those "dark moments" of major sickness and the "dizzy abyss" of death when he is losing hold of himself, and God is "painfully parting the fibers of my being in order to penetrate to the very marrow of my substance."

His wish is that in his death he does more than die while *communicating* with God. He wants to be able to treat his death as an act of *communion* with God.

Perhaps a word is in order about the difference between *communicating* with God, that is, praying to God as someone apart from you, and *communing* with God, becoming one with God, spirit to spirit. Our prayer of petition *(communication)* creates the image that God is somehow a being separate and distinct from us. An act of union *(communion)* creates the image that God and I are one, with nothing separating us.

To be able to make one's death an act of communion assumes that we have learned to let our diminishments be transfigured into a force that helps complete the Body of Christ within the divine milieu. To understand this process, however, you must understand the meaning of true resignation.

D. True Resignation

Because of the misleading way that Christian writers and teachers through the years have described Christian resignation, many reasonable people have denounced "resignation" as an opiate of believers because it seems to foster "passivity in the face of evil" and a "perverse cultivation of suffering." Resignation is also sometimes caricatured as a naïve and thoughtless "submission to the will of God." A religion that doesn't call people to live to the highest human ideals and is not committed to promoting the best of human values "is already condemned," writes Teilhard.

He stresses again that this inaccurate representation is not what is meant by true resignation. True resignation demands that we fight sincerely and with all our strength, "in union with the creative force of the world," to drive evil away so that nothing in creation is diminished. Even noble, nonbelieving humanists, who are part of "the creative force of the world," do this much. They fight evil, strive for the highest human ideas, and are committed to the best human values. For the Christian, says Teilhard, this noble human quest is also an essential part of our striving with the rest of humanity to realize the earth's potential for higher consciousness. We are called to fully engage in this struggle, no matter what setbacks we encounter and must endure.

Spiritual Practice: How to Deal with Sickness, Dying, and Other Diminishments _____

Ω This is how Teilhard might summarize his way of responding to sickness, death, and other forms of physical, mental, or spiritual diminishments. For Teilhard, it is how to live in submission to God in *an active way*. His approach is based on the law of attraction-connection-complexity-consciousness. Here are the steps:

+ *Resist sickness, evil, or other diminishments with all your strength.* As long as human resistance is possible, the total Body of Christ will be resisting it too.

+ *Even if you are defeated by the diminishment, still resist it inwardly.*

+ While continuing to struggle against it, *recognize that this hostile force can become for you a loving principle of transformation*, that is, it offers the opportunity for you to recenter your personality from yourself into the Total Christ.

+ *But leave this transformation to one greater than you,* namely, to the Total Christ.

+ When all your strength to resist the diminishment is spent, *you are to unite yourself to the will of God*, firmly believing that the total Body of Christ will ultimately find its fulfillment.

+ *Join God in communion* across (over and above) *the evil at a level of union stronger than the diminishment.*

+ *Let your communion in resignation coincide with your deepest fidelity to the human task* (of promoting complexity and consciousness and revealing the Body of Christ).

_____

Like the faithful hero in battle against the enemy, we each struggle and fight in order to advance our side until all our strength is spent and we are either wounded or slain. For the truly resigned warrior, it is not a question of whether or not I will get out of the fight alive, but in the end will *our side* win the larger battle. Teilhard's belief is that the forces of growth and development in the divine milieu (our side) will transform and transcend the forces of diminishment.

Whenever we meet with personal defeat in our various attempts to advance the Body of Christ, we must still continue to resist the diminishment. At the same time, each time we recognize that what defeats us and disintegrates us can become a "loving principle of renewal," if we accept our personal defeat with faith in the destiny of the Christ Body.

Perhaps an example at a more personal level will help clarify Teilhard's explanation of acceptance of personal defeat. Suppose, during a battle, the warrior is wounded, say, he receives a gash in his leg. As a result of that gash, his skin and many of his leg's cells will suffer. If those parts of his skin and his damaged cells had consciousness and free choice, they would willingly have endured those diminishments for the sake of the success and survival of the warrior. The diminishments we suffer may be compared to those parts of the warrior's skin and the damaged cells. Just as the cells accepted personal defeat with faith in the destiny of the warrior's body, so we can accept personal defeat with faith in the destiny of the Body of Christ.

From another perspective, I know a mother whose son was born with cerebral palsy. It was a passivity of diminishment for both of them, for she was committed to caring for her special child as long as he lived. It was an unplanned-for commitment that consumed, every day, a great amount of her time and energy. Yet she was convinced that her son was born to make a difference in the world. When doctor after doctor told her there was nothing they could do, she never stopped challenging them and making their life more complex and their minds more conscious. Even when they politely dismissed her, she kept searching elsewhere. She explored new advanced medications. She looked for cerebral palsy research studies in which she might get her son enrolled. She looked for alternative sources of healing. She never gave up. She searched the Internet for others in her situation. She shared with them the techniques she had tried with her son that seemed to help. Whenever a group would allow her to speak, she told her story. She made audiences more conscious of this devastating illness and the need for research for a cure. Her boy is over thirty years old now, and she still resists the diminishment, as he does. At the same time, she is aware that God is using her and her son to call attention to the need for more research on cerebral palsy. Even in pain and rejection, she and her son experience the "loving principle of renewal." With conviction and passion, she keeps pushing for human progress.

When defeat or failure is looked at merely from the experiential viewpoint, everything seems lost. The warrior lies dead on the battlefield. A thirty-year-old palsied son rocks helplessly in his wheelchair day after day. But from the supernatural perspective (that is, from the perspective of God and the Christ Body) there is a further dimension to the diminishment, one that transcends the defeat. On this higher plane, says Teilhard, your true resignation in faith allows you to reach the "required point," that is, where you are part of, and God achieves — perhaps without your knowing it — a larger victory. In this way, says Teilhard, God produces "a mysterious reversal of evil into good." I experience a "communion in resignation" with God, and in my personal diminishment the divine milieu grows in complexity and consciousness.

A Caution about Laziness and Indifference

Of course, Teilhard observes, if evil comes upon me through my own negligence or fault, I have no right to regard the diminishment that befalls me as a case where I am "touched by God." However, he adds, despite my shortcoming, at every moment God offers me an opportunity to "repent and correct my lazy or indifferent attitude of mind." God can take up everything, even our sins and faults, and recast them into something that will advance human progress.

French Editor's Note

At this point in *The Divine Milieu*, the editor of the French text includes a summary, drawn from other Teilhard writings, of what he means by "true and total renunciation" (passivity) and "complete Christian endeavor" (activity). In this way, we can see how detachment and endeavor are closely related.

True and total Christian renunciation must satisfy two paradoxical conditions:

* It must enable us, with faith and intention, to go beyond everything there is in this world or that the world has to offer.

* It must, at the same time, compel us to press forward, with conviction and passion, to ensure human progress and keep developing this world.

Complete Christian endeavor has three conditions:

* We are to collaborate passionately in the worldwide human endeavor with the conviction that our activities are helping achieve the fulfillment of the Body of Christ.

* As we pursue this lofty and ever-expanding purpose, we need to attain at least a rudimentary form of renunciation and some degree of victory over our narrow-mindedness, our selfishness, and our laziness.

* We must cherish both the "hollownesses" of life (all of life's passivities of diminishment that "empty" us) as well as the "fullness" of life (all of our activities that help build the Body of Christ).

Two Simultaneous Movements

In summary, Teilhard's spirituality combines two simultaneous movements, (1) the *natural personalization* of man and (2) his *supernatural depersonalization* in the Body of Christ.

By *natural personalization*, Teilhard means an individual's human fulfillment, human self-development, and human self-actualization through experience, education, and training. By *supernatural depersonalization*, Teilhard means what happens when individuals recenter themselves as a cell in the Body of Christ.

Actually, while Teilhard uses the word "*de*-personalization" here, as if this movement were intended to produce a *loss* of personality, he is really describing a process more accurately labeled "super-personalization," that is, moving the center of my life from my individual human personality into the super-personality of the Total Christ.

Here's how he might describe the two simultaneous movements in other words: (1) While we personally *animate* and put our mark on all that we do in fulfilling our human potential, (2) Christ *sur-animates* us by letting all that we accomplish become part of fulfilling the Total Christ's potential.

A Familiar Experience

The experience of sur-animation is not at all foreign to us. Athletes fulfill its definition every time they play on a sports team. True athletes let all that they accomplish on the playing field become part of fulfilling the team's potential. While each player personally *animates* and puts his or her personal mark on all his efforts on the playing field, the larger body — the "team" — *sur-animates* him by letting all that he does on the playing field become part of fulfilling the team's potential.

The same is true for any team, whether it be a scientific research team, an automobile assembly line, a hospital surgical team, or a protest march. Because we want the team to succeed, we are willing to put aside our personal wants for a time while the team is playing and live as a part of the team — for the team, with the team, and through the team.

Spiritual Exercise: Sur-animating Moments _____

Ω Think of those times when you have been sur-animated by a team and its purpose. It is much the same process in faith when we experience ourselves and others as part of the Christ team. In those sur-animated moments, we are living for the Christ Body, with the Christ Body, and through the Christ Body.

Conclusion to Parts One and Two

SOME GENERAL REMARKS ON CHRISTIAN ASCETICISM

Summary

In what Teilhard calls a conclusion to Parts One and Two, he sums up three main themes of his spirituality ("ascetical doctrine") developed so far: Attachment and Detachment, the Meaning of the Cross, and the Spiritual Power of Matter.

In "Attachment and Detachment," he shows how certain traditional contradictory pairs — activity or passivity, life or death, growth or diminishment, possession or renunciation — are really complementary pairs. Your self-development (growth) is pursued in order that you may be equipped to give your life (diminishment) in service to the Cosmic Christ.

In "The Meaning of the Cross," Christ on the Cross in its broadest meaning, for Teilhard, symbolizes a vast movement and stirring up of human life, guiding it on a forward and upward path. The Cross also tells us that personal happiness and the purpose of creation cannot ultimately be sought in the temporal visible world but will occur only in a total transformation of ourselves and everything around us. The Cross, therefore, is a call for us to break through, not to fear to cross a threshold into a future than we cannot yet see.

"The Spiritual Power of Matter" reminds us that we need to handle material things with a proper sense of reverence. On the one hand, matter — which Teilhard defines as all the assemblage of things, energies, and creatures that surround us — can sometimes weigh us down and produce wounds, suffering, temptations, aging, and death. On the other hand, matter, when we engage with it confidently and with reverence, can release in us exuberance, effort, joy, strength, attractiveness, and link us to everything else.

◆ ◆ ◆

Looking Ahead

Before Teilhard explores the "heavenly layers" of the divine milieu in Part Three of his book, he pauses to sum up a few new ascetical attitudes and practices that he has suggested or implied in Parts One and Two In this section, he takes up (1) attachment and detachment, (2) the meaning of the Cross, and (3) what he calls the "spiritual power of matter."

1. Attachment and Detachment

In the following section Teilhard will talk a lot about attachment and detachment. Based on the above definitions, you may consider whether, at the moment, you are reading these pages as one who is interested, uninterested, disinterested, attached, or detached.

Naturally Integrated

A traditional linear thinker might typically ask Teilhard, "Which is better for a Christian: activity or passivity? life or death? development or diminishment? possession or renunciation? attachment or detachment?"

Teilhard does not like either/or thinking, nor does he like to be forced into either/or choices, since he is more of a systems thinker. In this mind-set, he tends to look at the whole picture, seeing how things that seem to be opposites really fit together. When he looks, he doesn't see *either* human beings *or* the Body of Christ. He sees them both together — human beings *in* the Body of Christ acting *through* the Body of Christ.

Asceticism

"Ascetical" refers to the area of spirituality that deals with the *methodical use of behavioral practices or habits* that are meant to dispose a person to spiritual growth and union with God — such as prayer, meditation, chanting, liturgy, study of spiritual writers, biblical reading, fasting, almsgiving, penance, physical labor, and various forms of self-discipline and self-denial.

St. Anthony the Abbot, who lived as a monk in fourth-century Egypt, is considered the founder of Christian asceticism because he developed the first asceticism, that is, the first integrated system of ascetical practices for a group of people. Today, for instance, the distinct ways each Catholic religious order interprets the vows of poverty, chastity, and obedience reveal its specific ascetical tradition.

Teilhard in *The Divine Milieu* is laying the foundation for a new asceticism for our new century that is grounded in both Christian theology and an evolutionary interpretation of creation and religion.

Neither does he want to separate the naturally integrated phases of activity and passivity, life and death, attachment and detachment. Teilhard explains the way he thinks about these seeming opposites and how he sees them connected to each other.

The essential purpose of asceticism, he says, is to help you *to be united with God.* No one will disagree with that. But, he adds, before you experience being united with the divine, *you must first of all experience being yourself as completely as possible.* Not all spiritual writers would agree with that. For Teilhard, God's grace and the divine milieu

---

Clarifying Investment-of-Energy Terminology

To be *interested* means to invest your energy, or at least your attention, in a certain process. It may also mean that you contribute your *effort* so that the process will attain its outcome or purpose.

To be *uninterested* means you intend to contribute *no* investment of attention or energy to the process or its outcome. "I can't be bothered."

To be *disinterested* means you have an investment of energy in the process and you will see it through to its completion, but you are not attached to a certain specific outcome. Thus, a judge in a court of law is expected to be disinterested, that is, impartial, not taking the side of either the prosecution or the defense.

To be *attached* (attachment) means your energy and attention are invested in the specific predetermined outcome that you desire, and that is the only outcome you will accept. You are glued to it.

To be *detached* (detachment) means you will spend your energy and attention to achieve the outcome you desire, but you are not so glued (attached) to that outcome that you cannot let go of it if things don't turn out the way you wanted.

---

are always urging you toward ever more self-development and self-awareness. To cooperate with God's work in the world requires that you develop yourself and learn to manage your life and your environment. This you must do if you want to bring something special and unique to your union with God. Central to Teilhard's spirituality is human self-development in order to serve the Body of Christ.

You have to possess yourself before you can renounce yourself. Otherwise, you have nothing to renounce. You can't give away something you don't already possess. You can't be of service to the Body of Christ if you have nothing to offer. Once you have developed yourself, then there is some meaning and content in "accepting diminishment for the sake of being in another." The "another" Teilhard is referring to here is, of course, Christ. Only when you possess a self can you consider "dying to that self to live in Christ." As Teilhard says, "The fire of heaven must come down on *something*: otherwise there would be nothing consumed and nothing consummated" (Torchbook, 99, emphasis added).

So Teilhard's general ascetical principle is: *First, develop yourself. Then, once you possess something of yourself to offer, you can offer it to God. More precisely, you can let the Christ Body possess and use it in Christ, for Christ, and through Christ.*

But, of course, Christ can use your talents and capacities only in and through you. Which is why you have to develop them in the first place if you want to participate in Christ's work in the world.

Spiritual Practice: My Self-Development _____

Ω This idea of self-development is a key element in Teilhard's spirituality. Please be certain that you understand it. Think about it and how it applies to you. What would it mean *for you* to develop yourself? Each person will give a unique response to that question, so it is important that you begin to explore your unique answer to it.

Once you begin to grasp the meaning of self-development for you, the following sections of the text will be more significant to you.

═══

A. First, Develop Yourself, Christianity Says to the Christian.

Many Christian ascetical books fail to emphasize this point — possibly because self-development seems too "natural," too "secular" or too dangerous to be insisted upon. Nevertheless, from the standpoint of helping fulfill the Body of Christ, it is a duty to grow and develop

---

Nothing God Makes Is Profane

Yahweh! What variety you have made in your creation,
Arranging everything so wisely!
Earth is completely full of things you have made....
As you send forth your breath, they are created.
You keep renewing the face of the earth.
The Lord is glad that he made these works.
                              —Psalm 104:24, 30–31 [my paraphrase]

---

so as to make one's skills and talents bear fruit in the natural order. Development of the talents you enjoy is important for two reasons. On the one hand, those talents are part of God's gift to you, so they should be developed and used to their fullest capacity, if only to give glory to God. On the other hand, those talents, well developed, are also needed by God for the fullest advancement of the Body of Christ.

It is part of Catholic tradition, especially from St. Paul, to encourage self-development and the advancement of the whole human race. We are meant to discover and love everything that is true and beautiful in creation. Human effort, says Teilhard, even in areas that have been labeled "profane," must assume "the role of a holy and unifying operation."

"Profane" means whatever is secular and nonreligious, so for Teilhard this might mean anything from engaging in sports, making business deals, mopping floors, and being a bouncer in a night club to playing poker, dancing, gambling, selling used cars, or getting cosmetic surgery. For Teilhard, even these activities may become holy and unifying efforts if they are done in ways that promote attractiveness, connection, complexity, consciousness, and human bonding.

Time and effort expended in personal development and achievement is an essential first step in preparing the gift of ourselves to God for the development of the Body of Christ. When self-development is pursued in this light, Teilhard says, our apparent "attachment to creatures . . . melts imperceptibly into complete detachment."

Any attachments we make in life are always made with a view to transcending them or going beyond them. For example, if a young man and woman are attracted to each other on their first date (attachment), it is likely that both of them hope their relationship will develop (transcendence). Young couples who get married (attachment) plan to have a home, a family, and a happy future (transcendence). A young man studies diligently in college (attachment) in the hope that this will bring him a good job and a productive career (transcendence). A widow selects a dog for herself (attachment) in the hope that the pet will prove to bring companionship and affection into her life (transcendence).

From this same perspective, *attachment is always penetrated and dominated by detachment.* Attachments look to a brighter future (transcendence), but bring with them a certain price (detachments). The young couple delighted with each other on their first date will each undoubtedly have to make many accommodations and changes of plan (detachments) if they pursue their relationship. The married couples will have to forego many pleasures and freedoms they used to enjoy before they assumed a staggering mortgage, and they will have to totally rearrange their lives to care for their first baby. The college student will have to submit to all the academic demands of his professors if he hopes to get good grades and gain their support. The widow will have to make changes in her life to accommodate her new pet; she will have to give up some of her freedom to take care of her dog, walking it, feeding it, cleaning up after it, grooming it, and visiting the vet.

Teilhard says the idea of developing oneself only for one's aggrandizement or ego, which we are all tempted to do, shows a disregard for the Body of Christ. To guard against this dangerous illusion, he says, it is important to keep constantly alive the passionate vision of the Total Christ, which he names the "Greater Than All."

We contemporary people are so caught up in being separate individuals that even many spiritual writers are absorbed in this mentality and focus only on each individual's relationship to God, as if there were nobody else around except God and me. In his sections on activities and passivities, Teilhard wants to remind us that every single particle of matter and thought in the universe is intertwined with every other single particle of matter and thought. Separateness may sometimes feel very real, but a much truer approach is to see that everything around us is interacting with everything else. In the end, there is only one great big system of which we are all interacting parts. Teilhard wants us never to forget about the big system even when we are focusing on our part of it and our private, personal relationship to God.

Spiritual Practice: What and Who Is Involved in My Relationship to God? _____

Ω The very first section of *The Divine Milieu* stressed how important it was to get a sense of the universal pervasiveness of the divine milieu and how it provides the life force penetrating the great Body of Christ. In everything that Teilhard writes he assumes that you are reading his words in the light of the whole Christ Body. The same is true in this section.

Please check to see how strongly you are caught up in the attitude that there is only you and God, as if there was nobody and nothing else around, either supporting or hindering that relationship. For example, when you are in church, do you just go to your pew and pray, or do you notice others there and wonder if they need support or a smile? Do you think gratefully of the people who have cleaned the church, dusted and put things in order for you, the ushers who volunteered their time, those who planned the liturgy, the one who prepared a homily? Do you remember with gratitude the people who contributed to the church so that you might have a building to worship in?

Then check to see how strongly you believe that you are an interacting, totally intertwined cell of one great living divine system.

B. And If You Possess Something, Christ Says in the Gospel, Leave It and Follow Me.

For those persons who understand that attachments are meant to be transfigured (or sur-animated) through detachment, this second step — "Leave it and follow me" — will feel natural and automatic. It becomes a small part of the "great work," in Teilhard's words, subjecting "a little more matter to spirit."

This spiritual attachment-detachment process has a very natural and ordinary expression. For example, when a person dedicates his time, his health, and his life to something greater than himself, such as supporting and caring for a family, or a truth of science to be discovered, or a cause to be defended, he must give up many other things he might like to enjoy. But he does it willingly — even happily. These are all human examples of passing from attachment to detachment, as that person "faithfully mounts the ladder of human endeavor" (Torchbook, 98).

Reserved Forms of Renunciation

Teilhard advises here that there are two forms of renunciation that should *not* be used except by the clear and unambiguous urging of God the Creator, because neither of them in themselves can be otherwise justified without that divine impetus.

The first renunciation Teilhard cautions against is *a life dedicated to the evangelical counsels* — a vowed life of poverty, chastity, and obedience in a religious order or congregation. Remember, Teilhard himself is a vowed religious person who has made this renunciation, but he is very convinced that he is following a divine call and he lives it faithfully to the end of his life. So it is ironic that he presents such a

Transcend, Transfigure, and Sur-animate

Teilhard often uses the three terms "transcend," "transfigure," and "sur-animate" interchangeably, but each term has a slightly different nuance.

"To transcend" means to go beyond or to see something from a higher perspective. For example, I may work in the billing department of a hospital; but instead of seeing my job simply as getting this or that bill written up accurately and efficiently, I transcend that personal perspective and see it as my contribution to improving the quality of service we offer in our hospital.

"To transfigure" means to change the shape of something into a better or higher shape. For example, as the billing person, instead of seeing the fifty bills I have to prepare and pay this morning as fifty tasks to complete, I transfigure them and see each one as a way the hospital stays connected with the patient to whom it is being mailed.

"To sur-animate" means to obtain the source of your energy and reason for acting from a higher being or system than from within yourself. (For Teilhard, the preposition "sur" is like the English "super," so we might prefer to say "super-animate.") Instead of seeing the patient bills I'm preparing simply as things I am getting done on my own, I am sur-animated by the hospital's purpose and energy. I see what I do as an action that is my small part of the entire hospital's service to the patient, that is, something all the employees of the hospital — as a single living system — are trying to offer to our patients.

strong warning to anyone thinking about entering religious life. But he does.

Teilhard is very clear about ensuring a divine call before anyone makes a commitment to the religious life. One cannot dedicate his or her life, he says, to the practice of poverty, chastity, and obedience without an explicit invitation from God. This "vocation," he explains, is a divine call "to a flight beyond the normal spheres of earthly, procreative, and conquering humanity." A vocation to a monastery or convent should not be assumed or undertaken without that call. In a most radical sense, to choose to become a vowed religious is to choose to live one's life without ever embracing the responsibility of ownership (vow of poverty), relinquishing totally the right to use one's natural attraction to form a loving union with another person and raise a family (vow of chastity), and handing over those fundamental choices that shape one's productive life and career to another human being (vow of obedience).

Although in our day of very few vocations to religious life we may not need to hear this caution, we should remember that in Teilhard's day — the end of the nineteenth century and the beginning of the twentieth century — it was the cultural expectation and common social practice for a large Catholic family to strongly encourage one or more of their children to find their career in religious life. Other children were expected to join the military or take up the family business or, in the case of women, to get married and raise a family. In those days, a son or daughter in religious life brought special recognition and prestige to their family. In order to produce or preserve such social and religious prestige for their families, we may assume that many a teenaged boy or girl felt obligated to join a religious order or enter a convent, which motivation is exactly what Teilhard is cautioning against.

The call to live the evangelical counsels in a religious community is indeed a special and beautiful vocation, when it comes from God, but you cannot invent your own religious vocation. From Teilhard's perspective, no one has the right to choose for oneself, without a divine summons, to live such a humanly diminished life.

Teilhard certainly understood the diminishments he underwent from the religious vow of obedience he made to his Jesuit superiors. As a result of that vow, he could not teach what he wanted to, or follow a career he wanted to, or live where he wanted to, or publish what he wanted to. For example, he loved theology and spirituality, yet he was commanded not to teach it. He was hired as a professor at a famous college in Paris, but his superiors forbade him to accept the position. He wanted to live in Paris, but instead his superiors sent him to China, where he was forced to live for thirty years. He longed to share his many writings about God, spirituality, and evolution, but was denied the right to publish them. He had to trust that somehow God would find a way — which happened only after his death — to get his ideas out into the world.

In each of these unwelcome situations — passivities of diminishment — Teilhard, true to his beliefs, struggled against them and asked his few friends to help him. He never ceased to resist the diminishment of being forced to live in China. He never "surrendered" to this diminishment he believed was unwarranted. Again and again, while he continued to develop himself and refine his thoughts about spirituality, he wrote to his superiors, requesting permission to return to France. All through these decades of exile in China, he accepted their refusals with what he paradoxically called "true resignation," that is, while continuing to obey the explicit command of his superiors and remain in China, he continued to resist the diminishment they were imposing on him.

In his youth, Teilhard felt clearly the divine invitation to a vowed religious life in the Society of Jesus. He accepted that call with the diminishments he knew it might entail, but he was undoubtedly surprised and dismayed at those extra diminishments imposed by his superiors, ones that he never expected.

The Option to Refuse an Invitation, Even from God

Of course, if God offers you such a divine invitation, you may refuse it, since it is an invitation rather than a command. God would never command anyone to accept such a radical diminishment. God's call could only come as an invitation. It has to be freely chosen, just as it has to be freely offered by God — open to refusal. In the Gospel a rich young man came to Jesus and asked him what he should do with his life. Jesus recognized that the young man had received a vocation from God, so Jesus told him what that vocation might entail. Jesus said to him, "Go, sell what you possess, give the proceeds to the poor, then come follow me." We are told that the young man walked sadly away. He had made the choice *not* to respond to the divine invitation. His walking away was not a rejection of God, but only the turning down of an invitation. The appropriate response to any invitation, even from God, is a simple yes or no. God can work with either response.

Excessive Mortification

The second form of renunciation Teilhard cautions against is *the voluntary practice of excessive mortification* — those penances and sacrifices that diminish or threaten one's health or life. Here Teilhard is thinking about stories of "holy" people who, in a distorted sense of renunciation and a misdirected desire to please God, apparently tortured their bodies with extreme fasting, whips and chains and other forms of self-mutilation, enduring excruciating pain believing it would free them to live a higher, more spiritual life.

The word "mortification" literally means "making oneself dead." It is a kind of self-death. Since only God alone "can bring forth another life from every form of death," a human being, Teilhard argues, does not have "the right to diminish himself for the sake of diminishing himself." Teilhard is very strong on this point. "Voluntary mutilation, even when conceived as a method of inward liberation, is a crime against being, and Christianity has always explicitly condemned it" (Torchbook, 98).

In a word, this is *not* a way to follow Christ, unless God very explicitly invites one to it. To assume one is called to a life of extreme mortification would be a sin of presumption, a conscious *activity of diminishment*.

Rather, as Isaiah wrote, what is described above is not the kind of fasting and mortification God wants. If you want to die to yourself, if you want to practice true renunciation, here's how to do it so that it glorifies God and promotes the Kingdom of God:

> Is not this the fast that I choose: to loose the bonds of injustice, to undo the thongs of the yoke, to let the oppressed go free, and to break every yoke? Is it not to share your bread with the hungry, and bring the homeless poor into your house; when you see the naked, to cover them, and not to hide yourself from your own kin? (Isa. 58:6–7)

Instead of a spirituality that promotes the activity of *voluntary self-diminishment as a way to get closer to God*, Teilhard proposes a spirituality that promotes the activity of *voluntary self-development as a way to better serve God's people*, the Body of Christ. As we shall see, such self-development calls for its own renunciation.

C. Thus, in the General Rhythm of Christian Life, Development and Renunciation, Attachment and Detachment Are Not Mutually Exclusive.

Development and renunciation, just like attachment and detachment, work together in harmony, says Teilhard, "like breathing in and out in the movement of our lungs." Inhaling and exhaling may appear to be opposing movements, but in reality they are two necessary phases working together that keep us alive.

However, even breathing is "subject to an infinite number of subtle variations." Our manner of breathing changes when we are sitting and when we are standing, when we are sleeping and awaken, when we are resting and resume playing, when we are eating and then get back to working. Our breathing adapts to each different situation.

In a similar way, the dialectics between attachment (inhaling) and detachment (exhaling) have their own variations depending on the situation. In some people, human effort and self-development may be strong at some times with little demand for detachment or renunciation — when life is easy and smooth sailing. Others may find their attempts at self-development thwarted again and again by external diminishments, and so detachment plays the stronger role in their lives. You want to finish your education but your funds run out, you develop a serious illness, your spouse divorces you, or your child is arrested for possessing illegal drugs. No matter what happens, however, you need to keep breathing in and out.

Teilhard uses another example of an in-and-out dialectic where traditional spiritual writers stress only an opposition, that is, between asceticism and mysticism. They claim, and Teilhard agrees, that *asceticism* focuses one's attention on self-discipline and self-perfection, whereas *mysticism* focuses on being absorbed in God. One is human-centered, these writers maintain, while the other is God-centered. With this oppositional, either/or position, Teilhard disagrees, because he sees the two efforts, like breathing, as a single two-phased process. "There is nothing [inherent] in man's concern for self-perfection to distract him from his absorption in God," he writes, provided one's human life is seen, loved, and developed as a life moving toward an intimate union with the Body of Christ.

Such a movement is undeniable, if you accept the principle that evolution is always happening on every level of being — and has a direction. Evolution's direction in the divine milieu is always meant to move in an upward trajectory, from separateness to union, from complexity to higher complexity, from consciousness to higher consciousness, from matter to spirit.

In this sense inhaling symbolizes the enjoyment of self-development: learning to play tennis, perfecting a new recipe for lasagna, practicing the piano, learning a foreign language, traveling abroad, acquiring a college degree, or developing a new business skill. Exhaling symbolizes each action becoming part of a larger evolutionary process. It involves the movement from being centered in yourself to becoming centered in the divine self.

Teilhard wants you never to forget that, at every moment of its existence, every fragment of creation is constantly inhaling divine grace, which is the oxygen provided by the divine milieu, for that fragment's development. So as God takes possession of each active and self-developing human being, by his or her free choice in faith, this human creature eventually becomes "passive." Teilhard is using the term "passive" as a true mystic would. The true mystic has not become some helpless or inert puppet that cannot move unless someone pulls its strings. Rather, Teilhard uses "passive" in the sense that the person becomes consciously aware that his or her human self is being newly created and newly developed as part of a divine union, and freely chooses it. Asceticism is like inhaling, mysticism is like exhaling.

For Teilhard, mystics following his spirituality need not cease doing the "worldly" work they have been doing. They need to keep inhaling. Nor do they need to cease doing it with as much fervor, enthusiasm, and delight as they have always had. Nor does Teilhard's spirituality exclude laughter, merriment, and fun. The mystic's self-development need not cease at all. In fact, all of these factors might even increase because such persons realize consciously that their efforts are now, and always have been, part of a much larger and more important project, namely, the building of the Earth. That planet Earth, they now realize, is nothing less than part of the very divine Body of Christ.

To use another metaphor, their human roles as teacher, nurse, scientist, lawyer, or parent are not written out of their human script. Their script has been reenvisioned and rewritten and they have been "recast." They are still performing their human talents but are now acting in a *divine drama*.

Each of these images reflects Teilhard's way of describing the harmonious interaction of possession and renunciation, attachment and detachment. The life of faith always involves inhaling and exhaling, taking in and giving back, "growing for Christ and diminishing in him." In this process, what is natural and what is supernatural are

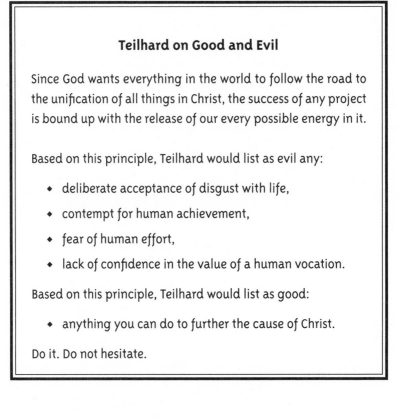

> ## Teilhard on Good and Evil
>
> Since God wants everything in the world to follow the road to the unification of all things in Christ, the success of any project is bound up with the release of our every possible energy in it.
>
> Based on this principle, Teilhard would list as evil any:
>
> - deliberate acceptance of disgust with life,
> - contempt for human achievement,
> - fear of human effort,
> - lack of confidence in the value of a human vocation.
>
> Based on this principle, Teilhard would list as good:
>
> - anything you can do to further the cause of Christ.
>
> Do it. Do not hesitate.

not in opposition, but are both forces in the divine milieu that are designed to work together in harmony.

Spiritual Exercise: You Can't Get Away from Renunciation _____

Ω List some of the ways your self-development also involves renunciation, how your attachment to your work or profession continually calls for detachment. Perhaps you are already a committed nurse, physician, salesperson, or investor or you are in some other line of work. Being true to your profession often makes demands on your time, your relationships, your finances, and so on, that you might like to enjoy elsewhere. But you must detach yourself from — let go of — these other enjoyments because of your commitment to your work.

Recognize how much your self-development and your work or profession are like breathing in and out. Think of breathing in as whatever
nourishes your mind or spirit, such as learning new things, closing new
contracts, or making others feel healthier. Think of breathing out as what
it costs you in terms of your own time and leisure in order to succeed.

The Use of "Creatures"

Just as it would be absurd to impose unlimited amounts of eating or
fasting upon the physical body, the same goes for development and
renunciation in the spiritual life. There needs to be a balance. More
importantly, just as each person must find the optimum amount of
food needed to stay healthy, avoiding either obesity or malnutrition,
so each one must find the optimum balance of self-development and
renunciation for a healthy spiritual life. Finding this balance is one
part of the self-discipline required in asceticism.

In the use of "creatures" — that is, the objects that are all around
us such as food and drink, house plants and pets, radio and television, telephones and computers, newspapers and magazines, cars and
homes, money and political connections — some spiritual writers promote the *minimum* theory, that is, to use these objects in the least
possible amount. The mistaken assumption behind this theory, Teilhard feels, is the belief that there is little or no spiritual yield to be
gained from involvement in material creation; moreover, to become
engaged with such "creatures" is to be distracted from God. If that is
true, the question arises, Why did God create all these possibilities in
the first place and bless them as "good"?

Teilhard proposes an alternative, a spirituality that teaches us "how
to get the *maximum* spiritual yield from the objects which surround
us — which is what the reign of God really means." A few pages
later in this general remarks section, Teilhard will explore the radically
revolutionary notion of the "spiritual forces in matter." For Teilhard,
we are called to love passionately all these objects in the world —

to love them as part of the Body of Christ — precisely because in Christ they may always become something "greater" than they are in themselves.

We see this happening in science and technology all the time. Grains of sand that had been lying on the seashore for centuries have become "greater" as scientists have used them as key components in a computer's silicon memory chip that now can hold for posterity the words of an important article on health or a photograph of your child. Through the human impulse to evolve, the sand has become more than mere matter. In its ability to help you preserve valuable ideas or memories, it has tasted spirit.

Iron and other metals that were hidden beneath the earth's surface for eons have become "greater" as engineers used them to build bridges over rivers, automobile frames, I-beams for holding up skyscrapers, medical equipment, airplanes, space stations, and a myriad of tools and utensils. In each case, through the impulse to progress, humans have made metals more than mere matter. These metals now allow complexity to increase and consciousness to rise. They have tasted spirit.

This same process of becoming "greater" happens on the human level also. Each athlete becomes "greater" as he or she becomes part of a team, since the whole can become greater than the sum of its parts. Acting in concert, the team operates at a higher level of complexity in their shared purpose than any one individual team member acting alone.

Wouldn't you feel "greater" knowing that, more than being merely one separate human animal among six billion or more walking the planet, you can become one of the memory cells in the mind of the Total Christ, or a cell in that heart, or a cell in the cornea of one of those divine eyes?

The point Teilhard is trying to make here is this. All these diverse elements of creation are living in the divine milieu. Hence, they are all driven by the law of attraction-connection-complexity-consciousness. This means that every fragment of creation feels the impulse and the longing, at some incomprehensibly basic level of consciousness, to become greater. Perhaps even more than us humans, the fragments of earth are willing to endure patiently whatever it takes to achieve "the laborious and painful bursting out beyond matter."

The spiritual principle at work here, especially for us human beings, is that, while "the supernatural awaits and sustains the progress of our nature," making us greater and greater, the supernatural Christ Body also "purifies and perfects that progress" by renunciation. Personal progress and renunciation, like inhaling and exhaling, form an inseparable alliance in God. But in the end, Teilhard notes, renunciation takes the ascendancy.

In another book, Teilhard paints the picture of a man climbing a high mountain. At the base of the mountain, the man begins his ascent loaded with much baggage. As he ascends, he realizes that toting all his baggage is holding him back from his goal. It is keeping him from reaching the peak as soon as he might. Little by little, as he climbs, he jettisons more and more of whatever he does not truly need to get to the top. Renunciation, getting rid of what he doesn't need, becomes a way of life.

However, Teilhard reminds us, any sense of loss or annihilation we may feel in this process of transforming ourselves into the Body of Christ is only apparent and temporary, not real or final. This idea Teilhard uses when he discusses the full meaning of the mystery of the Cross.

Spiritual Practice: Excess Baggage

Ω Reflecting on your life, can you name some of the ways God is "awaiting and sustaining" your natural gifts and talents, and at the same time "purifying and perfecting your progress"? Have you been jettisoning excess baggage in your pursuit of self-development?

For example, have you given up or changed the way you recreate? The way you eat? The way you relate? Have you had to follow a certain regimen or discipline in order to perfect your skill? For example, musicians or dancers must spend many hours a day practicing their art in order to become accomplished professionals. To maintain this discipline, they have to cut other things out of their daily schedules. What of your life and baggage have you had to leave behind?

Realize that when you leave something behind, it is not lost, but is held for you in the loving atmosphere of the divine milieu.

2. The Meaning of the Cross

For some Christians, the Cross is seen as a symbol of sadness, limitation, and repression. Their interpretation implies that the Kingdom of God can come about only through limitation and repression and that it, in effect, rejects purely human aspirations and energies.

Teilhard prefers to see the Cross of Christ from an evolutionary perspective. It is an evolutionary step, incomplete in itself. It is leading to a transformation somewhere up ahead — some new and beautiful purpose or aim. Through Christ and in Christ, we each must take this evolutionary step symbolized by the Cross. For Teilhard, the Cross calls for our adoration of it precisely as a symbol of the "sublime purpose to be attained" by humanity transcending itself in each person — and in all of humanity.

For Teilhard, the suffering of Christ is always tied to the Risen Christ. Christ always knew that the Resurrection would follow his suffering. Whenever he predicted his suffering and death to his apostles, he also gave them the assurance of his resurrection. In a very real sense, humanity is going through a period of evolutionary suffering now but Christ assures us that we will, collectively, experience a sublime culmination equivalent to his resurrection. Teilhard might say that the body on the Cross today is not merely Jesus of Nazareth, but all of us in Christ — the Cosmic Body of Christ.

Teilhard also ties the meaning of the Cross to ideas he discussed in the previous section. In other words, that sublime end that the Cross

---

Help with Our Passivities of Diminishment

Since all the human children share the same blood and flesh, he too shared equally in our human nature, so that by his death he could take away all the power of sin and death, and [by his resurrection] set free all those who felt enslaved all their lives by the fear of death. For it was not angelic nature he took to himself, but descent from Abraham. In this way he became completely like us so that he could be a compassionate and trustworthy high priest in service to God, able to atone for human sins. Because he has himself suffered and been tempted he is able to help us who suffer and are tempted.

—Hebrews 2:14–18 [my own paraphrase]

---

symbolizes will be attained, individually and collectively, through the ongoing two-phase process of possession and renunciation, of attachment and detachment. This is the meaning of the Cross for us today.

In a series of rather startling insights, Teilhard describes how the Cross is connected to a sublime purpose planned for humanity. These are insights few have ever voiced before. Some explanations flow from some of Teilhard's later thoughts.

1. The Cross and Creation's Sublime Purpose

In the most general sense, *the doctrine of the Cross supports the belief that all creation is part of an evolutionary movement.* The Cross tells us two things about this evolutionary movement.

First, it assures us that *evolution leads somewhere* — to a new state of evolving collective existence that Teilhard describes as a "sublime end." Here Teilhard is using the word "end" in his text as referring to a "purpose" or "aim," not as "the last day" or the *end* of the world.

Participating in the Cross

Through him God was pleased to reconcile to himself all things [the universe], whether on earth or in heaven, by making peace through the blood of his cross.... I am now rejoicing in my sufferings for your sake, and in my flesh I am completing what is lacking in Christ's afflictions for the sake of his body, that is, the church.   —Colossians 1:20, 24

Second, *this collective evolution is following a continually upward trajectory.* That is, it is evolving to a higher state, not devolving to a lower state. The Cross reveals, in Teilhard's words, that we are all called "toward the highest spiritualization of matter by means of the greatest possible effort" (Torchbook, 102). That is, this spiritualization of creation will come about by the basic processes of possession-renunciation and attachment-detachment, as these processes occur primarily in humans, but also in nature. After all, trees enjoy life, but their lives can be destroyed in a forest fire; yet through their seeds they may "resurrect" from their death.

Spiritual Exercise: Find Yourself on the Cross _____

Ω Traditional explanations of the "sublime end" of our existence have centered around a scene of the individual souls of the just being taken up to heaven, thanks to Jesus' suffering and death on the Cross, where they will enjoy the utter peace and happiness of contemplating God for all eternity.

From a different perspective on the Cross, Teilhard sees the body on the Cross representing the total Body of Christ evolving through time struggling toward its own "sublime end." If we are elements or cells of this total

Body of Christ, reflect on how this might enrich our understanding of the Cross and deepen the meaning of our own struggles and suffering.

The Body on the Cross — the Christ Body that includes all creation — is what is experiencing the total convergence. This includes the harmony, balance, and integration of all opposites, all polarities, and all apparent contradictions — total oneness.

Ask the Cosmic Christ for a deeper understand of the Body on the Cross.

2. The Word of God as an Element of the World

The Cross reveals the "moving and unfathomable reality of the historic Christ" as the pivotal figure in the evolutionary process. For Teilhard, the risen Christ is "the Master of this world, leading, like an element of the world, not only an elemental life, but (in addition to this and because of it) leading the total life of the universe, which he has shouldered and assimilated by experiencing it himself" (Torchbook, 103).

The fact that Jesus led an "elemental life" — starting as a fertilized egg in Mary's womb, being born as a helpless baby, and growing up like all of us had to do — was very significant for Teilhard. In taking upon himself a human body, Teilhard says, the Word of God accepted and acknowledged in his body all the "elements" of the universe. Like our bodies, Jesus' body was made up of minerals, metals, vitamins, water, chemicals, and oxygen. His body assimilated every layer of living things just as we do, grains from the fields, fruits and nuts from trees, vegetables from the earth, oil from olive vines, wine from grapes, proteins from fish, meat from animals and fowl. Like us, his body hosted in its organs all sorts of living bacteria and microbes that kept his biological systems healthy. Like us, his thoughts, his attitudes, his feelings, his opinions, his beliefs, and the images that filled his imagination were influenced and shaped by his family culture and history, his neighborhood, his teachers, religious leaders, and the people he encountered in his travels. Like us, he tasted and integrated into his personal life all the elements of the universe — from the most elemental, like oxygen and calcium to the highly complex like reasoning and calculating — so that he as the Christ might legitimately become the leader heading the "total life of the universe."

Spiritual Exercise: A Day in the Life of Jesus _____

Ω In your imagination, picture Jesus of Nazareth eating, sleeping, washing, getting dressed, playing games, running errands, conversing with neighbors — doing all the different kinds of things you do during your own typical day. Picture him listening and being influenced by his parents, boyhood friends, his grandparents and cousins.

Let yourself be filled by the awareness that because the Word of God tasted all the elements of the universe in his human body, he earned the right to be Lord of the Universe — maybe not unlike a son or daughter learning the family business from the bottom up.

In a very physical sense we are all connected to the body of Jesus of Nazareth. Scientists tell us that every time we exhale, we expel 10^{23} particles that had been inside us (10^{23} means 10 followed by 22 zeroes). Of course, when we inhale, we also take into ourselves about 10^{23} microscopic particles that had been floating around outside us. Many of those particles are partially the exhalation of other humans, animals, trees, and plants, since they too "breathe."

So for thirty or so years, Jesus was spreading 10^{23} particles from his body every time he exhaled. Everyone around him was absorbing little bits of Jesus. If all these particles he exhaled were not immediately absorbed, air currents would carry them gradually all around the earth, until probably every human being and every animal in every part of the globe had absorbed one or more particles from Jesus' body.

By the same token, over those same thirty years in each of Jesus' inhalations he probably absorbed exhaled particles from every other human being on earth as well as from the animals, trees, and plants.

Thus, each person on earth in Jesus' day was probably carrying particles exhaled by every other person on earth. So everyone was physically participating in Jesus' body, at least microscopically, and particles of them were also in him.

Since there aren't any new particles being made on our planet, those particles that came from Jesus' body are still floating around the planet today, so we each probably have in our bodies particles that were once a part of Jesus' body. His molecules are still with us.

3. An Unimaginably New State

The Cross symbolizes our thirst for deepest happiness and a transformation we cannot yet imagine. In this, the Cross reminds us that the final fulfillment of creation and exquisite happiness cannot be sought for in the visible world we know *today*, since the evolution of the cosmos is still going on as is the evolution of humanity. This is true even in merely human terms. For example, who in the Middle Ages could have imagined the transformation that has happened in science, technology, communication, and medicine that we enjoy today? Christ's resurrection, which completes the struggle through his suffering and death on the Cross, points to a state or condition "beyond a total transformation of ourselves and of everything surrounding us." It is a transformation of our very state of being that we cannot yet comprehend.

Jesus' own disciples could not comprehend the resurrected body that had all the aspect of a spirit — it could walk through walls, be in two places at one time, or apparently inhabit any body he wanted — but was still undeniably a human being, because he ate food, walked, talked, had visible wounds, cooked fish on the shore, and could be physically touched and felt.

The divine milieu, Teilhard reminds us, is always transforming everything within it into new states that a previous state could not imagine. Inorganic minerals could not imagine what the molecular structure of an organic state could be. Similarly, organic chemicals could not imagine what the dynamic structures of a living plant could be. Too, a bush or a tree could not imagine the mobility of a fish or a bird or an animal. A caterpillar cannot imagine being a butterfly, being able to soar in the air instead of just crawling around. An animal could not imagine the human ability to write a book or build a car. Nor can we humans imagine the state that the Body of Christ will reach when it is fully transformed. But the Cross points to it — because of the Resurrection.

Emergent Properties

In systems thinking, when all the parts of a new system come together properly, the system is usually able to do new things that none of the parts by themselves could do. These new abilities are called *emergent properties*. For example, plants can grow and reproduce, whereas rocks can't. The ability to grow and reproduce is an emergent property of plant life. Animals can move about, run, and jump, whereas plants can't. Free movement is an emergent property of animal life.

Many new properties have emerged during human history, as well. Two hundred years ago, how many people could have imagined that the human race would have communication tools like telephones, radios, television sets, cell phones, or the Internet? How many people back then would have envisioned medical breakthroughs like penicillin, polio vaccine, heart surgery, or organ transplants — or a field like anesthesiology? They couldn't even imagine having ether as an anesthetic for an operation. Teilhard sees all these advances in communication, medicine, biology, genetics, and all the other sciences as the evolutionary thrust of the divine milieu. These are emergent properties of human society and, of course, of the Body of Christ. For Teilhard, from now on, evolution's path and progress is in our human hands and minds. It is up to us to, first, dream each next step, then make it real.

For Teilhard, this cocreation of God with humans is what God had wanted to happen since the beginning of time. After all, how could God ultimately create anything less than the fullest expression of personhood? According to Teilhard, the final emergent property of creation in its evolutionary trajectory will be the divine personhood of the Cosmic Christ, fully conscious in all its elements.

Spiritual Exercise: Emergent Properties of the Body of Christ _____

Ω Even though we can't really be certain what future emergent properties of the Body of Christ might be, it is good to accept the imaginative challenge to dream up some of them. What are some of the properties you might like to see emerge next in the Body of Christ?

For example, some people are pushing to raise the ecological consciousness of everyone on the planet, so we can save our earth, which is, of course, part of the Body of Christ. Others are promoting ecumenical and interfaith dialogue among religions. Others are fostering world peace and want to start peace academies instead of military academies. Others are promoting the consciousness that the earth and everything on it is one big organism. Some scientists are hoping to uncover more and more dimensions of physical reality that still remain hidden from us. Others want to link many human minds together, much as people have linked hundreds of computers together, to conceive of new technology that no individual mind can now imagine. All of these are ways of expanding our present level of consciousness.

It's your turn.

4. A Law Common to all Life

The Cross reminds us that the "final ascent" of the Christ Body will compel us to cross a threshold, to go beyond a critical point, where, as Teilhard puts it, "we lose touch with the zone of the reality of the senses" (Torchbook, 103). In other words, we cannot ground this "final ascent" in anything we currently know or experience, no more than the caterpillar in a cocoon can imagine turning into a butterfly that can fly.

But this transition, which will be unimaginably new to us, is only "the sublime aspect of a law common to all life." Transitions from old states to new states have always been happening. Although the inorganic gases of oxygen and hydrogen could not imagine what an organic state could be like, when their molecules were brought together under the proper conditions, they entered the higher life of water. As part of their ascent to a higher life, they left behind their inert status and now enjoyed the capacity to change form, from a liquid to a solid or to a vapor. Again, water of itself could not imagine living any higher state than its own, but once it was absorbed into a plant, it became an element in something that could grow and produce blossoms, flowers, fruits, nuts, or grains. The water had crossed a threshold where it lost touch with its normal zone of experience, and was living an unimaginably transformed life. And so on, from plants to animals to humans.

There is no reason to doubt that, as this evolutionary thrust keeps pushing forward, we humans will, in turn, be assimilated into a higher unimaginable being. Teilhard's point is that, because Jesus came to earth and taught us, we have some inkling of what that next state — after human life — might be.

For Christians, Teilhard would say, one of the reasons Christ appeared on earth when he did was that we humans were finally ready to hear the Creator's evolutionary message about the next state of life we are being called to and what that state will be like. Jesus called that state the Kingdom of God or the Kingdom of Heaven, and he used many symbols and stories to describe what this next state would be *like*. He could only tell us what it would be *like*, because, to humans then and now, that state remains as unimaginable as the butterfly to the caterpillar.

The first Christians had three images they used for the development of the Body of Christ — a *human body, a building,* and *a grapevine.* They believed that, if they were to describe that new Kingdom state as a *human body,* Christ would be its head — where the brain and major sense organs, like eyes, ears, nose, and mouth are located — and we would be the members or organs of his body. Today, since we humans number in the billions, we might better name us each as a tiny cell in the Christ Body.

If that new state was described as a *building*, Christ would be the cornerstone of it, and we would be the living stones and bricks that made up the rest of it.

If that new state was described as a *grapevine*, Christ would be the vine with all its roots — the source of its life — and we would be the branches and the grapes.

Spiritual Exercise: A Cell? A Brick? A Grape? _____

Ω Choose one or two of these descriptions of the Kingdom of God found in the images and parables of Jesus and consider how they might help us glimpse the future workings of the Body of Christ.

We humans often use metaphors to try to describe indefinable experiences, like falling in love, being awestruck, enduring chronic pain, feeling delighted, made helpless by fear, and so on. Teilhard asks you to stretch your imagination and try to describe this great Christ Body and how the Cross fits into its growth and development.

One person suggested that the Body of Christ might be the Internet. Christ might be the brains and memory of it, and we individuals tap into it and use it. The diminishment of the Cross might symbolize the hackers who try to plant viruses into the Internet system to diminish its potential. What do you think? How about another image?

---

5. Revealing the Path of Evolutionary Transformation

For Teilhard, *Jesus on the Cross is "both the symbol and the reality of the immense labor of the centuries which has, little by little, raised up the created spirit and brought it back to the depths of the divine milieu"* (Torchbook, 104). Different from the Divine Spirit, the created spirit, implanted in the first fragments of matter in the Big Bang, remained dormant in the evolutionary trajectory for billions of years. It clearly appeared during the human stage of evolution. Humans were definitely a created and creative spirit. However, before the arrival of Christ, humans did not recognize this long path of their evolutionary transformation. They were confused, misdirected, detoured, rerouted, frustrated, unknowing. They did not understand how the human race and all of creation fit into a greater divine plan. They couldn't envision, as we can today, the "immense labor of the centuries" that struggled to push spirit through the stages of evolution from gas to mineral to metal to plants to invertebrate life to fish, birds, reptiles, mammals, and eventually humans. It still took Jesus Christ, fully divine and fully human, to tell us where we and the rest of creation were headed and what God's plan was for us.

The Cross, More Than a Deliverance from Sin

In early Christian theology an original fall from grace was revealed — symbolized by original parents eating a piece of forbidden fruit — that attempted to explain a reason for all the generations of sin and suffering in the world, and thus a need for the saving Cross. But since the early Christians didn't have the sciences of geology and paleontology to guide them, they couldn't identify the evolutionary process that had been going on for eons in its upward thrust. They could only see the Cross as a deliverance from sin, but this was only a small part of the Cross's symbolism. For Teilhard, more importantly, Christ on the Cross showed us how to plunge our human spirits into the depths of the divine milieu.

Christ showed that his death on the Cross was not simply a human event, but a superhuman one. The Cross was revealed as the "critical point" on the hundred-million-year journey of human effort and endeavor. Teilhard says that Christ on the Cross clarified a number of things for us humans. It corrected the older misconceptions we might have held about the purpose of creation and human life, it redirected our thinking to creation's ever-climbing evolutionary path, and it provided a light guiding us forward. Teilhard discusses these ideas more fully in Part Three of his book.

Spiritual Exercise: Some Misconceptions _____

Ω Each of us possesses a created spirit (the source of our life) that, hopefully, we have used creatively. Teilhard said that Christ's Cross clarified older misconceptions we might have held about the purpose of creation and human life. For example, many Christians for centuries believed that God's plan was simply to save individuals one by one. Others thought that the earth was just the testing grounds for us humans and had no place in the final Kingdom of Heaven. Others believed that the material things God created — sun, moon, stars, oceans, mountains, winds — were merely kinds of teaching tools to humble us and demonstrate the immense power and majesty of God.

What do you think some other misconceptions might have been? Teilhard will give some answers to this question in later sections of *The Divine Milieu*, but, since you are already beginning to use your mind like an evolutionary-thinking Teilhardian, enjoy exploring and reconceiving some misconceptions.

---

3. The Spiritual Power of Matter

In the previous section, "The Meaning of the Cross," Teilhard emphasized the Incarnation of God — how the *divinity* of Christ was humanized and immersed in matter. In this section he explains how the "matter" or physical elements of the *Cosmic Body* on the Cross — which includes us with all our materiality — can be spiritualized. For Teilhard, the two processes are not separated or opposed.

Remember, when Teilhard looks at the figure on the Cross, he sees not only the body of Jesus of Nazareth hanging there but also the

---

The Spiritual Power of Our Earthly Bodies

And now we groan with great longing to be clothed in our heavenly garment [a spiritual body (see 1 Cor. 15:44ff)]. By being clothed in this way we shall never be found without a body.... It is not that we want to get rid of our earthly body, but that we want it to be wrapped and protected in a heavenly garment, so that whatever in us must die will be swallowed up in the life of Christ.   —2 Corinthians 5:2–4 [my personal paraphrase]

---

entire Body of Christ — which includes all humanity, all life, the entire planet, solar system, and universe. So the challenging task assigned to the divine milieu is not merely to spiritualize the materiality of Jesus of Nazareth but the materiality — the *matter* — of the whole cosmic Body of Christ.

Any Christian spirituality must consciously incorporate this two-sided challenge, that is, to explain not only how the divinity of Christ becomes humanized, but also how the materiality of the body of Christ (whether the body of Jesus of Nazareth or the cosmic Christ) becomes divinized or spiritualized.

Some Christian traditions preempt this two-sided challenge. In their eagerness to make distinctions, they contrast soul and body as well as spirit and matter, as if the two could somehow be separated in reality — not merely in their minds. Thus they tend to cultivate one side and eliminate or disregard the other. Once mentally separated, these two sides get stamped with labels, soul and spirit labeled as *good*, body and matter as *evil*. For Teilhard and the Catholic tradition, matter and spirit are inseparable in reality.

So a valid spirituality must acknowledge this inseparable union. For instance, our sacramental elements are examples of spiritualized matter. The physical matter of wheat can become the most spiritual Eucharistic bread. The physical matter of grapes can become the most spiritual Eucharistic wine. The physical matter of olives from the olive tree are crushed to become the sacramental oil for baptism and the anointing of the sick.

When Teilhard uses the term "matter" he means it in the widest possible sense. Matter, for him, is "the assemblage of things, energies, and creatures which surround us insofar as they are palpable, sensible, and 'natural' [as opposed to supernatural]." And again, "Matter is the common, universal, tangible setting...in which we live" (Torchbook, 106).

That "setting in which we live," Teilhard notes, is "infinitely shifting and varied." It is never the same from moment to moment, since at every moment billions of humans on the planet are making decisions and acting, and each of those decisions and actions changes the setting. This is to say nothing of how the weather and other natural forces are constantly changing the "matter" of earth. Since the material world is constantly changing, spirit must also match it in its dynamism. The two, matter and spirit, are always interacting and always creating new relationships and new beings.

Spiritual Exercise: The Shifting Setting of Life _____

Ω Reflect for a moment on Teilhard's idea that matter and spirit are always interacting and always creating new relationships and new beings. How has this process been lived out in your life?

For example, a man and a woman (both dynamic systems of matter and spirit) meet and interact to form a new relationship. If they marry and have children, their interaction has created new beings. The cook in the family kitchen is always interacting with matter, and from time to time can come up with a new dish (a new being). The physical brain with all its neurons firing combines sensory experiences and continually creates new ideas and concepts or generates new information.

Find your own examples of creating new relationships and new things, as well as how the constant shifting of the "setting in which you live" has challenged and inspired you.

You may thank God for putting the law of attraction-connection-complexity-consciousness into the divine milieu and into your life.

Matter's Two-Sided Power

Matter can both drag us downward *and* lift us up. It can be both a burden *and* a blessing, painful *and* pleasurable, threatening *and* enhancing, heavy *and* light, growing old *and* ever young, running us down *and* recharging us.

Traditional spiritual writers tend to emphasize how matter can drag us down and even entice us to sin. No one needs to remind us about this *de*volutionary power of matter. We all know the aches and pains of our material bodies, food that spoils, metals that rust, motors that wear out, soil that loses its richness, organisms killed by disease.

Instead, Teilhard wants us to acknowledge the second side of matter's power, the vitalizing and energizing capacities of physical things — expressions of life that could not ever happen without our material bodies. Consider the physical exuberance of the athlete, the dancer, the clown, and the child taking her first eager steps. Think of the ennobling contact when people meet face-to-face to share ideas, interact on teams, or work together for certain causes. Look at the vigorous effort of humans toiling in fields, factories, and buildings. Recall the joy of growth, watching a child learn to walk and talk, to swing a baseball bat or ride a two-wheel bicycle. These are all examples of matter's vitalizing power. To be deprived of such power, says Teilhard, would be "intolerable," yet how many spiritualities of the past, especially religious and monastic traditions, have deliberately turned away from the energizing capacities of matter!

Or think of the matter of berries that are crushed to make ink with which the artist sketches the lines of a beautiful drawing or that

Defining "Spirit" and "Matter"

Here is a summary of Teilhard's revolutionary ideas about the relationship of spirit and matter, taken mostly from his book *How I Believe* in the essay "Faith in Spirit."

Spirit is NOT the antithesis of matter.

Matter is merely spirit made concrete and physical.

Spirit is NOT an entity independent of matter.

Spirit is NOT antagonistic toward matter.

Spirit is NOT locked up in matter trying to escape.

Spirit is NOT floating somewhere outside or above the physical world.

Spirit is born within matter and acts as a function of matter.

Spirit expresses itself in and through matter.

Spirit is the origin and term or goal of matter.

In the beginning, spirit gave birth to matter.

Spirit helps matter to recognize its spiritual beginnings.

Spirit is continually leading the universe toward a more spiritual state.

Spirit is driving everything to be more conscious and more spirit-filled.

Spirit is the force driving everything toward integration, synthesis and sublimation.

Spirit is the power of unity scattered throughout the innumerable fragments of matter in the universe.

the composer uses to put on manuscript paper the musical notations that will eventually be heard as a symphony. Or the matter of petroleum turned into plastics used to make sound recording tape, CDs, or DVDs. The material wood transformed into a violin. The material brass transformed into a trumpet. This is the creative and spiritual power of matter, matter redeemed from its inert state in service to a more spiritual purpose.

Didn't the Word of God, Teilhard asks, plunge himself into matter in order to redeem it and reveal its more spiritual purposes?

Teilhard's Way of Handling Matter

The main point of this section, for Teilhard, is "how we should touch and handle matter with a proper sense of reverence." His ascetical suggestions about spiritualizing the "matter" of your life call for a personal evolutionary process that includes at least seven stages or steps.

To prepare us to understand the transition stages in becoming aware of the spiritual power of matter, Teilhard offers two images.

The first is a deep-sea diver rising from the depths of the ocean to the clear light on the surface. At any point in his ascent, the sea below him and the sea above him have opposing properties. What is below him looks ever darker, while what is above looks ever brighter.

The second image is of a hiker on a fog-bound mountain climbing upward to a peak that is bathed in light. Again, like the case of the deep-sea diver, the fogged area below the hiker always looks darker than the area toward the peak. Also, in the fog the hiker's success depends upon using everything around him — the rocks, the branches, the wind, a pathway, and the sunlit peak — as leverage to assist his climb.

Teilhard wants you to keep these images in mind as he describes the seven stages in discovering the spiritual power of matter.

1. Realize when handling the matter of your life that you are, symbolically, climbing a slope, on which *you can go upward as well as downward*. The choice is always yours. However, Teilhard cautions, "as a result of original sin," there is always a perpetual impulse or pull

to go downward toward the darkness or fog. But implanted in us also is the law of attraction-connection-complexity-consciousness, that is, the impulse to climb upward.

2. Realize that, as a result of the Incarnation and the thrust-toward-consciousness of the divine milieu, *matter also "contains the spur or the allurement to be our accomplice towards heightened being."* Matter can help us upward. It can energize and inspire us. This is perhaps one of Teilhard's greatest insights, that matter is not only helpful but is also essential if we are to reach the heights of spiritualization.

3. Realize that *each one of us is placed at a certain starting point on this slope* at a specific place, defined, among other things, by the present time in the history of the earth, the culture, country, and city we were born in, our personal aptitudes or career, and the tasks assigned to us.

4. Realize that in the process of attaining God, *we are each given a certain set of created things (matter), which are meant to be not obstacles but "footholds" to assist us in our climb toward consciousness of the divine.* Teilhard uses other metaphors to describe these "created things." They may be viewed as "opportunities," "intermediaries to be made use of," or "nourishment to be taken" for the journey, "sap to be purified." Of course, some things will inevitably involve diminishments, but all are "elements to be associated with us and borne along with us." Such associated "elements" might include the people in our lives, the groups we belong to, the places where we work. Remember that these are also on the upward journey with us.

5. Realize, like the hiker, that as a result of each position we subsequently occupy in climbing the mountain, *the matter of our lives will reflect two different areas,* (1) the level already left behind, "to which we should not return, or at which we should not pause, lest we should fall back" (Teilhard calls this the area of matter in the *material* sense — the downward pull of gravity), and (2) the areas of the climb that await us. The sunlit mountain peak.

This step in the climb — which is every step of the climb — marks a continuing crucial moment of decision for the hiker. At every higher step, the hiker asks, "Shall I keep on making the struggle to advance higher, or shall I decide to stop here and settle for what I have so far attained, or perhaps I might even turn around and return to a lower level where it seems safer and less threatening?"

Teilhard's image of the hiker turning around and going back down, or "pausing" as if this is where the hiker will stop climbing — these choices are all about *falling behind* in the spiritual quest. This can happen in a number of ways. The most obvious one is to give up the quest to reach the top, that is, striving for everything I am capable of attaining.

In the expression "falling behind," Teilhard is also referring to those people whose lives are strangely focused on the past. Instead of climbing higher, they spend their effort not in climbing but in trying to deny their past or wishing to change it. Still others — there are many of these — seem to "love" the past and continue to replay it or remember it as a state more desirable than the present or any possible future. They would happily return to the past. In either case, because of their preoccupation with the past, that is, some "lower level of the mountain," they cannot appreciate the opportunities of the present or plan to utilize the potentials of the future. Remember, Teilhard's spirituality focuses on the *not-yet* — what I can still do for Christ.

6. Realize also *our current position presents an opportunity for our "renewed efforts toward progress, search, conquest, and 'divinization'"* (Teilhard calls this the area of matter in the *spiritual* sense). Granite and marble remained inert matter buried in the earth, but served a spiritual purpose when they were made into cathedrals. Lead remained an inert metal in the earth until it was put inside a pencil and could capture the experiences of a person on a piece of paper. Olives hung helplessly on a tree until someone squeezed out the oil and it became the oil used for sacramental anointing. Matter is constantly being spiritualized.

7. Realize that *the frontier between these two areas is always changing*, or in Teilhard's words, is "essentially relative and shifting." In other words, those material things that might serve as good, sanctifying, and spiritual for the person who happens to be climbing below or beside

me can be misleading and bad for me. "What I rightly allowed myself yesterday, I must perhaps deny myself today." Thus, I can only reach my spiritual destiny "after having traversed a *specific path* through matter" (Torchbook, 108). Each one must find his or her own specific path through matter.

In the end, according to Teilhard, no one comes to be as God destines him or her to be without having acquired certain possessions and skills in the material realm and without having experienced certain victories and certain defeats in that realm.

Spiritual Practice: Helpful or Not?

Ω Think of a few people you know quite well. They may be family members, fellow workers, other students, or close friends. Can you think of any "material things" that might be spiritually helpful for one or other of them that would *not* truly be helpful for you at your present location on your climb toward God?

Conversely, can you think of any "material things" that might be helpful to you that would not be helpful for one or other of them?

Thank God for this awareness.

For example, in the physical order, if you are a diabetic and your friend is not, perhaps certain foods that are dangerous for your health might provide at this time the precise nourishment your friend needs. On the intellectual level, perhaps taking certain university courses might be helpful to you for what you will eventually contribute to the Body of Christ, while for your friend taking these courses would be of little use or even wasteful.

Jacob's Ladder Dream

Teilhard recalls the famous ladder dream of the biblical Jacob (see Gen. 28:10–22). For Teilhard, the rungs of that ladder stretching from earth to heaven symbolize "a series of material objects." We climb to heaven on the *material* rungs of a ladder. *We get to God through matter.* That is a basic principle of Teilhard's spirituality. Thus, Teilhard concludes, "it is not our business to withdraw from the world before our time; rather let us learn to orientate our being in the flux of things" (Torchbook, 108). We reach our spiritual destination by using physical things and relating to people in the "setting in which we live."

In Teilhard's spirituality, we are always climbing toward the mountain peak, just as Jacob's dream foreshadows his call to climb the ladder, material rung by material rung, to heaven.

If we use material objects well, Teilhard points out, they can help us to climb and see better in a number of ways. They can

- enlarge our horizons
- snatch us away from our petty and selfish thoughts
- impel us toward a broadening of our vision and awareness
- urge us to renounce some of our no-longer-useful pleasures
- support the desire for ever-more spiritual beauty

When used in this way, matter becomes spiritualized. This is Teilhard's discovery. This is one of his unique gifts to the ascetical tradition in Christianity. While from some perspectives matter seems to compel us to *devolve* toward maximum pleasure and minimum effort, matter in its *evolutionary* potential "now emerges as the principle of minimum pleasure and maximum effort" (Torchbook, 109). Instead of being merely an instrument of *entropy*, matter in Teilhard's spirituality becomes an instrument of evolutionary *synergy*.

Perhaps Teilhard's approach to matter as an "evolutionary potential" flip from entropy to synergy needs a bit of explanation. Entropy is a physicist's term. Physicists have discovered a principle that they call the second law of thermodynamics, which roughly means that, over time, physical matter tends to decay into states that are less and less useful, productive, or valuable. For example, while we might be able to use a log of wood in many ways, once we burn it in our fireplace all we have left is a pile of ashes. That's entropy at work. Similarly, powerful radioactive substances like uranium will eventually lose their power. Our sun will probably burn itself out in another billion years. Even human beings grow old as our parts wear down. The law of entropy seems cruel, enough to discourage any optimist's hope in the future, but not Teilhard.

Where physicists tend to see only entropy, Teilhard prefers to see a blossoming of synergy. To synergize means to combine the energies of mind and matter to produce a higher form of energy — something more useful, more productive, and more valuable. Usually synergy is most easily recognized at the human level, where a team of people can accomplish a task that no single member of the team could have accomplished — or even envisioned. Teilhard was stunned by the synergy of the team of scientists and engineers who were called upon in the early 1950s to develop the cyclotron, the machine that could get an atom going so fast that the atom could be split into its components. None of the members of the team could envision or see how to build the cyclotron or make it work, but *together* they could!

Teilhard recognized that humans were — and have been through the centuries — using the human mind and imagination to create synergy with different kinds of inert matter. For example, two pieces of different metals, when strapped together, can act as a hydrometer that measures humidity in the air. Others discovered that if they put mercury in a slender glass tube, it could tell us the temperature of the air with tremendous accuracy.

More importantly, humans have been finding continuously more effective ways of turning entropic processes into synergic ones. Entropy tends to make our eyes grow weaker as we age, but humans have taken glass and plastic to make eyeglasses or contact lenses, thus reversing the natural entropy through the synergy of human minds and inert elements. While entropy causes iron and other metals to rust, human minds have used various products to remove rust. For metal parts that tend to wear down, humans have invented from fossil elements ways to rejuvenate machines by lubricating them. When human organs get diseased by entropic forces, humans have learned through synergy of mind and matter to mend and replace them. Even at the emotional level, we might see psychological depression in a human being as a kind of entropy. Instead of letting depression cause a person to spiral downward, chemists through synergy of mind and matter have found substances derived from plants to counteract depression and recharge people with new energy. The examples can go on and on, since humans have become better and better at turning entropy into synergy. For example, instead of wasting the energy in river water, humans have built dams and hydroelectric plants. Instead of just letting the wind blow away, humans have created sails for boats, windmills to grind grain, and wind turbines to generate electricity.

These are a few examples of what Teilhard means when he says that matter "now emerges as *the principle of minimum pleasure and maximum effort.*" Instead of seeing matter as dragging us in a downward trajectory of entropy, we completely turn our perception of matter around, so we now see matter as useful and even essential to human progress and the full development of the Body of Christ. For only matter can enable people to maximize their human energy. Only matter gives humans the ability to work with synergy, to keep the evolutionary trajectory continually moving upward toward spirit. Without the gasoline to run our cars, without the Freon to keep our refrigerators cold, without the sand and metal to make light bulbs, without the metal wires to bring us electricity, without the solar panels on our satellites to bring us television programs, weather reports, and other signals, we would remain totally subject to entropy. Synergy makes life more complex and us more conscious. It's the law of attraction-connection-complexity-consciousness at work, the law that governs the divine milieu.

Spiritual Practice: Making Me More Complex and Conscious ____

Ω Consider each of the bullets in the list on page 162 and reflect on how material things and events have led you toward a more complex and conscious, that is, a more spiritual life. For example, what events or people have enlarged your horizons? What project has captured your attention so as to lure you away from petty and selfish thoughts? What people or events have helped you to look at things with a broader perspective? What happenings have helped you give up enjoyable pursuits that no longer serve you or the Body of Christ? What events or people have inspired you to aspire to more spiritual growth?

Thank God for each of these people and events that have conspired to make you more conscious.

The Progressive Sublimation of the Universe

Just as each individual has a trajectory or path to discover and follow before attaining union with God, so the world itself has a trajectory or path to follow before it finds its fulfillment. The world's destiny is the theme Teilhard takes up in the final pages of this section.

Even though the material world has some energies in it that humans have not yet found a use for in fostering spiritual transformation, and even though other physical energies may appear "perverted," there are many physical energies that, in the evolutionary process, are slowly being separated from their simple material reality and used to move us toward spirit. Still other physical forces already possess a "certain quantity of spiritual power." The basic metals, plastics, silicon chips, and wiring that make up my computer have been separated from their simple material reality and joined together to serve a spiritual power such as writing this book. The material plants and trees that provide fruits, grains, and vegetables for our food are transformed in us as energy to feel, think, act, imagine, and dream The material bodies of our pets already possess "a certain quantity of spiritual power" in their companionship and their ability to faithfully love and protect us. Teilhard maintains God is progressively sublimating all the physical energies on earth.

At present on earth, spiritual power is still in a diffused state almost everywhere, especially in material objects. For example, we

---

Clarifying Some Consciousness Terminology

"Suppress" means to put out of conscious awareness some thought or feeling; however, with conscious choice the suppressed thought can be retrieved.

"Repress" means to force into unconsciousness a feeling or response that then cannot easily be retrieved.

"Sublimate" means to redirect the energy of a lower drive to a higher cause. For example, I turn my moneymaking skills from making profit to philanthropy.

"Sur-animate" means to obtain your life-force and reason for living from a higher being than from within yourself.

---

have hardly tapped the energy of the sun. It has available, if we ever get around to capturing it in useable forms, enough energy to power all our electrical needs for centuries to come. We haven't learned to draw upon the energy available in the ocean currents. Thus, the spiritual potential of the sun and the oceans remains in an unused state.

However insignificant or crude some object or energy may appear to us — a pebble by the seashore, dead leaves fallen from a tree, a piece of fruit that has become rotten, a vicious animal, or a serial killer — it is not without some trace of this spiritual energy, if only because it exists in the divine milieu. In each age, the task of the Body of Christ is patiently to sort out whatever can be spiritualized, and to extract that energy without letting any of it get lost. We cannot do it all, but we can at least do our part.

Because of the many individuals currently extracting those "heavenly forces" from the world, the spiritualizing energy of the divine milieu can insinuate itself everywhere. For Teilhard, this is how the "general 'drift' of matter toward spirit" is happening.

The law of attraction-connection-complexity-consciousness is constantly urging humans to raise what is inert matter into a more spiritual
form than where it started. The tree in the forest becomes more spiritualized when it is turned into building materials to make homes, furniture, telephone poles, and works of art. Wood is also transformed into
pulp to make paper to bring more consciousness through newspapers,
magazines, and books. When we take vitamin pills, inert minerals like
calcium and magnesium become fuel for our bodies and brains. Feathers
from ducks become pillows for the human mind and body to rest. Wool
shorn from sheep may be woven into all manner of attractive clothing. Inert iron ore and aluminum ore become thousands of things —
automobiles, airplanes, bridges, skyscrapers, home appliances, audio
equipment — that make our lives more complex and conscious.

Eventually, by the relentlessly loving power of the divine milieu,
whatever of matter can be divinized will be transformed first by the
human spirit, and from that state into the Body of Christ. When all
matter has been reclaimed by spirit, then our world will be ready for
the Parousia — the summary and fulfillment of the world. (See the
epilogue for a greater discussion of the Parousia.)

How will this happen? The gradual evolutionary transformation
will happen through a series of twofold yet single movements.
Among these dialectical evolutionary movements are "immersion and
emergence," "participation and sublimation," "possession and renunciation." It is by means of these movements that we enter into matter
in order to save it.

The Christian always remembers that, because of the Incarnation,
the life and force of Christ have passed into all matter. All material
creation is capable of being spiritualized for two reasons: first, because
the Creator loved it and, second, because Christ entered it fully.

Two Pitfalls

In a final footnote, Teilhard reminds us that the challenge to spiritualize matter has its pitfalls, because it requires the completion of two
stages, both of which are essential: (1) enter fully into matter and

---

Immersion and Emergence

Teilhard looks at the "immersion and emergence" experience of Jesus in his baptism by John in the River Jordan, and asks, "Who can fail to perceive the great symbolic gesture of this baptism in the general history of matter?" The waters of the river symbolize the forces of the earth, and by his immersion in them he sanctifies them. And by his emergence from the water he spiritualizes them. St. Gregory of Nyssa used this same imagery and said, "With the water that runs off his body he elevates the whole world."

---

(2) enter into spirit. However, some people want to forget about or omit one or the other.

Those who go no further than the first stage — *entering fully into matter* — can fall into the error of "seeking divine love and the divine Kingdom on the same level as human affections and human progress," never sublimating these experiences to a higher purpose.

On the other hand, those who omit the first movement and concentrate only on the second phase — *entering into spirit* — tend to believe that spiritual perfection is built on the destruction of nature and matter. They try to suppress any awareness of matter's influence on the process.

Neither of these two pitfall groups understands the nature of transformation. Because of the first group's assumption that nothing exists but the material world, the work of the spirit eludes them. Even when a thing is transformed into spirit, they still see it as the same old thing unchanged. For them, the graphite in the pencil is still graphite in a pencil; it is not capable of being transformed into spirit — even as they read the loving words on a note to them that a piece of graphite has made.

For the second, the essential need for matter and its evolution in this transformation process eludes them. Being only a purely spirit-focused group, they see in a transformation only the part that is new, that is, the spiritual part. They see only the loving message in the note, and disregard the graphite from the pencil that holds the message.

True Christians, explains Teilhard, understand both stages of the transformation process required to spiritualize matter and creatures. In the transformation, they neither leave the creature where it is, on its own plane, nor suppresses it. In Christ, they sur-animate it. They delight in the loving message and they treasure the graphite and the paper that carries the message, because it holds a promise of the spiritual transformation of all things.

Spiritual Exercise: Spiritualized Matter

Ω Look around you and identify at least five pieces of matter that contain, sustain, or manifest some element of spirit. (Without even trying, I can name at a dozen, all within arm's reach: a lamp, a book, an audiocassette, a telephone, my computer, its printer, a clipboard with notes on it, a cup full of ballpoint pens and pencils, computer discs, a photograph of my wife and me, an icon of the Pietà, a letter from a friend.)

Say thanks to God that someone has found a way, in each case, to spiritualize some small amount of matter.

Can you do the same for others?

Part Three

THE DIVINE MILIEU

Summary

Teilhard begins by reminding the reader of his spirituality's foundational truth, namely, that we live and move and have our being in the divine milieu. Everything in the universe is surrounded, penetrated, and shaped by this divine loving presence.

In the first section of Part Three, Teilhard spells out many of the attributes of the divine milieu, such as its ability to assemble and harmonize apparently contradictory qualities and to serve as a center or point of convergence, while managing the process of its own growth and fulfillment.

In the second section he defines the nature of the divine milieu and shows that the divine milieu and all it contains forms the Universal or Cosmic Christ. He explains how from the first moment of creation a single event has been developing and unfolding in the universe, namely, a divine incarnation being realized in each individual and in the whole universe. Teilhard understands the Eucharistic process at Mass—Christ becoming incarnate in the physical matter of bread and wine—as an expression of the sacramental action of Christ sanctifying and incarnating in all matter. Christ is carrying out this transfiguration process everywhere, not merely at Mass.

The third section explains what Teilhard means by the divine milieu growing, that is, what the Cosmic Christ is slowly accomplishing in the collective mass of humanity, how the holy presence is being born and revealing itself within us, individually and collectively. But this transformation does not modify the way things ordinarily appear, no more than the Eucharistic consecration at Mass modifies the appearance of the bread and wine.

For Teilhard, individual progress in the divine milieu happens by developing purity, faith, and fidelity. He gives each of those virtues a special meaning. Collective progress in the divine milieu happens through the development of charity, a bonding in compassionate and unconditional love for one another.

◆ ◆ ◆

After a sermon, a little girl asked her mother, "Didn't the priest tell us that God is bigger than anybody?"

The mother replied, "Yes, dear. That's right."

The girl asked again, "And didn't he say that when we receive communion, God comes to live inside us?"

"Yes," the mother said.

"Well," asked the little girl with a puzzled look on her face, "Shouldn't God show through?"

The simple logic of this child was wiser than most. All around her she was seeing grumpy-faced parishioners and wondering why they weren't letting God show through, at least in smiles and gestures of openness and joy. She knew that if God permeated the material world and that if God was truly present in our flesh and blood, our bodies ought somehow to manifest that energy of divinity *tangibly*, in the various ways we think, choose, act, and relate to each other.

From all we have studied and reflected upon so far in *The Divine Milieu*, we realize that we have only to use our new eyes to see a bit beyond the limits of tangible reality in order to detect the divine energies showing through everything. Teilhard hopes that by now we have developed our spiritual sight to the degree that we can begin to see the divine bubbling up in things and people — showing through.

Always a Part of Christ

The life and death of each of us is not just about us or the influence we have on others. Whether we live or die, we do it for the Lord. Alive or dead, we are a part of Christ.

—Romans 14:7–8 [my paraphrase]

What we discover about the divine milieu is that it is not only inside us and outside us, but, as Teilhard says, it is so universally present that "we find ourselves surrounded and transfixed by it." In fact, there is no place outside of the divine milieu "to fall down and adore it, even within ourselves" (Torchbook, 112). No matter how hard we might try, we cannot put ourselves outside the divine milieu, because there is nothing outside the divine milieu. For centuries, no human could get far enough outside the earth to take a picture of it, until astronauts went into orbit around the planet in the 1960s. Even if we were to be transported to the outermost reaches of the galaxy, we would not be outside the divine milieu. Even if we delved into the deepest microscopic levels of microbe life, the divine milieu would be penetrating every atom of those life forms. So if we want to worship this source of our lives — this divine milieu — we have to do it from within itself.

We were taught to imagine the divine as distant and inaccessible, "whereas we live steeped in its burning layers," says Teilhard.

As Abraham's grandson Jacob said when he awakened from his famous Ladder Dream, this world we live in that we tend to treat with boredom and disrespect is "indeed a holy place." Teilhard hopes that we, like Jacob, will come and adore. *Venite adoremus!*

In this third and final major section of his book, Teilhard wants to take us on an inventory tour of the divine milieu, exploring (1) its attributes, (2) its nature, and (3) how it is growing. He does this in the hope that "we can open ourselves evermore to its penetration."

1. The Attributes of the Divine Milieu

In this first section of Part Three Teilhard is simply going to name a number of the qualities, properties, attributes, and capacities of the divine milieu. He will begin by stepping back, as it were, looking at the divine milieu "on the surface." He will list more than a dozen of the divine milieu's qualities, with only a quick sentence or two for each (Torchbook, 113–15). Next, he will dive deeply into the divine milieu and look at its attributes "beneath the surface" (Torchbook, 115–16). Finally, he wants to assure his readers that what he is writing in *The Divine Milieu* is Christian spirituality to the core, since some people have misinterpreted Teilhard as a pantheist, a pagan, a Modernist (a generalized heresy condemned by Pope Pius X in 1907), or even one of the Illuminati.

An On-the-Surface View of the Divine Milieu

Here Teilhard identifies many of the obvious attributes of the divine milieu that he can see "on the surface." Although Teilhard does his listing in the book as if it were just a quick review to remind us of the divine milieu's many dimensions, exploring them is so new for most of us that I have taken the liberty of suggesting a spiritual exercise after each one, if only to underline the need to develop a familiarity with each attribute.

1. The divine milieu reconciles opposites. The first marvelous emergent property of the divine milieu to notice, Teilhard says, is the "ease with which it assembles and harmonizes within itself qualities which appear to us to be contradictory." For example, the divine milieu just as easily comprehends two galaxies that are separated by billions of light years, as it does two events in a computer's microprocessor that occur merely nanoseconds apart. It just as easily holds in its hands a moon as a microscopic bacterium. It embraces and absorbs millions of contradictions and confusions — both sides in a war, opposing sports teams, competitive businesses, feuding families, the thousands of different spoken and written languages, and so on.

Spiritual Exercise: Reconciliation

Ω What are some conflicts and adversarial relationships in your life that you would like the divine milieu to reconcile? Perhaps you are the child of divorced parents who are still fighting each other and using you as their weapon. Perhaps you are the parent of children who have left the church and the faith that you hold dear. Perhaps you plan to marry a person who adheres to a faith tradition different from yours, and you both are strongly religious people. Perhaps you and your spouse have continual disagreements about what to do with the money you have both earned.

Could you stretch your mind to view those conflicts you personally experience from the perspective of the divine milieu and imagine how the divine milieu might suggest a reconciliation?

2. *The divine milieu possesses a particular personal identity.* Despite the vast energy and the complexity and even chaos that seem to be living and operating within the divine milieu, it has "in a supreme degree that precise concentrated particularity which makes up so much of the warm charm of human persons." Although we might like to describe the divine milieu as an immense but vague reservoir of energy, says Teilhard, it is as individually identifiable as any person in your life.

That is quite a claim Teilhard makes about the divine milieu. It may be valuable to attempt to see if Teilhard is really correct. For example, we usually identify people by their looks, the color of their eyes, the color, design, and amount of their hair, the curl of their lips, how tall they are, how much they weigh, the color of their skin, the date they were born. We also identify them by name and family, by the country in which they were born, and so on. But these are only the external, visible qualities that identify them. More import are the inner qualities that shape their personality and character, their seriousness or sense of humor, their compassion or cleverness, their suggestibility or level of self-esteem.

Teilhard is asking you to begin listing the qualities of the divine milieu to realize how uniquely identifiable it is. You might start by noting its history, guiding laws, functions, and relationships.

Your best hope, however, is to use metaphors the way Jesus did when trying to describe the Kingdom of Heaven to people who had never been there. To convey the experience of heaven, Jesus used the metaphors of yeast, seeds, grain, fields, farmers, merchants, landholders, kings, bridegrooms, children, and even a storeroom. Explore some metaphors for the divine milieu. With each image you choose to compare, ask yourself: How is it like this thing? How is it different?

Spiritual Exercise: The Personalized Milieu _____

Ω In this section, Teilhard is trying precisely to describe what makes the divine milieu "individually identifiable." Read each of the numbered thirteen statements in bold italics on the previous and following pages, put them together, and see if you begin to get a distinctive, personalized picture of the divine milieu.

3. The divine milieu achieves a paradoxical "concrete transcendence." When we think of the billions and billions of creatures sustained and sur-animated by the divine milieu, we assume the divine milieu must be so transcendent as to be ungraspable and unimaginable. Yet despite the complexity of it all, it brings all these creatures together along with all the elements of the world into a personal unity, and does it without the least confusion. At the same time, while the divine milieu continually unifies all of us creatures into a transcendent whole in Christ, we still continue to see each other concretely, as distinct individuals. As part of the body of Christ, we never lose our individuality.

Spiritual Exercise: Reminders of the Divine Milieu _____

Ω Can you think of human organizations where the organization as a system unifies all of its members, while the members continue to see themselves as distinct individuals? Think of as many as you can—teams, committees, groups, businesses, congregations, etc.—because each system can suggest some aspect of the work that the divine milieu is trying to accomplish with everything and everyone on earth.

It is just as important to identify those groups or organizations that, unlike the divine milieu, tend to split their members and pit them against one another, or other organizations you may belong to that try to destroy your distinct individuality. For example, our school classrooms often pit students against one another in competition for the highest grades. Or certain sales offices split their salespeople up into competitive units. Among organizations that care little about your individuality might be manufacturing plants where workers on an assembly line are expected to do their operations exactly the same way as everyone else.

═══

4. *The divine milieu, so near and perceptible, constantly eludes our grasp.* Yet if we raise ourselves up "to the extreme limit of our effort," we can begin to feel ourselves being drawn by the divine milieu into the depths of each creature that lives and moves in it. For example, it may be easy for us to understand the fascination and wonder that the study of the planets and galaxies might bring to scientists as they continue to discover the endless and inaccessible depths of our universe. However, a similar fascination and wonder may be felt by individual biologists who have devoted their lives to studying some tiny animal or insect that the ordinary person might find boring or perhaps even disgusting, such as flies, beetles, mosquitoes, or spiders. No matter

what creature we may choose to explore, as we delve more and more deeply into that creature's life, makeup, history, habits, functions, and relationships, we can find ever-new revelations about it and about our world.

The divine milieu wants us all to become conscious of the spiritual richness and potential of every created thing, even the rocks buried in the earth and the gasses swimming in our atmosphere.

However — and this is the point Teilhard is trying to make here — imagine, as we move more deeply into each creature's depths and perhaps its evolutionary forebears, we start to think that we are beginning to grasp the divine milieu itself. At that moment, the divine milieu "withdraws always further, bearing us along with it toward the common center of all consummation." God is not playing a teasing game with us here. God is merely inviting us to go deeper and deeper. If we are awestruck at how deep we discover some insignificant creature can be, we might ask ourselves, "How deep must be the uncreated God?"

Teilhard simply wants us to know, as St. Paul centuries earlier discovered, "How teeming with riches are the depths of God! How deep runs his wisdom and knowledge! How impossible to penetrate the motives for his decisions or comprehend his methods! Who could ever fathom the mind of the Lord?" (Rom. 11:33–34 [my paraphrase]).

Spiritual Exercise: A Sense of Wonder

Ω List at least one or two things, preferably pursuits that required training and effort, where, as you got deeper and deeper into your subject matter, you began to feel the awe and wonder at what you were dealing with. This is not an exercise only for research scientists, microbiologists, or astronomers. For example, most mothers have experienced this sense of wonder during pregnancy and birth. Where have you felt it? For more ideas, read on.

Thank God for your ability to experience a sense of wonder.

Footnote on Spiritual Growth

In a footnote at this juncture, Teilhard tries to explain this ever-deepening process we call spiritual growth. We do it, he says, in two basic ways: (1) through ordinary ways of loving or (2) through art and scientific research.

First, the ordinary ways. Teilhard says, "I attain God in those whom I love to the same degree in which we, myself and they, become more and more spiritual." For example, the less selfish and more honest my expressions of love become, the more spiritual they are. If I am conscious and have eyes to see my love as a response to the inner movements of the divine milieu, I get closer to understanding who God is and what his motives are. Growth in spirituality and growth in deeper awareness of God run a proportional path. The same is true in outward expressions of ordinary love — love in action. St. Scholastica, the twin sister of St. Benedict, was wont to say, "The more you love, the more you show it in action." As your loving feelings grow and improve, so do your actions.

Now for the artistic and scientific way. "In a similar way," Teilhard says, "I grasp him in the Beautiful and the Good in proportion as I pursue these further and further with progressively purified faculties." Pursuit of the Beautiful is the mission of the artist. As artists progressively purify their pursuit, toiling not for selfish or petty reasons but for the revelation of the beauty of God's creation, they progressively grasp God.

The sculptor Michelangelo, who was able to visualize the final statue, say, one of Moses, as soon as he saw a certain piece of raw marble, described his work as "merely chipping away from the stone what was not Moses." In fact, he was so absorbed in this particular work that when he was almost finished, he shouted, "Moses, come out!"

The same spiritual growth is waiting for the dedicated scientists who search for the Good and True in creation, not primarily for the rewards and prestige new discoveries or inventions might bring, but for the revelation of the truth and goodness in creation, whether they

---

The New Human

Put on a new man, one who grows in knowledge as he is formed anew in the image of his Creator. There is no Greek or Jew. . . . Rather, Christ is everything in all of you. . . . Whatever you do, work at it with your whole being. Do it for the Lord rather than just for yourself.

—Colossians 3:10 –11, 23 [my paraphrase]

---

realize it or not. As Teilhard says, they "progressively grasp God." This paragraph describes Teilhard's own life and work as a scientist, his journey of seeking the truth at the heart of the universe.

You must realize these observations Teilhard makes about the divine milieu are radical and revolutionary statements about spirituality and spiritual practice. How different from generations of spiritual teachers who said things like, "Nothing of the world is of any significance or worth. Only heaven itself is worth pursuing."

5. *Through the transforming power of the divine milieu, touching matter can become a purification.* For example, says Teilhard about the transforming power of matter, physical expressions of love can be transfigured into expressions that reflect a spiritual purity akin to chastity. (Teilhard has written an entire treatise called "The Evolution of Chastity," which is a topic far too complex to explain fully in a few sentences, but here are some ideas from that treatise.) Teilhard is certainly not recommending that married spouses cease having conjugal love experiences and, instead, become celibate. Rather, he is saying that even the most physically and emotionally passionate expression of human love, when seen as immersed in the divine milieu, can become an activity of spiritual growth and development. Teilhard simply didn't have another word than "chastity" to describe physical love when

it approaches this pure state. One couple I know described a love-making experience where they felt in their moment of most intense physical pleasure a desire to experience becoming "one flesh." They asked me if I thought that's what Teilhard might have been talking about here.

Envious of them, I answered, "Yes, I think so."

Spiritual Exercise: A Purifying Touch _____

Ω Have you ever had an experience of "touching something" — hold-ing a newborn infant, tending a flower garden, kneading dough for bread making, picking fruit from a tree, working on a car's engine — with such intensity that it began to focus you so deeply that you became one with the object of your attention? When this happens, it "purifies" your motives, your response, and your responsibility. If you've ever felt this way, this is the experience Teilhard is talking about when he says, "Touch-ing matter can become a purification." This intense purity of experience is what he means by chastity.

Thank God for the sense of touch and what it can awaken in you.

6. **When we are immersed in the divine milieu, personal development culminates in renunciation.** For example, while we may form strong attachments within the divine milieu, the power of the same milieu gradually separates us from everything within these attachments that is "disintegrating." In this way, by our immersion in the divine milieu each attachment to life we have culminates in a resurrection.

As an example, suppose the married couple were in their earlier days "attached" to the sensual pleasures of lovemaking. As they gradu-ally let go of always seeking the pleasures of this attachment to redirect their attention to their union — becoming one flesh — this union that was always there, but remained unrecognized by the couple, is now born again, "resurrected." The intense pleasure *that used to be there as an attachment* remains, but it is there now purified and chaste. The sensuous pleasure doesn't leave. It is the *attachment* to the pleasure that is removed, not the pleasure itself, which in itself is holy and purifying.

Spiritual Exercise: Without Loss of Satisfaction _____

Ω Teilhard used this example of attachment to sensuous pleasure as a case where the "attachment" can be renounced without loss of personal spiritual development. Could you perhaps describe the same purifying process for motherhood, or parenthood, or the pursuit of a career, or scientific research, or an artist's work?

Begin by asking, "What are the feelings or rewards that a mother, a parent, a businessperson, a scientist, or an artist can get attached to?" Once you have identified the attachment, explore some of the ways your focus of interest might be redirected without losing the satisfaction or pleasure involved.

For example, one young mother I know sees herself as having been given a sacred trust by God when she gave birth to each of her children, to nurture and protect them. Again, I know a physician who sees each patient that comes into her office as a divine gift to the world, and her task is to cooperate with God in keeping that person healthy.

Most of the attributes described above, says Teilhard, stem from one fundamental property of the divine milieu:

7. **"God reveals himself everywhere...as a universal milieu, only because he is the ultimate point upon which all realities converge"** (114). Mathematicians and geometers understand intuitively this insight about convergence to a point, since they are always dealing with infinities, shapes, lines, and single points and how they are related. It is no surprise, then, that as a scientist Teilhard describes

this divinizing convergence and grand evolutionary process — from the first moment of the Big Bang to the final Parousia — using the image of a geometric cone. The base of the cone sits at the bottom (the Big Bang symbolizing the beginning of the process there) and culminates in its singular point at the top (the Parousia symbolizing the convergence point of the process).

If you just think of the shape of the cone for a moment, any and all points at the base of the cone that move upward must find the apex of their movement at the uppermost point of the cone. All paths or lines starting from the bottom and moving upward lead to the same point.

The circular area at the bottom of the cone represents the first moments of creation, where fragmented creation is scattered far and wide in the universe. From that fragmented state, it starts its evolutionary ascent toward God from below. The cone's uppermost point represents divinity, the ultimate convergent point. According to Teilhard's evolutionary premise, all the elements of creation will continue to evolve, through attraction and connection, to ever-higher levels of complexity and consciousness, eventually meeting at the cone's top. Each person and thing will reach its individual perfection there at the top, at the same time as the world as a whole will reach its own general perfection. In the divine milieu all paths lead to God. Even if some of our paths are not straight lines, but go wandering about, sometimes backward, sometime in circles. Still the constant push or pressure of the divine milieu is urging all things upward with an irresistible force.

Spiritual Exercise: The Cone of Creation _____

Ω Take a sheet of paper and draw a large cone. Everything within the cone is immersed in the divine milieu. Write the word "GOD" at the top point of the cone. Then with your pen or pencil, starting from the bottom, write or sketch the different layers of creation as they appeared through evolution. Primary elements such as elemental gases like hydrogen and helium at the bottom; more complex inorganic elements like minerals and metals come next; then organic elements, followed by primitive living microbial life; then plant life, insects, fish, birds, reptiles, mammals, more intelligent animals, and finally humans.

As you study what is within the divine milieu, get a sense of the evolutionary lines of growth and development as they appear. Notice how each new layer of creation evolves to something more complex and a bit higher in complexity and consciousness than the layer before it. Notice also that nothing good and useful of any previous layer is lost. It is always somehow integrated into the next higher layer and all those above that one.

---

8. The divine milieu tells us that each created thing cannot be looked at simply in terms of its own nature and action. But that created thing — in fact, every created thing — must be looked at from the perspective of the ultimate point (the apex of the cone). That point serves as the source, support, and guide for each created thing in its path to its personal perfection, and it is joined to all others in the general perfection of the entire creation, which is, for Teilhard, the Body of Christ. Beneath and above this incredible fragmentation and multiplicity is the One, the divine Single Point. Even from the first moment of the Big Bang, the divine Single Point has been operating beneath, behind, or permeating the incredible fragmentation, because creation is nothing more than the Word of God expressed "outside Itself," as it were. The divine Single Point is also above, or out in front of, creation calling it, urging it, and leading it onward to its unique fulfillment.

Teilhard called the Single Point that started creation "the Alpha," and the Single Point that will be creation's culmination "the Omega Point." Teilhard uses this symbolism because Alpha and Omega are the first and final letters of the Greek alphabet.

Spiritual Exercise: Lines of Convergence _____

Ω Working with the cone you drew and filled in during the previous exercise, begin drawing convergence lines from the bottom of the cone. At the bottom of the cone, most of the lines at their origin are clearly separate from one another. But as they rise, they get closer and closer to each other, until they reach the incredible density of a single point at the top.

By the law of attraction-connection-complexity-consciousness, every created thing wants to ride those convergence lines upward to the top. That is the driving force of the evolutionary process that God implanted in the heart of every smallest fragment of creation. As you walk around today, look at each object and acknowledge that in its deepest reality it wants to follow that law to the Omega Point.

_____

9. *The divine milieu is also spiritual beneath its materiality.* Because of this, says Teilhard, "No object can influence us by its essence without our being touched by the radiance of the focus of the universe." In other words, nothing can have a physical effect on me without my being touched by the divine milieu at the same time. For example, no one can genuinely smile at me without my being touched, through that smile, by the radiance of God in the divine milieu. No one can give me a genuine hug or kiss without my being touched by the radiance of God.

For this reason, Teilhard adds, my mind is incapable of fully grasping any reality without being compelled, *"by the very structure of things,"* to go back to the first source of its perfections. If you want to truly understand any person or thing, you can trace any of its qualities, talents, or gifts back through an evolutionary line to where it first emerged. Ultimately it will lead you back to the beginning of creation and the divine milieu.

Because of the divine milieu, God is simultaneously broad and deep, yet somehow only a single point. Because of the divine milieu, Christ can be both infinitely near and yet dispersed everywhere. It is precisely because Christ is a center of light and love that he fills all of creation.

Spiritual Exercise: A Symbol of Light ⎯⎯⎯⎯⎯⎯⎯⎯⎯

Ω In olden days, a candle or an oil lamp might be a symbol of the light of God. If in a dark room you lighted a candle, though the light was centered in the candle, it dispersed itself everywhere throughout the room. Today, a light bulb serves the same purpose. Your task is to show how this light bulb is "spiritual beneath its materiality."

Hint: What can you now do in that lighted room that you couldn't do while it remained dark?

Thank God for the spiritual light in your life that enables you to see whatever you can of the Cosmic Christ.

10. *The divine milieu unites and completes all beings within it.* To Teilhard, the most important attributes of the divine milieu are those properties of a center, the most important of which is to unite and complete all beings within its powerful love.

Thanks to the influence of the Eastern philosophies, almost everyone in the United States is familiar with "getting centered." Very many of the Eastern spiritual practices begin by asking the person to "get centered." Perhaps we all intuitively know what this means. Perhaps we don't. A friend once described getting centered as "bringing all your faculties back home." Though I happen to be sitting in this room, my mind may be miles away, and my spirit may be wandering somewhere else. To become centered, the challenge is to bring the body, mind, and spirit to one place. Usually practitioners recommend one spot in your body to serve symbolically as your *center*.

In a similar way, it is the task of the divine milieu to get all the parts of creation centered in God. The divine milieu has been working at this task for billions of years, trying to get all of the beings that live in it, first, to realize they are meant to be one being, and then to get them to act consciously and lovingly as that one being.

Spiritual Exercise: Acting as One _____

Ω If you were on a small team of people assigned to get all of the people on earth to realize they are meant to be one body and then to get them to act consciously and lovingly as one body, how and where would you recommend starting the process? What would be the first step?

This is perhaps one of the most important exercises in this book.

After your recommendations to the worldwide committee, move to a team assigned to get all the people in the organization where you work to realize they were meant to be one body and to act consciously and lovingly as one body. How would you recommend starting the process? What would be the first step?

If you were following Teilhard's spirituality, he would say starting and maintaining this "one body" process within the groups you are part of should be one of your main spiritual practices.

Since you are not likely to get the worldwide assignment described above, nor the one for your work organization, you might start with your family. Doing whatever would help make them one body and acting as one body is another of your main spiritual practices in Teilhard's spirituality.

═══

11. *Because all beings live in the divine milieu and because of it, "all the elements of the universe touch each other by that which is most inward and ultimate in them"* (Torchbook, 114). Although Teilhard says nothing more about this attribute here, we can find expressions of it, for example, in the power of prayer that happens in the divine milieu. Today, research has shown that when people make a prayerful

connection with the intention of healing a sick person, good results happen. Patients who are prayed for in this way tend to heal faster and with fewer complications or infections than those who are not specifically prayed for. As Teilhard observes, all of us in the universe touch each other at the soul or spirit level.

Spiritual Exercise: Healing in the Divine Milieu _____

Ω Think about the power of prayer and its ability to produce healing at a distance. Science can't yet explain how a small group of people in Chicago can pray for a specific sick patient in a California hospital and effect some degree of healing. How might you begin to explain that healing in terms of the divine milieu?

12. *In the divine milieu, each being concentrates, little by little, all that is purest and most attractive in it without loss and without danger of subsequent corruption.* Again, in the text Teilhard says nothing more here about this insight. However, we all know the experience of "concentrates" when we walk along the frozen foods section of the supermarket. We can buy a small can of orange juice concentrate. In its eight ounces it contains "all that is purest and most attractive" from the orange. Very little has been lost in this process and it is certainly not likely to be corrupted. As soon as we add water and mix, it becomes a quart of orange juice.

This is perhaps a crude image to use, but the divine milieu is slowly turning you into a concentrated form, saving all that is purest and most attractive in you, without loss of your essence and without danger of subsequent corruption. As the matter of your life becomes more and more spiritualized — or concentrated — you become less and less vulnerable to the possible downward pull of diminishment and death. We do not wish to escape matter, but rather to bring it to the Cosmic Christ in as pure a form as possible.

Spiritual Exercise: Concentrate of You _____

Ω What would it mean to you personally to become a you-concentrate? Make a note of what you think is "purest and most attractive" in you, so that as long as the you-concentrate were saved there would be no true loss of you.

═══

13. In that milieu, in their meeting each other, individuals shed their mutual externality and those incoherencies that form the basic pain of human relationships. By turning to that divine center, those who are saddened by separation, misunderstanding, distance, indifference, desolation, or the stupidity, the meanness, and the wastefulness of the world will find refuge. All that pain is only on the surface.

Spiritual Exercise: Shedding Externality _____

Ω Can you begin to explain, or give an example of, what Teilhard means when he says that the basic pains of relationships will begin to cease when people in relationships can "shed their mutual externality"? What would be left of us if we were to shed all that makes up our externality?

═══

These are some of the attributes of the divine milieu that Teilhard sees from the surface. More "inexhaustible wonders" await us as we plunge beneath its "surface."

A Beneath-the-Surface View of the Divine Milieu

Paradoxically, the divine milieu allows us to plunge beneath its surface and into God *without leaving the world*. This is the kind of assertion Teilhard makes that scares traditional spiritual writers. Yet from what we have learned so far, his assertion makes much sense.

The more traditional idea of "leaving the world" while we are immersed in it seems even more paradoxical and self-contradictory. Yet for centuries spiritual people have tried to create environments in caves and monasteries and on mountaintops that are "otherworldly," that have the least amount of "world" in them. Next, they tried to eliminate the elements of the earth that they carried in their bodies and minds, through penance, fasting, abnegation, mortification, self-denial, and special forms of meditation and prayer.

For Teilhard, all of these worldly things, including us, are swimming in the divine milieu. Why would God have created this divine milieu if then God wanted us to escape it, disregard it, or be disgusted with it? Why would Jesus tell us that God so passionately loved this world that he would give to it his only-begotten Son, and then want us to withdraw from that world, reject it or even hate it? How can we do anything but love this creation and help bring it to its fulfillment? How can anyone tell us, says Teilhard, that the world God loves is evil and is intent only on leading us into sin?

Rather, says Teilhard, "Let us establish ourselves in the divine *milieu*" (Torchbook, 115). For him, there is "where the soul is most deep and where matter is most dense."

Spiritual Exercise: Why, God? _____

Ω Take a moment to ponder the question: Why would God have created this endlessly fascinating divine milieu if God wanted us simply to escape, disregard it, or reject it? It is not a silly question, since many deeply religious and faithful Christians appear to have done just that, and have counseled others who sought spiritual growth to do so as well.

Where Desires Are Fulfilled

One of the most fascinating attributes of the divine milieu, in Teilhard's view, is that when we truly get to see it in its depths, we shall

---

When the Time is Right

God's secret plan, which he will complete in the fullness of time, is to bring all creation together, everything in heaven and on earth, with Christ as head....The church is Christ's body, the completion of him who himself completes all things everywhere in the universe.

—Ephesians 1:10, 23 [my paraphrase]

---

discover all the brilliant flowers and parts of nature that in the busyness of daily living we didn't have time to stop and admire. We didn't contemplate the lilies of the field perhaps because we had to be faithful to our calling as students, parents, administrators, laborers, scientists, researchers, teachers, physicians, and so on. All those beauties we missed, Teilhard assures us, will await us in the depths of the divine milieu. In other words, it's not too late. The divine milieu will see that you eventually will have your chance to enjoy all these beautiful things, since they will remain in the divine milieu forever.

Think, says Teilhard, of all the people you have wanted to meet and talk to and perhaps even influence, but they weren't in the same place or time that you were. Those people will be in the divine milieu awaiting your contact. The divine milieu will lose nothing of importance — ever! — though it may be preserved in concentrated form.

There, too, says Teilhard in a burst of incredible optimism, "the least of our desires and efforts is harvested and tended." Think of all those things you wanted to accomplish in the world while you were living but never had time for because you were faithful to the work that was assigned to you. All those desires, suggests Teilhard, will have been accomplished and will have had their good effect in the world, just as you wished. All those good intentions that you felt in your heart and fully wished you could accomplish were also felt and carried out in the divine milieu in ways unknown to you.

Teilhard never explains how these wished-for good effects could possibly happen. Perhaps the explanation is contained in his personal experience of the divine milieu, which was not made explicit in his book.

For example, Teilhard desperately wanted his spiritual and philosophical writings to be published, especially *The Divine Milieu* and *The Phenomenon of Man*. Teilhard died with no assurance that publication would ever happen, But it did happen. It was carried out by the divine milieu in ways unknown to Teilhard.

Again, Teilhard longed for humans to develop a reverence for the earth, but nothing seemed to happen while he was still alive. But the divine milieu had not forgotten his prayer and his intention. Since his death, the science of ecology has arisen as well as the entire ecological movement. Laws have been passed to protect endangered species. The Society for the Prevention of Cruelty to Animals (SPCA) has flourished. Books, funds, and world organizations have appeared to further this cause. Rev. Thomas Berry, a past president of the American Teilhard Association, has been a strong advocate for reverence for the earth.

Psychologists currently researching the power of prayer and intentionality remain puzzled but still publish the results of many double-blind studies, such as prayer groups on the East Coast successfully intending the healing of patients unknown to them in a West Coast hospital. Teilhard would have attributed this healing work — at long distances with healers unknown to healees — to the many interconnections within the divine milieu all unknown to the people being healed.

Spiritual Exercise: Things Missed but Not Forgotten _____

Ω Here you have three different lists to make.

The first list includes all those beautiful things in nature that you had wanted to visit and spend time contemplating but never got around to doing. Perhaps Niagara Falls, the Grand Canyon, the roses in a neighbor's garden by the house where you lived as a child, the trees in Central Park, and so on.

The second list includes all those people you had wanted to meet and talk to or maybe ask questions of. Perhaps, your grandfather who died when you were an infant, your brother who died before you could be reconciled, or some famous people like Thomas Jefferson, Rosa Parks, or St. Augustine. It's *your* list.

The third list includes some of the things you wanted to accomplish during your lifetime but never got around to doing. Perhaps write a book, play an instrument, create an organization to help victims of crime, and so on. Or some simpler things like writing some thank-you notes that you never had time for, visiting and consoling sick friends, volunteering to coach a Little League team, taking your children outside on a summer night to watch and wonder at the stars.

Enjoy making your lists and realizing that our benevolent God assures us that nothing will be forgotten in the divine milieu.

When we fully enter the divine milieu, says Teilhard, "we shall feel the plenitude of our powers of action and adoration effortlessly ordered within our deepest selves."

To grasp this idea, imagine stepping outside your room one day, leaving behind a messy desk, piled high with years-old layers of papers, and when you returned a short time later, you found everything is in total order just the way you would have done it. In this same way the divine milieu will rearrange the powers and actions of your mind and heart so that everything is "effortlessly ordered within our deepest selves."

The fact that the divine milieu will totally coordinate and harmonize all the physical elements of the world is one marvelous thing. By a complementary marvel, "the man who abandons himself to the divine milieu feels his inward powers clearly directed and vastly expanded by

The Lilies of the Field

We do not cease to march towards heaven by stopping before the lilies of the field. On the contrary, by allowing our souls to vibrate in unison with created things, we make our hearts more human, and reproduce the action of the Incarnate Word, who himself stopped before these created splendors to contemplate there the traces of an eternal love.

—Emile Mersch, S.J.,
The Theology of the Mystical Body of Christ

it with a sureness which enables him to avoid . . . the reefs on which mystical ardor has so often foundered" (Torchbook, 115–16). That's the kind of good things that happen when you consciously and fully enter the divine milieu. The divine milieu is a true guide that will keep you from damaging your mind on such reefs as pantheism, paganism, and illuminism, which Teilhard discusses in the following pages.

Spiritual Exercise: Expanding Inward

Ω If you were to abandon yourself to the divine milieu, how do you think your inward powers would be more "clearly directed and vastly expanded"? What might that mean to you, practically speaking? What would you be able see or to do that you can't do now?

What Teilhard's Spirituality Is NOT

Some have warned that if you go swimming in the beauties of the world, you are likely to fall into trouble, which might include temptations to pantheism, paganism, illuminism, and others evils. Teilhard, because of what he taught, has been accused, at different times, of all of them. He shows clearly that he falls into none of these "serious errors," as the church called them.

Teilhard is not a pantheist. There is a very subtle but important difference between pantheism and what Teilhard teaches. The pantheist believes that all of creation is God; there is no difference between what we see and what is God. Teilhard is a pan*en*theist, which means that every created thing exists in God. Teilhard's divine milieu is indeed divine but it is also a milieu, an atmosphere, an environment that contains and nourishes all that is in it. If you think of the divine milieu being like the air we breathe, you can easily see that you and the air are not the same thing. The atmosphere may contain you and nourish you, but you are quite distinct from the air itself. So it is with the divine milieu. We all exist and move around in it, but we are not the same as it. While the air around us happens to be a fine metaphor for understanding the way the divine milieu is omnipresent and permeates everywhere, the air we breathe is also living in the divine milieu.

Furthermore, many religious pantheists believe that at the end of time all material reality will dissolve into one spiritual substance, much as individual raindrops all dissolve and lose their identity in a lake. In the end, for these believers, all will dissolve into an unconscious fusion of spirit.

On the contrary, says Teilhard, "Our God . . . pushes to its furthest possible limit the differentiation among the creatures he concentrates within himself" (Torchbook, 116). In true Christian mysticism, we become united with God (that is, we become one with the Other) while remaining ourselves. Teilhard assures us that we can plunge into the divine milieu as deeply and as mystically as we want without the risk of finding ourselves dissolved into nothingness. The divine milieu will never allow us to disappear. Our personal identity lasts forever.

All this is fundamental Christian theology, says Teilhard, easily found in the writings of John the Evangelist, the letters of St. Paul, and many of the early Greek Fathers. Teilhard is merely using his own scientific language and insights to describe for intelligent people today what have always been core Christian beliefs — and clear to the Christian with eyes sensitized to see the divine milieu.

Teilhard is not a Modernist. Modernists worship science and want the church to stay out of the way of scientific advancement. For Modernists, the church and science should be forever kept separate. Teilhard is trying to do just the opposite, namely, to show how the church has nothing to fear from any present or future discovery of science, nor does science have anything to fear from divine revelation that the church proclaims. In the divine milieu, as Teilhard discovered, both institutions, science and religion, are working together to shape and reveal the cosmic Body of Christ. In a very real sense, science and the worldwide scientific enterprise in general may be seen as a reflection of the power of God in evolution, especially in the divine milieu's Department of Discovery and Development.

Because the Modernists promoted evolution as the scientific explanation of all things, and Teilhard was also a great proponent of evolution, some in the church accused Teilhard of being a Modernist. At that time, in the first half of the twentieth century, the church found the theories of evolution very threatening (as did Darwin himself, a very religious man). Teilhard, who understood evolution better than most and had more deeply explored it, saw that it offered no threat to Christian theology, but rather confirmed what St. Paul envisioned as the growth and development of the total Body of Christ. Today the church has come to recognize that evolutionary theories offer no threat to Christian living, but can even be a helpful guide.

Teilhard is not one of the Illuminati. "Illuminati" is a Latin term that literally means "enlightened ones." Various mystical, Gnostic, and esoteric sects within the Christian tradition have built their religious beliefs and practices on ancient spiritual texts (different from the canonical books of the New Testament) that were very cryptic and deep. They were understood only by those few who were "deemed by God worthy of enlightenment." Other groups of Illuminati, without

Modernism

Avowed Modernists are united in the common desire to adapt Catholicism to the intellectual, moral, and social needs of today and to live in harmony with the spirit of the age. This includes:

- the emancipation of science from ecclesiastical interference in every field of investigation;

- the emancipation of the state from interference by religious authority;

- the emancipation of private conscience from papal definitions;

- the emancipation of the universal conscience, to which the church should bow, ever in agreement;

- a spirit of reconciliation among all people and all religions through feelings of the heart, without the limitations and demands of ecclesiastical doctrines;

- a commitment to a sweeping form of evolution that abhors anything fixed and stationary, even religious and moral truths.

- In general, Modernists would put the responsibility for managing the universe entirely in the hands of scientists rather than in the hands of the Creator or the church.

Pope Pius X in his encyclical *Pascendi* (1907) summarized the teachings of the Modernists and condemned them. For many years during the twentieth century, the church even required all teachers of philosophy and theology in Catholic seminaries and colleges annually to swear an oath against Modernism and in their classes to present modernism as a heresy.

resorting to ancient texts for support, claimed to have received direct revelation from God for their spiritual practices and theological ideas.

Teilhard's accusers in Rome saw his teachings as related to the spiritual Illuminati, as if in his writings, revolutionary as they were, he were reporting personal divine revelations. As far as we can tell, Teilhard never had any special heavenly visitations that revealed to him the elements of his spirituality. Rather, as he describes in the introduction to *The Divine Milieu*, they came from his intense love for both God and physical creation, and his desire to integrate those two loves, instead of doing what traditional spirituality told him to do — choose one (God) and reject the other (physical reality).

While Teilhard's often mystical and convoluted writing may, to some, read like a Gnostic text, that was more a fault of his writing style and the apparent radical newness of his ideas than anything else. They were quite grounded in the historical Jesus and the canonical scriptures.

"If you suppress the historical reality of Christ," Teilhard clearly states, "the divine omnipresence which intoxicates us becomes... uncertain, vague, conventional" (Torchbook, 117). He emphasizes, "The mystical Christ, the universal Christ of St. Paul, has neither meaning nor value in our eyes except as an expansion of the Christ who was born of Mary and died on the cross."

You may be drawn into mystical heights, Teilhard says, but if you leave out the Jesus of the Gospels, You could end up among the Illuminati.

Teilhard is not a pagan naturalist. If you read Teilhard superficially, you might find a striking resemblance to the tenets of paganism. After all, the pagans love the earth, they highly value human endeavor, they call for an awakening of adoration of the world, and they respect the spiritual powers still latent in matter. So far, it all sounds very Teilhardian. But in each instance there is a major difference.

Pagans love the earth in order to enjoy it; Christians love the earth in order to make it purer for God.

The Illuminati

Illuminati is a Latin term that literally means "enlightened ones," and several unrelated historical groups have identified themselves as Illuminati. Some, including the twelfth-century *alumbrados* of Spain, claimed to possess ancient Gnostic texts of divine revelation or other arcane information not generally available — and quite unintelligible to the ordinary person — that guided their often-secret spiritual practices.

The designation Illuminati was also used in the fourteenth century by the Brethren of the Free Spirit, who claimed that illuminating light came, not from an authoritative secret source like ancient texts, but from within. Illumination, for them, was the result of exalted consciousness, or "enlightenment."

A different group of Illuminati were the fifteenth-century Rosicrucians, a secret society that claimed to combine esoteric principles of religion with the mysteries of alchemy. Rosicrucians also claimed heritage from the Knights Templar.

The church denounced each of these forms of Illuminati.

Later on, the Freemasons, a secret society, became associated with these mystical and spiritual sects, probably because each of their ascending ranks were named Illuminati. Instead of seeking divine enlightenment, however, Masons were much more interested in using the wealth, property, economic power, political influence, and social prestige of their members in creating a New World Order. For example, it is reported that all but a few of the original signers of the Declaration of Independence were Freemasons.

Pagans wed themselves to sensible things so as to extract delight from them. As Teilhard says, the pagan *"adheres to the world."* In contrast, the Christian *"pre-adheres to God."* That is, Christians multiply their contacts with the world so as to harness (activities) or submit to (passivities) the energies they will take bring to the Body of Christ.

Pagans believe that humanity will divinize itself. They envision the final act of human evolution to occur when the individual and the totality of humanity "constitutes itself within itself." On the contrary, Christians believe their divinization will happen only in the Other assimilating them and their achievements. For them, the culmination of life is living in union with God.

The pagan believes that what is perceptible is the full extent of the real. For the pagan, reality is defined as perceptible and multiple. The Christian believes in the reality of perceptible things, the same as the pagan does, but doesn't stop there. The Christian prolongs and pushes physical reality along the common evolutionary axis that links all things to God. According to Teilhard, this push toward God is "the natural and spontaneous reaction of the soul to the stimulus of a milieu which is exactly, by nature and grace, the one in which that soul is made to live and develop itself" (Torchbook, 119).

Summary

The divine milieu is full of paradoxes that we will never quite understand until we reach heavenly consciousness. Here is one of them.

* *The divine milieu has need of everything and yet has need of nothing.*

Teilhard takes a moment to explain this paradox.

"Everything is needed," he says, "because the world will never be large enough to provide our taste for action with the means of grasping God [activities], or our thirst for undergoing with the possibility of being invaded by him [passivities]" (Torchbook, 120). Simultaneously, nothing is needed except the only reality that will satisfy us, God.

Becoming More Than Human

What interest have we, then, in the moderate maxim of ancient wisdom: *a healthy mind in a sound body!* It is all over with these low aims since our nature forms only one person with God in Christ. Certainly, one must be a human; but not to dream of being more is, henceforth, to refuse to be totally human. Our dust can, by grace, resemble the Only-Begotten, and the divine goodness can transfigure our smile. It is finished then: the naturalist idea is a profanation.

—Emile Mersch, S.J.
The Theology of the Mystical Body of Christ

"Everything is God to me and everything is dust to me: that is what a human being can say with equal truth," explains Teilhard, depending on our point of view at the moment.

After listing all the attributes of the divine milieu, Teilhard now wants to explore the very nature of the divine milieu. What is it? Or WHO is it?

2. The Nature of the Divine Milieu, the Universal Christ, and the Great Communion

The Divine Omnipresence

As a first approximation to the exploration of the divine milieu's *nature* or character — in contrast to its *attributes* (discussed in the previous section) — Teilhard says that the divine milieu is formed by the divine omnipresence. "The immensity of God is the essential *attribute* which allows us to seize him everywhere, within and around us" (Torchbook, 121). *Immensity* is an attribute, while *omnipresence* is an aspect of the divine *nature*.

This omnipresence has what Teilhard describes as a "mobile homogeneity," by which he means that the divine milieu is equally intensely present in every square inch of the universe. But it is not an inert presence; it is active and dynamic. It is at work, if you can imagine it, moving in and out of every corner of earth, heaven, and hell.

One of the richest symbols of the omnipresence of the divine milieu may be found in the omnipresence of radio waves and other invisible signals actively alive and operating in each separate cubic inch of space in your home. For example, choose some precise location in any room of your house. Carry a radio to that spot. The signals from every radio station, AM, FM, and short wave, are present in that spot. If you held a portable television set with an antenna in that exact spot, it would be able to capture the signals from all the broadcast channels in your area. If you assembled all your neighbors from blocks and blocks around your house who had personal cell phones, each cell phone signal would be accessible simultaneously in that exact spot in your home.

If you then took all these electrical components to another room in your house, all these hundreds — maybe thousands — of signals would be alive and active in that tiny space as well. In fact, no matter where you went with those components in your neighborhood, no matter in what precise spot you chose to turn them on, those same hundreds of invisible signals would be there actively ready for you to tune into them.

And all those signals are in every space equally and simultaneously. You know this because you may be driving along the highway at sixty miles an hour, yet the passenger in your car talking on a cell phone experiences the voice of the caller without interruption as your car speeds along.

The divine milieu is like those radio, television, and cell-phone signals — omnipresent, always actively operating. The divine milieu is different from these electronic signals, however, in that the message and the power of the divine milieu never get out of range. Even if you were to be transported to the farthest reaches of outer space, the

---

The Work of Grace

The Word of God was made human; thereby, humanity, in Christ, is united to the Word. A change has occurred, not merely in our relations with God, but within our race itself. We, the members of Christ, are no longer simply humans. An elevation is given to us which changes us into divine humans, and that is grace. It is grace appearing in our nature as an ennobling of our nature.   —Emile Mersch, S.J.

The Theology of the Mystical Body of Christ

---

divine milieu would be there alive and actively operating for you, just as powerfully as it is right here and now.

However, Teilhard finds this description of the divine milieu as omnipresence less than truly satisfying. So he asks a further question: How is this divine immensity relevant to humanity? In other words, under what form does it manifest itself to us? How does it adapt itself to the evolving universe and to the human mind and senses?

Sanctifying Grace Circulating Everywhere

One thing we can add about the nature of the divine milieu is that it is charged with what the Catholic Church calls sanctifying grace, the divine gift continually being poured upon us helping to make us holy. Since it has a direct effect on our whole being, this sanctifying grace can be compared to the sap that runs through a living tree circulating everywhere in the tree, from its deepest roots to the outermost leaf on the highest branch.

But sanctifying grace is basically another word for a certain expression of the permanence of divine love, or charity. "Remain in my love," says Jesus to his disciples. Actually, Jesus' words, from the original Greek text, are better translated, "Remain in my delight." The word "love" by itself connotes a kind of quiet solicitude, but "delight" adds the extra note of being happy to have you there, resting in my arms.

Grace has many ways of expressing itself, as does human love. Sanctifying grace — a universal, unconditional gift — is only one form of expression of God's love. Sanctifying grace refers to that kind of love that urges, nurtures, invites; it is an attractive love that is almost irresistible. It supports the law of attraction-connection-complexity-consciousness.

Consider some other expressions of human love. Sometimes love is very active and energetic. Sometimes love is patient and waits. Sometimes it just listens. Sometimes love is healing and comforting. Sometimes it is just a gentle kindness. Sometimes it is humorous and teasing. Sometimes it suffers. Sometimes it rejoices. Sometimes it disciplines those it loves. Sometimes it must be stern, as in "tough love." These are only a few of the many faces of human love. God's love is not unlike that. God's love adapts to any situation, and never leaves the scene.

True love never departs. That is why the divine milieu's love — or sanctifying grace — is omnipresent and equally active everywhere.

Teilhard is still unsatisfied with the description of the nature of the divine milieu so far. He wants to know, What is "the concrete link which binds all of these universal entities together and confers on them a final power of gaining hold of us?" (Torchbook, 121–22). Those "universal entities" are all those attributes of the divine milieu that we have studied so far in this section.

If we can find that concrete link, says Teilhard, we will have found the essence of Christianity.

The Concrete Link

Of course, for Teilhard, as for St. Paul, the concrete link is our Lord Jesus Christ, who called himself the Son of Man. Now Teilhard wants to take us, step by step, to show how he validated this "prodigious identification of the Son of Man and the divine milieu" (Torchbook, 122).

Christ the Divine Milieu

He [Jesus Christ] is the image of the invisible God, the firstborn of all creation; for in him all things in heaven and on earth were created, things visible and invisible, whether thrones or dominions or rulers or powers — all things have been created through him and for him. He himself is before all things, and in him all things hold together. He is the head of the body, the church; he is the beginning, the firstborn from the dead, so that he might come to have first place in everything. For in him all the fullness of God was pleased to dwell.

—Colossians 1:15–19

Step one. We recognize the divine milieu's omnipresence as an *omnipresence of action*. While the normal air we breathe waits for us to inhale it, the divine milieu is proactive. It keeps creating us and preserving us, says Teilhard. It enfolds us and penetrates us, so much so that we participate in its very life.

Step two. The divine milieu as a field of loving omnipresence fills us with itself so that we aspire to be like it, to belong to it, even to be one with it. Its action on us is a transformative action. And the aim of that transformation is personal union of us with the divine milieu. Each one of us is destined to become one with the divine milieu.

Step three. This step takes the unitive transformative power of the divine milieu to a much more complex level. Beyond transforming each individual (step two), the divine milieu is transforming the total system of all individuals, past, present, and future, into a single divine union.

Insofar as we humans carry elements of all of creation with us at all times, that unified human system includes all the rest of the universe, since it too exists, lives, and moves within the divine milieu.

The Pleroma

Pleroma is a Greek word that is variously translated into English as "fullness," "completion," or "perfection." St. Paul uses it many times in his letters to describe the fullness or completion of the Christ, that is, Christ filling the entire cosmos with the creative presence of God (see, for example, Rom. 15:20–28; Eph. 1:10; Phil. 2:10–11 and 3:21; Heb. 2:5–8; Col. 1:18 and 2:9).

Teilhard also preferred the word *pleroma* and used it in the Greek without translating it throughout his writings. For him, the word *pleroma* represented the "Christification of the total universe" or "the fulfillment of the Cosmic Christ."

Theologically, the Christian tradition has always held that Jesus Christ had two natures. He was fully human and fully divine. In the *pleroma*, Paul is assigning a third nature to Christ, one not clearly accounted for, a "cosmic nature" that enabled him to center all the elements of creation in himself. For Teilhard, this third nature of Christ, expressed as the *pleroma*, is central to his spirituality. For Teilhard, the *pleroma* was the only true point of view from which our evolving world could be understood.

Teilhard points out that this supreme union is nothing else than what St. Paul and St. John talked about when they try to describe the fulfillment of God's divine plan for creation, what St. Paul calls the *pleroma*.

Step four. What else can be the active center of this divine milieu that can unify and unite everything within it? St. Paul proclaims: It is Christ who died and is risen, who fills all things, and in whom all things remain in being.

The Secret Hidden Revealed

I became a minister of this church through the commission God gave me to preach among you his word in its fullness, including that secret hidden from ages and generations past but now revealed to his people. God's plan is this: to make known his secret to his people, this rich and glorious secret that he has for all people. And the secret is this: Christ is in you, which means that you will share the glory of God. This is the Christ we proclaim...hoping to make every person complete in Christ.

—Colossians 1:25–28 [my paraphrase]

The divine milieu, the loving, active, transforming, unifying omnipresence is translated into Christian language as "the network of the organizing forces of the total Christ" (Torchbook, 123).

That Total Christ includes all the powers of heaven, earth, and hell, in the act of forming, saving, sur-animating, and consummating all of creation. Christ unifies all those energies, leading the universe back to God through his humanity.

The divine milieu assimilates us into itself, but what is really happening in this assimilation is the unification of the Body of Christ. The divine milieu is Christifying us and everything else in the universe. This is the secret Paul talks about, that was hidden from all ages past and finally revealed.

Christification

The Incarnation of Jesus of Nazareth marks the beginning of the process of our Christification. As Teilhard explains, "All the good that I can do [by my activities] . . . is physically gathered in, by something of itself, into the reality of the consummated Christ [the *pleroma*].

Everything I endure [passivities] with faith and love by way of diminishment or death makes me a little more closely an integral part of his Mystical Body" (Torchbook, 123).

Teilhard, echoing St. Paul, says our activities and passivities no longer belong primarily to us, since they are happening in Christ. Through them we are being Christified. It is Christ whom we make or whom we undergo in all things. In Jesus' own words, "Whatever you did for one of the least of these, you did for me.... What you did not do for one of these least of these, you did not do for me" (Matt. 25:40, 45).

Paul says that to those who love God all things are converted into goodness. He also says they are converted into God and, quite explicitly, into Christ.

Some people, Teilhard believes, will feel it is going a bit too far to picture the divine milieu as a real personal Body, with arms, legs, eyes, ears, and a nose. But Paul was very explicit. The Cosmic Christ Body enjoys all of the capacities that we give to arms, legs, eyes, ears, and so on.

And if you think about it for a moment, says Teilhard, if you really examine what the Eucharist is — the Body of Christ today — you will come to the very same conclusion. It is a real personal Body. If the Eucharist is the Body of Christ *as that Body is today,* it contains all of us. We as cells of that body make up its arms, legs, eyes, ears, and all the rest.

Spiritual Exercise: What Would You Like to Be? _____

Ω If you are a member of the body of Christ — or more likely a cell — in what part of the Christ Body would you like to be located and working? In one or other of the body's organs? In its nervous system? In its muscles and tendons? In its circulations system? In its breathing system? In its digestive system? Or some other part? Imagine you are in the part of your choice. What kinds of work would you be doing?

The Eucharist and the Body of Christ

At the moment of consecration, the priest addresses the bread on the altar with the words, "This is my body." His words fall onto the bread and directly transform it, says Teilhard, into the "individual reality of Christ."

At each Mass, the consecration is experienced as a localized and momentary event happening here and now. But Christian doctrine has always taught that there is only one Mass and one communion. I may attend Mass and receive communion every day for many years, but each Mass and each reception of communion is merely a unique act that is split up in time and space, because that is the way we experience it. Today's communion participates in the one communion. The theological fact is this:

All the communions of a lifetime are one communion.

All the communions of all people now living are one communion.

All the communions of all humans, present, past, and future are one communion.

The influence of that one communion radiates out from the Cosmic Christ, and through us touches the entire human family. In this way, the human layer of the earth is continually under the self-organizing influence of the Incarnate Total Christ.

For Teilhard, the Body of Christ we receive in the Eucharist at each Mass is ever the same, yet ever changing and evolving in many

---

An Ineffable Bond

In the Holy Eucharist the faithful are nourished and strengthened at the same banquet and by a divine, ineffable bond are united with each other and with the Divine Head of the whole Body.   —Pope Pius XII, *Mystici Corporis*

God Became Flesh

In his encyclical *Mystici Corporis* (1943), Pope Pius XII says that the point of the Incarnation was to bring us to the divinity. To do this, God became flesh—flesh he took from the Virgin Mary. This flesh he offered up on the Cross to his eternal Father for our sins and to purchase for us all the graces we would need to be saved. This same flesh he offered to us as food, and as the principle of our divinization.

---

ways. The idea of something ever the same yet ever changing is not incomprehensible. On their wedding day, the couple make a promise to be faithful to their union. Each day, when they say "I love you" to each other, it is a renewal of that promise. For them, all the promises of a lifetime are really one promise. Their union is ever the same, yet ever changing and evolving in many ways.

Spiritual Exercise: Everyone in the Host

Ω The next time you attend Mass, at the consecration imagine that the entire congregation is in the consecrated host and that the entire congregation is present in the consecrated wine. How does that change your perception of the people sitting around you?

Thank God for your new perception of the congregation.

The Human Layer of the Earth

Before leaving this section, Teilhard wants us to take a look and ask ourselves: "How does the human world itself appear within the structure of the universe?"

Build Your Life on Him, in Him

As you therefore have received Christ Jesus the Lord, continue to live your lives in him, rooted and built up in him and established in the faith, just as you were taught, abounding in thanksgiving. For in him the whole fullness of deity dwells bodily...and you have come to fullness in him, who is the head of every ruler and authority.   —Colossians 2:6–10

Here's how Teilhard sees it.

First, he says, we notice that the human layer is a "zone of continuous spiritual transformation." All the "inferior realities and forces"—the metals and minerals of the earth, the seas, the atmosphere, the weather, all biological life, insects, plants, animals—without exception are, in the human community, "sublimated into sensations, feelings, ideas and the powers of knowledge and love" (Torchbook, 125).

In other words, humans are always taking "inferior realities and forces" and transforming them into higher realms, mental and spiritual. A man gives a rose to his beloved. In itself, the rose is just a rose. But, as a gift, the rose is transformed both mentally and spiritually: mentally, into a message to his beloved, and spiritually as an act of love.

Whether you want to talk scientifically or theologically, humans form the link between matter and spirit, and between matter and God.

Though we may be able to separate plant life and animal life from human life mentally, we cannot draw a clear line between them in any real sense, since all of those "inferior realities and forces" are absorbed without loss in us humans and in fact sustain us in life on earth. We couldn't exist without air, water, food, vitamins, and minerals. We carry them at all times within our bodies. And through us—through

---

One Bread, One Body

St. Augustine asks, "Why is this mystery accomplished with bread?" He answers himself. "Let us offer no reason of our own invention, but listen to the Apostle speak of this sacrament, 'We are one bread, one body.' Understand this and rejoice. . . . What is this one bread? It is one body formed of many. Remember that the flour of the bread is not made of one grain of wheat. At baptism water was poured over you, as water is poured into the flour. Then the Holy Spirit entered into you like the fire that bakes the bread. Be what you see, and receive what you are."

---

our bodies, brains, and spirits — all these "inferior realities and forces" can be transformed into powerful emotions, sacred thoughts, kind actions, loving gestures, and insightful ideas.

What Teilhard didn't know then, but science knows now, is that all the "inferior realities and forces" are also in continuous transformation. For example, your own body alone contains an estimated 75 trillion cells; it is creating two billion new blood cells every second, and every drop of your body's blood passes through your heart every minute. Every time you stand up, sit down, climb a set of stairs, or ride a bicycle, about six hundred muscle systems inside your skin are adapting to your movements. And each time you think, the billions of nerve cells in your brain can be making up to ten thousand connections every split second.

If the Eucharist is the sovereign influence upon our human natures, then its influence necessarily extends in continuity into those "less luminous regions that sustain us," including the ground you walk on, the air you breathe, the water you drink, and the sunlight you count on to see where you're going.

The Cosmic Christ as Temple

In him the whole structure is joined together and grows into a holy temple in the Lord; in whom you also are built together spiritually into a dwelling place for God.

—Ephesians 2:21–22

Thus, we may truthfully say that at every moment the Eucharistic Christ sustains the whole movement of the universe.

Extending the Eucharist

Teilhard is leading up to the insight that the Eucharistic Christ and the Cosmic Christ are one and the same. In other words, the bread consecrated during Mass becomes far more than merely Jesus of Nazareth at the Last Supper, and even more than the Christ who died on the Cross and rose from the dead.

We can believe that the sacramental action of Christ in the Eucharist extends its influence beyond the purely supernatural, precisely because the consecration is an action that sanctifies matter — the bread and wine. Thus, the Eucharistic presence extends its influence over "all that makes up the internal and external ambience of the faithful." In a word, the Eucharist makes its mark on everything that we humans call "our world."

Just as our humanity assimilates the material creation, and as the Eucharistic host assimilates our humanity, this assimilation process goes on beyond the transubstantiation of the bread and wine on the altar. As Teilhard puts it, "It irresistibly invades the universe."

The Eucharistic bread becomes also the Cosmic Christ, since Christ is all in all. Then it follows that the nourishment we receive in the Eucharist is of the same nature as the nourishment we receive by living in the divine milieu.

One and Indivisible

For if we all eat of the one bread we all become one body, since there can be no division in Christ. For this reason is the church called the body of Christ, and we individually and collectively are called his members, according to the teaching of St. Paul. Since we are all united with the one Christ through his sacred body, and since we all receive him who is one and indivisible into our own bodies, we ought to look upon our members—we and all others—as belonging to him rather than to ourselves.

—St. Cyril of Alexandria

But the Eucharistic Christ is the Incarnate Word of God and, as we have seen, the Word of God spoken at the beginning of creation has become the divine milieu, and the divine milieu is the Cosmic Christ.

But if the Cosmic Christ is evolving and growing toward its fullest completion, the *pleroma*, then in a very true sense the sacramental species of the Eucharist must be evolving — that "one communion" will need the entire duration of God's continuing creation for its complete consecration. For Teilhard as well as for St. Paul, that "one communion" is far from over. It is still in process.

Teilhard's Prayer

The final pages of this section appear in the form of a prayer that Teilhard, the priest, makes to God standing at the altar at Mass.

He asks that God grant him the ability to "discern the infinite perspectives hidden beneath the smallness and nearness of the host" in which Christ is hidden.

He also asks, as so many Christian have done before him, that instead of his consuming the host that the host consume him.

Teilhard asks us to let the bread represent all the efforts and activities of his life — personal and linked to all others.

He sees the wine as representing all the diminishments of his life — personal and linked to all others.

Addressing Christ in this prayer, he says that others have told him that if he wants to increase the attractiveness of Christ, he should make the focus of his meditation "almost exclusively the charm and goodness of your human life in the past...in Judea two thousand years ago."

But Teilhard finds the evolving Christ, the Body of Christ that lives today, far more absorbing and attractive to him than Jesus of Nazareth. We can understand this, since as parents we are much more concerned and absorbed in the lives of our adult children as they are today, rather than remaining absorbed in memories of their childhood events. Even more, as parents we would also be concerned about our adult children's future and what they will become. In a similar way, if Teilhard is going to give his total heart and soul and mind to Christ, he wants to give it to the Christ that lives today, the evolving Cosmic Christ. Thus, for Teilhard, it is most satisfying "to give one's deepest to that whose depth has no end." Teilhard would rather fix his eyes on the Christ of today and the Christ of the future — the Christ who is "not-yet." Instead of meditating exclusively on the historic Jesus, he wants to contemplate "the glory of the world that is coming into view" — the evolving Universal Christ.

Spiritual Exercise: Loving the Not-Yet _____

Ω In a very wise comic strip about family life called *For Better or for Worse,* the mother is looking through some favorite baby photos of her children, as a teenage daughter observes her intense absorption in them. The daughter asks, "Do you wish we were all little kids again?" The mother says no, and the daughter asks why. The mother turns to her and says, "These pictures say where you've been. And I want to know where you're going."

All parents know this experience of looking into the "not-yet" of their children. Their dreams are always positive, and they are willing to do whatever it takes to make their children successful and happy. Teilhard is simply asking you to take that "not-yet" viewpoint with the world and with Christ. Give it a try. Envision the world in its optimum positive potential — in Christ.

Christ's "Third" Nature

Inspired by St. Paul, Teilhard is here trying to formulate a new theological position with his understanding of the Cosmic Christ. This understanding has always been implicit in the Christian tradition, but never really brought into such clarity before Teilhard. Since its beginnings, the church has always taught that Jesus Christ is the Word of God, the Second Person of the Blessed Trinity. In his incarnation, this Person who was fully God also became fully human — body and soul — without losing the fullness of his divine nature. In other words, in Jesus Christ who walked the earth two natures, divine and human, coexisted. Teilhard is suggesting, that in the evolving Body of Christ that has been growing and developing since the Resurrection, there is a third "nature" coexisting in Christ, namely, his *cosmic nature.* That cosmic nature is clearly different from his human nature as Jesus of Nazareth, and very different from his divine nature as the Second Person of the Trinity. That cosmic nature is characterized by its ability to subsume and integrate into its "nature" all the various "natures" of creation, from the "natures" of the most inert and lowly rocks to the "natures" of the creatures with higher and higher levels of complexity and consciousness. Thus, for Teilhard, as for St. Paul, there are three natures in Christ. Christ is fully human, fully divine, and fully cosmic.

And for both Paul and Teilhard, the "nature" of Christ that is most important for us to explore today is the evolving Cosmic Christ and, specifically, the "not-yet" of that Cosmic Christ. When Teilhard thinks of the not-yet of Christ, he asks himself — and us — the fundamental spirituality question: "What can I still do for Christ?"

3. The Growth of the Divine Milieu

Teilhard wants to hasten the coming of the Cosmic Christ, so he suggests we concentrate on a better understanding of "the process by which the holy presence is born and grows within us," so we can cooperate with it. Teilhard looks at the birth and growth of the divine milieu, first, within individual humans and, then, in the relationships formed by all humans interacting.

A. *The Coming of the Divine Milieu. The Taste for Being and the Diaphany of God*

Some Psychological Observations

Teilhard again reminds us that in these pages he is not writing a theologically rigorous treatise, but rather offering a psychological description of what happens in human beings when they experience the omnipresence of being or the oneness of life. So don't demand strict theological reasoning from Teilhard in the following sections.

He begins his observations by what you can't do if you have had this transcendent experience. First, you cannot compel or wish the divine spirit to descend upon you at will, but one day you may discover you have been blessed; you have become conscious of the divine all around you. Second, if I question you about it, you can't tell me where it came from, what prompted it, or why it came at this time.

But what can you say about it?

You can say that you have acquired a new sense — new eyes that can see things your normal eyes never noticed. With those eyes you can now perceive a new quality or a new dimension in whatever you observe. Of course, you can still see everything the way you always did. More importantly, though, a transformation has taken place within your whole being in the very way you perceive things. It has almost produced a reversal of the ways you think. You are drawn to employ these new eyes more and more, until you become almost intoxicated with what you can see with them. What is most fascinating is that this change appears to have occurred within the very natural parts

---

The Whole

The fundamental truth is that God has created everything, that Christ has redeemed all of us, and that, in him, human nature forms only one person with the divine nature. Union with God, union with Christ, union with all men in Christ and in God, that is the essential, and in a certain sense, the whole thing.

—Emile Mersch, S.J.,
The Theology of the Mystical Body of Christ

---

of your humanity — it feels like your human senses and your human brain are doing it.

At least this is how it was for Teilhard.

Next, he realizes that this kind of transcendent perception could happen to anyone. It feels like a "natural taste for being." You don't have to be a Christian for it to occur. There have been many non-Christian mystics. Unitive vision could happen just as powerfully to a pagan or a pantheist. For this reason, Teilhard feels there is an "immense need for some revealing word to come from the mouth of him who is" (Torchbook, 130). We want to have some divine framework in which to ground our transcendent experience. For this, Teilhard turns to his Christian faith.

Guided by divine revelation, he says, we come to realize that "the divine milieu discloses itself to us as a modification of the deep being of things." This gives rise to two observations, says Teilhard.

First, the manifestation of the divine doesn't modify our normal perception of things, no more than the Eucharistic consecration modifies the appearance of the Sacred Species for us. Even as we perceive the divine milieu operating in the "within" of all things, the relationships among all these things remains exactly the same as before. In the divine milieu "they are merely accentuated in meaning."

So what does such a person actually see that is new or different? What kinds of changes have happened to him? The change happens in two ways, says Teilhard, in the way the perceiver of the divine milieu *describes* the differences, and in the way the perceiver *understands* them and treats them. That, he says, is where the differences are most noticeable.

For Teilhard personally, the change appears as an "enhancement," he says, akin to a kind of *radiance* in things. "The great mystery of Christianity is not exactly the appearance, but the *transparence*, of God in the universe" (Torchbook, 131). This is what Teilhard means when he uses the expression the "diaphany of God." The person can somehow see through the thing to the presence of God within the inner layers of the thing. It is an "incandescence of the inward layers of being" that we can now see.

Second, the perception of the divine omnipresence is a gift, like life itself. No one can prevent anyone who can see in this way from enjoying the capacity. They can see the diaphany, "because it happens at a deeper level than any human power" can stop. Furthermore, "no power in the world — for the same reason — can compel it to appear."

It cannot be gained directly by any process of reasoning or human equipment — though, as science has discovered, psychotropic drugs can mimic it, and brain scans can reveal the activity among the neurons in the cortex of the person exercising this special perception.

As a gift, Teilhard would call this perception of the radiance in things a treasured "passivity of growth." We may want and desire this new perception with all our hearts, but in the end the initiative for it and the awakening of it must always come from God.

Spiritual Exercise: "Lord, That I Might See!"

Ω This doesn't mean we can't pray and ask God for this gift, since it is most desirable. Teilhard says we should want it with the intensity of the blind man in the Gospel. When Jesus asked Bartimeus what he wanted, he answered without hesitation, "Lord, that I might see."

But if even after persistent prayer for new eyesight it is not forthcoming, you can still pray, "Lord, send forth your Spirit and renew the face of the earth." You can still want life to keep evolving toward the Parousia with ever increasing intensity.

B. Individual Progress in the Divine Milieu: Purity, Faith, and Fidelity — the Operatives

In this longer section, Teilhard explores three virtues "that contribute with particular effectiveness toward the limitless concentration of the divine in our lives." These three sources of energy in the divine milieu are *purity*, *faith*, and *fidelity*. Teilhard realizes that when you just look at these three words, they don't sound very inspiring or exciting. But when he describes how their energies work, you will see that they become "the three most active and unconfined virtues of all."

i. Purity

Most people, says Teilhard, see only the negative or passive side of purity, that is, merely staying away from what is forbidden or what keeps us from God. But the positive side has tremendous energy. Purity, by the way, is often confused with chastity, but it is a much larger source of energy. Purity, he says, is "the impulse introduced into our lives by the love of God" to seek "the unification of the universe in God." In other words, for those who understand the central importance to God of the building up of the Christ Body, living with a pure heart means that the Christ Body is your main preoccupation, the main focus of your energy.

Perhaps the closest approximation to purity of heart might be a young man who has searched all his life for the perfect life partner and has finally found her — or she has found him. Being in love has flooded him with energy and happiness. His mind becomes occupied with her — even preoccupied with her. He could never have willed this preoccupation, nor can he will it to stop. He wants to be with her. He would drive five hours just to spend a few hours with her, and feels torn inside the moment he must leave her. He wants the best for her. He wants her to be safe, to be happy, to grow and develop all her talents. He works hard at his job because he wants her to be proud of him. Whenever his mind has a moment to rest from his daily work, it spontaneously turns to thoughts of her, wondering where she is or what he might do to make her happier.

For Teilhard, the one who has a pure heart for Christ will be like that young man. Whenever the mind is at rest, it spontaneously turns to the Body of Christ, asking, "What more can I do for Christ?"

Notice that this Teilhardian definition of purity is moving beyond tradition. Traditional spiritual writers would agree with Teilhard that purity is a grace given to us by the love of God, but they would say that the grace is to "seek God alone." In other words, those with a pure heart will have their eyes focused on God alone.

St. Paul seems to echo this thought when he writes, "So, whether you eat or drink, or whatever you do, do everything for the glory of God" (1 Cor 10:31). But Teilhard has caught something more in Paul's expression.

Teilhard, on good theological grounds, is going beyond "to seek God alone" to saying that those with a pure heart *who understand the divine milieu* will keep their eyes focused also on *whatever God loves.* The same holds true of the young man and his beloved. Besides loving her for herself, he also loves and wants to foster whatever she loves. If she loves flowers, he will bring her flowers. If she loves her dog, he will bring treats for her dog. If she loves astronomy or archery, he will read up on astronomy and ask her to show him how to use a bow and arrow.

In Teilhard's spirituality, he also asks, What is it that God loves more than anything?

St. John tells us, "God so loved the world [the "cosmos" in Greek] that he gave his only-begotten son. . . ." So if we love God we also love what God loves, namely, the divine milieu and all that is in it — the cosmos that God created.

What would give more glory to God — "do it for the glory of God" — than to help complete what God is trying to do in the world through his Son? This Son happens to be evolving in and through the world, where these pure hearts happen to be serving as the hands, feet, eyes, and lips of his Son.

Teilhard also gives a new meaning to the word "impurity." Those are spiritually impure, he says, who hinder or create division in God's great project, that is, the unification of the universe in Christ. The impure do it by "lingering in pleasure or shut up in selfishness" or seeking their own promotion and advantage, and encouraging others to do the same, instead of doing all they can to promote and intensify the Christ project.

"Still purer and more pure," says Teilhard, "is he who, attracted by God, succeeds in giving that movement and impulse of Christ's an ever greater continuity, intensity, and reality."

You can be pure of heart in Teilhard's sense even if your situation in life involves you in the most worldly and mundane pursuits. Purity in people is measured "by the degree of attraction that draws them toward the divine center," or also by their nearness to the Center in their love and intention.

"If we want the divine milieu to grow all around us, then we must jealously guard and nourish all the forces of union, of desire, and of prayer that grace offers us" (Torchbook, 134).

Spiritual Exercise: Fertile Purity

Ω Teilhard says that all he has to say about purity is summed up in the mystery of the Annunciation. When God wanted to make the Incarnation happen, God needed a mother who would engender the Divine Word in the human sphere. We usually say he created the Virgin Mary. But in Teilhard's spirituality what happened was that God "called forth on earth a purity so great that, within this transparency, he would concentrate himself to the point of appearing as a child." What Teilhard realizes is that purity (in his sense) has the power "to bring the divine to birth among us."

The challenge is to realize that your purity can have that same fertility as Mary's, as you help nurture the Cosmic Christ to his fullest maturity. Much mothering and fathering is still needed by the Body of Christ.

Teilhard observes that the church has always said of Mary that she was to be counted as "blessed" not primarily because of her purity but because of her deep faith. "For it is in faith," says Teilhard, "that purity finds the fulfillment of its fertility."

ii. Faith

Again, Teilhard will take the understanding of faith beyond its traditional meaning of "intellectual adherence to Christian dogma." (One might observe that even the Blessed Virgin Mary would have failed the test according to that definition of faith, since she didn't yet know any of the Christian dogmas.) For Teilhard, faith is an active virtue rather than merely an intellectual one. It involves saying yes to God and following through that yes with appropriate words and deeds.

Simple reflection will tell you that faith in God, whatever its dogmatic contents may include, is a response of the "whole person," not merely of the intellect. Mary as well as any believer knows from personal experience that in a real act of faith — as in marriage or parenthood — you put your whole self on the line. As Teilhard describes it, faith is the outward expression of a very "practical conviction." It is "an operative power." The responses required by that "yes" are something individual and personal and will vary with the situation. The responses called for from Mary the mother of Jesus were different from the responses called for from Teilhard during his life and will be different from the responses called for from you and me.

Nor is faith an act made once in a lifetime to last a lifetime. Rather, for Teilhard, faith is called upon to reaffirm itself thousands of times, each time an opportunity occurs and a choice must be made to act or not act to promote the growth of the Body of Christ, that is, to vitalize the forces of nature for God.

"[Faith] means the practical conviction that the universe, between the hands of the Creator, still continues to be the clay in which he shapes innumerable possibilities according to his will" (Torchbook, 134–35).

Teilhard observes, "All the natural links of the world remain intact under the transforming action of 'operative faith.'" That statement has two sides to it.

First of all, praying in faith, as important as it is, does not replace human effort. God is not going to give us, simply because we pray for it, all the new knowledge and skills we may need for the future, things that up till now have been gained by human industry and research. No, God counts on us continuing our search to vitalize and improve all the forces available to us in science, medicine, art, literature, and all the rest of our human endeavors. In other words, even in the domain of faith, "all the natural links of the world remain intact" and wait for our energy and effort to make an ever-new world from them.

Second, the word "operative" also means that our faith in the Body of Christ gives the world "one might almost say an additional soul." Teilhard explains: "Under the influence of our faith, the universe is capable, without outwardly changing its characteristics, of becoming more supple, more fully animate — of being sur-animated."

Sur-animation works in a variety of ways, observes Teilhard. Sometimes, though not usually, sur-animation expresses itself in miraculous effects, as in healings that could not be accomplished by human science or medicine. At other times, more usually, sur-animation is manifested "by the integration of unimportant or unfavorable events within a higher plane and with a higher providence" (Torchbook, 136).

Here Teilhard is talking about how God works with *passivities of diminishment*, recasting our failures, our faults, and even our death into "something better and transformed in him." Just as God took the torturing and deadly passivities of diminishment Christ suffered on the Cross and transformed them by a "higher providence" in the

Resurrection, so God promises that our passivities of diminishment will somehow be transformed by a "higher providence" into some form of resurrection that we cannot now imagine. Perhaps if we call to mind someone we know who is enduring inescapable pain and suffering, we might picture Christ on the Cross embracing that suffering member of his body and assuring it that it will be with him in paradise. Though the person's pain is not removed, he or she is healed and made whole.

But what role does our personal faith play in all this divine "higher providence"?

Teilhard paints a picture of the priesthood we all share. Imagine, he says, that our world and our lives are placed in our hands, much as the Host is placed in the hands of a priest at the altar. What we hold in our hands is "ready to be charged with . . . a real presence of the incarnate Word." The transformation will be accomplished, but only on one condition, that we believe with our operative faith that what we hold in our hands has "the will and the power to become for us . . . the prolongation of the Body of Christ."

If we believe, then everything we hold in our hands gets illuminated — sur-animated. What seemed to be only the chaos and confusion of our planet has turned into order; we see how each little success of ours overflows into more successes and connects with the little successes of others; even our suffering is experienced as a consoling hug from God. If we believe. If I believe that I am a cell sur-animated by the Body of Christ and I believe that, whatever happens, I will still be a cell in Christ, then the energy I expend in all my successes and failures will be used by Christ to bring his Body to a blessed end, and I will be a part of it.

However, if we fail to believe, the rocks at our feet remain impenetrable, the sky above our heads remains ominous, the seas dangerous and unpredictable. Our successes are empty, our suffering is unendurable, and life itself is just one bungling attempt to succeed after another. That is when we hear the voice of the Master saying, "Oh, you of little faith, why did you doubt?"

For Teilhard, faith is a central force in the shaping of the Body of Christ. "We have only to believe," he says.

When reality seems to be overwhelmingly threatening and progress seems impossible, he says, "the more firmly and desperately must we believe." When we can keep faith strong in those almost unbearable times, then, little by little, we shall see what has threatened us begin to give way.

It is not the laws of chemistry and physics that give the universe its consistency, but "the subtle combinations of the spirit." As the Apostle Paul says, "faith is the substance of things hoped for." Faith is what keeps the universe together and growing.

Spiritual Exercise: Illusions?

Ω Teilhard ends his treatment of the power of faith with this statement: "The immense hazard and the immense blindness of the world are only an illusion to one who believes" (Torchbook, 137).

Ponder this statement for a while and ask yourself, "If those immense hazards and blindness are just illusions, then what does the person of faith see there?"

iii. Fidelity

If our faith consecrates the created world, says Teilhard, then our fidelity readies us for our communion with it.

In that communion, fidelity is able to release "the inexhaustible resources" of our every passion and our desire for divine communion. Through fidelity we open ourselves "intimately and continuously to the wishes and good pleasure of God." As at Mass, in response to our act of consecration in faith, we receive Holy Communion in our fidelity. In our fidelity, God's life penetrates and assimilates ours to nourish our activities and fortify us for the diminishments we may have to endure.

> ### Practical Results of Fidelity
>
> You will always have your trials but, when they come, try to treat them as if you were a lucky one, because you know that when your faith succeeds in facing such trials, you develop the ability to endure. Be sure that your endurance carries you all the way, without failing. It will produce some practical results, too. You become fully developed, complete, with nothing lacking.   —James 1:2–4 [my paraphrase]

By fidelity, we situate ourselves in each moment at that point where all the energies converge for us, where the divine milieu can "be made real for us."

"Through fidelity and fidelity alone can we return to God the kiss he is forever offering us across the world" (Torchbook, 138).

Just as there is no limit to the effectiveness of purity and faith, the same is true of fidelity. Fidelity operates limitlessly in at least three dimensions.

First, in our fidelity to the divine milieu there is no limit to the physical effort we can expend or the diminishments we can endure on behalf of the work we are given to accomplish.

Second, in our fidelity there is no limit to the quality of our inward intention in terms of greater conformity to the divine will, greater detachment, and greater love. Just as the quality of our work can be continually improved, so the quality of our intention can be continually purified and more clearly focused.

Third, in our fidelity there is no limit to the depth of our adherence to the divine object, the Cosmic Christ. Regarding this point, Teilhard reminds us, "God does not offer himself to our finite beings as a thing all complete and ready to be embraced. For us, he is eternal discovery and eternal growth." In and through us, the Christ Body never ceases to make new discoveries and never ceases to develop more fully in complexity and consciousness.

By similar reasoning, Teilhard sees no limit on any dimension regarding the quality of our fidelity to the Cosmic Christ. Every process that helps move Christ forward, every spiritual practice, every form of prayer, every scientific advance, every way of offering human service — whether in healthcare or business, at home or in school — can be continually improved to further enhance the "quality" of the Body of Christ. Whatever the human race has attained in knowledge or ability in our quest so far will not be rejected, but merely outstripped and increased. This is Teilhard's way of describing our fidelity's commitment to strive for continual improvement and continual evolution of the Cosmic Christ through the pursuit of ever-higher levels of complexity and consciousness.

Teilhard introduces as his image for this the star the Magi followed to find the Incarnate Son of God in his crib. The Magi's star appeared in the heavens two thousand years ago. There is a star in the heavens that shines for each of us today. Each one's star will lead each of us in a slightly different way. All the paths that those stars indicate to the billions of us walking the earth will have one thing in common. "They lead always upward." Teilhard explains "upward" for us with a few examples.

If you have fidelity, greater desires for Christ will follow your lesser ones; renunciation gradually gains mastery over pleasure; you cease to fear death; egoism gives way to selflessness, and so on. Eventually, fidelity brings you to where you begin to live only for Christ.

In this, Teilhard reflects the Jesuit motto and the Jesuits' fundamental life intention, *Ad Majorem Dei Gloriam*, Toward the Greater Glory of God. This motto reflects the attitude of a never-ending pursuit, since there will always be new levels to discover and explore, and new ways to live for the greater glory of God.

Summary

Teilhard's integrative mind-set says, "Under the converging action of these three rays — purity, faith, and fidelity — the world melts and folds" (Torchbook, 139).

Teilhard says that God will take all the tensions that happen in the encounter between God and humanity "and make them all, equally, serve the cause of union." God will do it "like the jet of flame that effortlessly pierces the hardest metal" or "like a mighty torrent, which is swelled by the very obstacles placed to stem it."

But immediately Teilhard changes his mind about having used these two images of fire and flood. He finds them too destructive, not unitive. They do not convey the point he is trying to make. So in the end of the section he says that God's love acting in the divine milieu "does not destroy things, nor distort them; but it liberates things, directs them, transfigures them, animates them. It does not leave things behind but, as it rises, it leans on them for support; and it carries along with it the chosen part of things" (Torchbook, 140).

Spiritual Exercise: Continual Improvement _____

Ω This "no limit" idea, which is so dear to Teilhard, is a central principle in systems thinking, the mind-set that has made the quality products of many Japanese automakers the envy of the world. In their approach, there is no such thing as a perfect process or a perfect product or a perfect service — only processes, products, and services that can be continually improved. For these quality auto manufacturers, there is no stopping point where they say, "We have done it as perfectly as possible. Let us stop here."

Rather they see what seems to be a perfect product today as merely a plateau on their climb to unattainable perfection.

Using this quality principle, consider how some of your processes, products, or services can be improved. Make a list of some possible improvements in your life and work that you can make. Which of them can you begin to implement today?

Thank God for the potential you have to improve yourself and the Christ Body.

C. The Collective Progress of the Divine Milieu. The Communion of Saints and Charity

i. Preliminary Remarks on the "Individual" Value of the Divine Milieu

Most of what Teilhard presented in the previous pages of Part Three has to do with the spirituality of the individual, as if that person were "alone in the world in the presence of God."

Now Teilhard deals with the question, Where do other people come in?

He replies that we must remember that despite our human solidarity, each person is a responsible natural unit charged with his or her own responsibilities and incommunicable possibilities within the ever-developing Body of Christ. And it must never be forgotten that each individual, though totally intertwined and involved with the rest of the universe, presents an independent perspective on that universe. So there are as many minicenters of divinization as there are individuals. Furthermore, even though there is one divine milieu for all of us, each of us experiences our own mini–divine milieu surrounding us in our local world.

We each encounter God according to many variables — our intelligence, our upbringing, our socioeconomic status, our nationality, and especially our level of development in purity, faith, and fidelity. Even though we all live in the same Christ Body, God has as many different ways of sur-animating us as there are individuals.

So before we jump into involvement in the entire Body, and even before considering others, we must be responsible for pursuing our own sanctification, that is, accomplishing the tasks assigned to us to divinize our little corner of the world.

Just as each cell in my human body must do its part well, each cell must always cooperate and integrate its activities with the functions of all those billions of other cells. In a similar way, even in the most private moments of our personal relationship to the Christ Body, we must always keep others in mind, since in one way or another we are connected to everyone and everything else. As St. Paul counseled the Corinthians, "Never do anything that would cause offense to anyone — to Jews or Greeks or to the church of God. Try to be helpful and respectful to everyone at all times" (1 Cor. 10:32–33 [my paraphrase]). For Teilhard, this advice of Paul's is especially important. For, people who are not members of the Christian religion may be contributing things important to the building of the Body of Christ, things that no one in the church is capable of doing.

The task of the divine milieu to integrate and systematize all our interactions with one another — with over six billion people on the planet at present — requires a constant flow of an almost infinite amount of grace from the divine milieu. The divine milieu must not only sanctify each of the six billion of us individually, but must also coordinate and sanctify the trillions of interactions that occur among us daily — no matter what our religious preference might be.

This showering of grace upon everyone occurs through the action of love, or charity.

Spiritual Exercise: Nothing Excluded from the Divine Milieu ____

Ω It is important to remember that everyone and everything that exists and has existed is eternally immersed in the divine milieu. Christians need to acknowledge that all the Jews, Muslims, Buddhists, Hindus, Shintoists, as well as people of other religious persuasions, plus the agnostics and atheists are immersed in the divine milieu and can have a positive impact on building the Body of Christ.

According to Teilhard, the law of attraction-connection-complexity-consciousness is the force that primarily builds the Christ Body.

Begin to think of the names of people who have fostered *attraction* (like sports coaches, counselors and therapists, florists, furniture makers, clothiers, restaurant cooks and waiters, and so on). How many of them are non-Christians? Be thankful for them.

Next, think of people whose work is making *connections* (like Realtors, brokers, salespeople, marketers, webmasters, programmers, telephone operators, customer service personnel, etc.)

Next, think of people whose work is building *complexity* into our lives (teachers, parents, government officials, corporation owners, auto manufacturers, computer manufacturers, and so on).

Next, think of those who build *consciousness* into us (teachers, therapists, writers, singers, actors, artists, scientists, philosophers, spiritual teachers, publishers, radio and television producers, and so on). Again ask, How many of these people building our planet and making us more conscious are non-Christian? Be grateful for all they have done to help build the Body of Christ.

---

ii. The Intensification of the Divine Milieu through Charity

First of all, Teilhard reminds us that, from God's perspective, through the ages of time and across the multiplicity of interacting individuals, "one single operation is taking place," the building up of the Christ Body. This means our salvation and the fulfillment of Christ must be pursued and achieved in solidarity.

In a very real sense, only one person will be saved, "Christ, the head and living summary of humanity" and in him the universe. Heaven, then, will be all of us humans and all of creation living in this One Person. Teilhard says, "In heaven we ourselves shall contemplate God, but, as it were, through the eyes of Christ" (Torchbook, 143). In other words, we will get to experience God most completely only when we manage to get the entire Christ Body there.

Therefore, Teilhard wants us to realize that our prayers, our efforts, our activities and passivities are interacting together with those of all others. No matter how individually connected to God we may feel, it always remains for each of us to link our particular work on earth to that of all those who surround us.

Teilhard's spirituality is totally ecumenical, totally interfaith, and all-encompassing. Moreover, it is interplanetary and intergalactic.

One way to rekindle our own zeal for the Christ is by contact with the zeal of all those other minicenters surrounding us or passing through our life. We do all we can to "propagate movement and life for the common benefit" and to adapt ourselves to "the common temperature and tension."

Charity is the only force available and strong enough to help "merge and exalt our partial rays into the principal radiance of Christ" (Torchbook, 144). Charity — or unconditional love — is the beginning and end of all spiritual relationships, says Teilhard.

We are involved in the greatest love story that could ever happen in the universe.

Teilhard defines charity as "the more or less conscious cohesion of souls engendered by their mutual convergence in Christ Jesus." He feels it is impossible to love others in human communion without moving nearer to Christ, and it is impossible to love Christ without loving others, at least in proportion as they are moving, consciously or unconsciously, toward Christ.

Another way to picture charity is as many mini–divine milieus flowing among us, and in this atmosphere of love people find an increase in their ardor for the fulfillment of the Cosmic Christ.

It is this love and ardor that enable us to tolerate the "tension of communion," that is, the inevitable passivities of diminishments that occur whenever people are joined together in attempting to accomplish a great task. In any evolving process, there inevitably occur conflicts about how to accomplish this or that, confusion in instructions, disagreements about what is important, sickness, accidents, errors, tempers boiling over, different personalities, misunderstandings, and so on.

Perhaps the hardest to bear for a person "on fire" for Christ is to be surrounded by those who are tepid and uncaring, selfish and cold, whiners and victims, cynics and bystanders who won't lift a finger to make a project succeed. This person on fire knows that the only human endeavor capable of worthily embracing the divine milieu is "that of all men opening their arms to call down and welcome the Fire." And yet, says, Teilhard, so few seem to care about the divine Fire — about that "One Person who will be saved."

Teilhard emphasizes that it is only that One Person who *can* be saved. "The only subject ultimately capable of mystical transfiguration is the whole group of mankind forming a single body and a single soul in charity" (Torchbook, 144). In other words, for Teilhard, we get to heaven only in and through the Body of Christ. But — and this is the core of Teilhard's spirituality — it is up to us humans, with God's grace, to get that One Person, that Christ Body, to the place where it is ready to step into heaven once and for all. "What can I still do for Christ?"

Teilhard ends this subsection with a long prayer to God, in which he admits his own slowness to love his neighbor in charity. Acknowledging his upbringing among the upper social classes and the best intellects, he confesses to God: "I have always felt an inborn hostility to, and closed myself to, the common run of those you tell me to love.... Would I be sincere if I did not confess that my instinctive reaction is to rebuff him? And that the mere thought of entering into spiritual communion with him disgusts me?" (Torchbook, 145).

How many of us would be willing to admit our biases and prejudices? To admit that there are large numbers of people in the world to whom, at present, our hearts are closed off?

Teilhard affirms that he knows God is not asking him to be hypocritical and fake a charity that does not yet exist. So he prays that God, through divine revelation and grace, will "force what is most human in me to become conscious of itself at last."

Teilhard recognizes that most other people are like him, unconscious and asleep to their deepest humanity. He prays, "Humanity was sleeping — it is still sleeping — imprisoned in the narrow joys of its little closed loves."

In the divine milieu, he says, a tremendous spiritual power is slumbering in our midst. We will be able to see it and recognize it when we break down our egotistical barriers and see things from the perspective of the entire creation and its longing for fulfillment.

Finally, he addresses Christ as Savior: "Compel us to discard our pettinesses, and to venture forth, resting upon you, into the uncharted ocean of charity."

Spiritual Exercise: Admitting Prejudice _____

Ω Can you be as honest as Teilhard in naming those groups of people you might have a hard time loving, or those you might not like to have working at your side in the Body of Christ? Can you name some of the kinds of people that annoy you or disgust you or that you avoid or disapprove of?

To bring it closer to home, the next time you are in church, look around and see if there is anyone you would not want to be next to you, someone you would be unwilling to join spirits with, or even give a hug to?

---

iii. The Outer Darkness and the Lost Souls

On this very final subsection of Part Three, Teilhard spends less than one page of instruction and almost three pages of prayer to Christ. Here he tries to deal with the topic of hell or the "outer darkness" where those who dwell there do not feel God's presence.

In previous parts of *The Divine Milieu* Teilhard tended to present sin and evil as imperfections, merely as steps backward, a temporary devolution in a more primary evolution. Up till now, Teilhard hoped that these turnings away from Christ would cease to exist, the further we penetrated into God.

Here he must face the fact that in the scriptures, Jesus Christ is presented not merely as a center of attraction and beatification, but also as a point of rejection and disbelief. Teilhard says that Christ, "because he is the one who unites that he is also the one who separates and judges." The Gospels continually point out that there is good seed and bad, wedding guests who come to the feast and those left outside, the sheep and the goats at the Last Judgment, and so on. The fire of Christ that unites in love can also destroy in isolation. "The whole process out of which the New Earth is gradually born is an aggregation underlaid by a segregation" (Torchbook, 147). Using this imagery, Teilhard is trying to reframe what the Gospel presents as the final judgment of God. It looks like the human race gets divided into two groups, the deserving and the undeserving. Those who do not deserve heaven are, first, separated from those who deserve it (segregated) and then sent into hell. Next, the deserving group will be gathered (aggregated) and welcomed into heaven.

For Teilhard, the optimist, hell is a very difficult concept to digest — especially thinking of it as being filled with people enduring eternal suffering uselessly. The more we are aware of the treasures hidden in each individual, he says, "the more lost we feel at the thought of hell. We could perhaps understand falling back into in-existence...but what are we to make of eternal uselessness and eternal suffering?" (Torchbook, 147). If there were truly undeserving people, Teilhard says, he could see God simply making them cease to exist in any shape or state of being, but not keeping them in existence only to let them languish uselessly for all eternity. Teilhard prefers to believe in an empty hell.

Teilhard's only consolation is this: "You have told me, O God, to believe in hell. But you have forbidden me to hold with absolute certainty than any single human has been damned." That is enough for Teilhard. He feels that he is free to believe that though there is a "structural element in the universe" called hell, maybe there is no one in it. An empty place. In line with this thought, a famous theologian once said that very few people, outside of the angels, had the clarity of consciousness and the freedom of will to be able to meet the moral conditions to commit a truly mortal sin.

Teilhard reminds himself in his prayer that though there are clearly powers of evil in the world and people who sin, they can do nothing, ultimately, to trouble or upset the divine milieu. He also knows that sin and evil can be caught up and twisted by God's irresistible energy and "converted into good to fan the fires of love."

Teilhard reminds himself that there is nothing that exists that is not held within the divine milieu, so he consoles himself by saying, "the damned are not excluded from the Pleroma, but only lost from its luminous aspect, and from its beatification. They lose it, but they are not lost to it" (Torchbook, 148).

It is not easy to grasp what Teilhard means by this last image of the final beatific state of the Cosmic Christ. Perhaps, by analogy, we could say that the blind people on earth are not excluded from the beauty of earth but only from being able to see it as it truly is. So the damned are not excluded from heaven; they just can't see it for what it truly is.

Thus, for Teilhard, the existence of hell does not destroy anything or spoil anything in the divine milieu. The Christ Body will keep inevitably progressing toward its completion.

Teilhard, then, has an important insight of why hell — the negative pole — may be important. Knowing that hell exists doubles for us the intensity and urgency of the power with which the divine milieu comes upon us, almost as if Christ was a jealous and greedy Master, proposing the existence of a hell as a way of ensuring that he would not lose anything that he could possibly obtain and integrate into himself.

"The fires of hell and the fires of heaven are not two different forces," Teilhard concludes, "but contrary manifestations of the same energy" (Torchbook, 149). Once again, Teilhard the systems thinker is aware that everything is part of the great system that God initiated in the first moment of creation. In the mind of God, everything, even opposites and enemies, find themselves eternally connected — and loved.

Spiritual Exercise: An Empty Hell? _____

Ω It is so easy in our country, where we put in jail and conveniently out of our sight those who disgust us or whom we disapprove of, to see hell as a place where all those in prison—plus a lot of others—ought to spend eternity. It is very difficult to imagine that God loves all these people, when we find it so hard to do so.

Take some time to reflect on your own concept of hell. Would you be happy to think of it as a place with no one in it? If not, who would you naturally think of as being there or deserving to be there? Can you find some way of seeing these people being used by the divine milieu for revealing or helping develop the Body of Christ?

Epilogue

IN EXPECTATION
OF THE PAROUSIA

Summary

The theme in these final pages is segregation and aggregation. In the last, climactic moments of creation and in its final crisis of development in the Cosmic Christ, Teilhard says, the evil elements will be removed (segregation), and the good will be unified (aggregation). The presence of Christ silently accruing in all things will be revealed.

Even though this final moment of segregation and aggregation may be far in the future, our task is to keep the flame of desire for this brilliant future of the Cosmic Christ alive in the world. We must keep evolutionary progress going forward on all fronts. "We must try everything for Christ," says Teilhard. We are to love the world and give ourselves over to its development with passion for its fulfillment in Christ.

◆ ◆ ◆

Three Key Terms

If Teilhard's religious superiors had allowed him to publish his books, which they didn't, the editors at the publishing house would have made some suggestions for clarifying parts of his manuscripts. For example, in this epilogue, they would have asked him to clarify the similarities and differences among three key Greek terms he uses that could easily be confused — *pleroma*, *Omega*, and *Parousia* — and to show how they are related in his thought.

238

So I have tried to do what Teilhard's editors would have asked him to do, namely, to show the relationships among those three Greek words.

Here are short descriptions of those terms in Teilhard's thought:

Pleroma refers to the process involved in achieving the fullest development of the Cosmic Christ. It is a term that emphasizes process and development. If the *pleroma* idea were applied to an artist's painting, it would refer to the process and development of the painting, a summary of all that would go into its completion. If Isaiah had known that Christ was the Word of God, his prophetic voice of God would be telling of the *pleroma*. "My Word that goes forth from my mouth shall not return to me void, but shall do my will, achieving the end for which I sent it" (Isa 55:11).

Omega refers to a culminating point of development in Christ's Cosmic Body; it indicates that the *pleroma* process has been completed. If the Christ Body were a painting, this would be the point at which the painter signed his painting and declared it finished.

Parousia refers to that moment in earth time of Christ's Second Coming at the end of world, or at least to close the period of human history as we know it. In terms of the artist's painting, the *Parousia* would refer to the day the painting was removed from the artist's studio where it had come to its fulfillment and taken up a new identity, perhaps in an art gallery

From a biblical perspective, the three Greek words each have their differences, too.

Pleroma was first used in scripture to describe the fullest development of the Body of Christ by St. Paul; he uses the word many times. (See page 241 on *pleroma* in St. Paul.) Teilhard picks up on Paul's understanding of *pleroma* and expands it.

Omega is found in scripture only once, in Revelation 1:8, referring to God, who is the Alpha and the Omega, the first and last. Teilhard expands *Omega's* meaning in a unique and evolutionary way, mostly in his other later writings, especially *The Phenomenon of Man* (or, as it is now called, *The Human Phenomenon*). For Teilhard, *Alpha* refers to the Absolute, the Creator God. *Omega* refers to the Cosmic Christ proudly bringing all of creation back to the *Alpha*.

Parousia appears always translated into English in New Testament writings, e.g., in Matthew 24:3 as "your coming." Of course, the event itself of Christ's Second Coming is described in many ways in the New Testament (see page 248 below). Teilhard preferred to keep the Greek word *parousia* in his text to maintain the richness of its meaning in Greek.

Let's review in more detail the three ideas, one by one.

Pleroma

Pleroma is the concept most developed by Teilhard in *The Divine Milieu*. It is also the concept most developed by Pauline thought in the later letters, especially Colossians and Ephesians. Teilhard's thought about the *pleroma* is rooted in the Pauline development of this term.

Here is Teilhard's one-sentence description of the *pleroma* taken from an earlier section of *The Divine Milieu*.

> It is the quantitative repletion and the qualitative consummation of all things: it is the mysterious *Pleroma*, in which the substantial *one* and the created *many* fuse without confusion in a *whole* which, without adding anything essential to God, will nevertheless be a sort of triumph and generalization of being. (Torchbook, 122)

A Teilhardian statement like this overwhelms most readers, which is probably why many tend to give up trying to understand him. But by now you should be able to put flesh and bones on it. I recommend it to you as a spiritual exercise to find some of the richness in this quotation.

As a hint, I will take you through this sentence as if Teilhard were talking about an automobile coming off the assembly line of an automaker of the highest quality.

Pleroma in St. Paul

The Greek word *pleroma* means "fullest development" or "completeness." St. Paul applied the term to the development of the Cosmic Body of Christ. Not only will the human beings in the Cosmic Christ Body—when that body reaches its fullest development—be filled to completeness with the divinity that filled Jesus, but the entire cosmos will also be filled with that same divine presence.

Paul teaches that the Incarnation and Resurrection make Christ head not only of the entire human race, but also of the entire created cosmos, so that everything that was involved in the fall of the human race is equally involved in its salvation. His greater body, or Cosmic Body, is made up not only of all humans but also of the entire cosmic reality, including the earth, seas, plants, animals, planets, the stars, the angels—everything! (see Rom. 8:19–22; 1 Cor. 3:22ff and 15:20–28; Eph. 1:10 and 4:10; Phil. 2:1011 and 3:21; Heb. 2:5–8).

In Paul's day, much Greek non-Christian religious thought held that matter (the human body as well as physical reality) was evil and that the spirit must be delivered from it. Paul says no. For him, matter itself was enslaved in the fall, just as humanity was, and was set free, just as humanity was, by Christ's Incarnation and Resurrection (see Rom. 8:19–22.)

Paul writes of the Cosmic Christ, "In his body lives the fullness [Greek *pleroma*] of divinity, and in him you too find your own fulfillment [*pleroma*], in the one who is the head of every Sovereignty and Power [i.e., the highest grades of angelic beings. Thus, in Christ lives the fullness of all possible categories of being.]" (Col. 2:9).

"quantitative repletion" means that the vehicle is replete (or filled) with every single necessary element and part, all of them in place, all of them working, no defective pieces. In terms of quantity, everything necessary is all there and ready to operate.

"qualitative consummation" means "highest quality," or, in other words, that all the parts are interacting perfectly with each other, and all processes involved in the automobile's proper functioning have been tested and continually improved until they are now working with optimum efficiency and effectiveness.

"the substantial one" in this case would refer to the automobile as a whole assembly. (In the case of the *pleroma*, it would refer to the oneness of Christ's Cosmic Body's divinity.)

"the created many" in this case refer to all the elements and parts of the automobile that have been created and manufactured separately and in different places. (In the *pleroma*, the created many include all the elements of the human family and of creation, originally all spread out but now brought together by the Cosmic Christ and in the Cosmic Christ.)

"fuse without confusion" means that, though the parts are many — up to five thousand or more elements in an auto — and their interactions complex, they are all in motion carrying out their functions in harmony with everything else in the auto and without interfering with any other parts or processes in the vehicle.

"in a whole." They form a whole system because every part and interactive process in the auto serves a single purpose, namely, to carry human beings from one place to another comfortably, quietly, and safely.

"without adding anything essential to God" in the case of the automobile might mean that all the little nuts, bolts, belts, pieces of cloth, glass, metal, and plastic as well as the car itself add nothing essential to the person who originally designed or created the car.

"will nevertheless be a sort of triumph and generalization of being" means that the automobile coming off the assembly line is something the designer and manufacturer can view as an accomplishment to be proud of — as they do all the other cars coming off that line.

Now it's your turn.

Spiritual Exercise

Ω Take each of the phrases of Teilhard's definition of the *pleroma,* as I have done for an automobile and its creator, and apply it to the Cosmic Body of Christ and the divine Creator.

For special credit, you might also try to explain how you think the divine milieu fits into this description of the *pleroma*.

Omega Point

For Teilhard, Alpha, the first letter of the Greek alphabet, refers to the Creator God before the creation of the world. Alpha is the one who made the Big Bang happen and set all things into motion in their evolutionary trajectory.

Omega is the last letter in the Greek alphabet. "Omega Point" simply refers to the final stage of evolution, the fullest accomplishment of the divine milieu in the Cosmic Christ.

While *pleroma* is mainly focused on the *process* of development of the Cosmic Christ, the Omega Point marks the culmination or *completion* of that process. Omega is the moment when Christ is ready to present his fully developed Cosmic Being to the Alpha, the Creator God who set the universe in motion.

In the grand scheme of things, for Teilhard, evolutionary transformation has gone about as far as it can to develop human beings

Toward Omega

Observing the evolutionary progression from inanimate matter through primitive life and invertebrates to fish, amphibia, reptiles, mammals, and finally humans, Teilhard noticed a continual increase in consciousness. With humanity, a threshold is crossed — self-reflective thought, or mind, appears.

But even humans do not represent the end-point of evolution, for this consciousness process will continue until all humans are united in a single divine Christ-consciousness, the "Omega Point."

Teilhardian cosmology is based on the idea of an evolutionary progression towards greater and greater consciousness, culminating first in the appearance of self-conscious mind in humankind, and then, in the Omega Point, of the divinization of humanity.

In *The Phenomenon of Man* Teilhard says that because space-time contains and engenders consciousness, it must possess a convergent nature, and somewhere in the future must become involuted to a point that he calls Omega (p. 259). In other words, as the envelope of thought evolves and converges around the planet, it inevitably reaches a single focus — just as all the lines from a cone's base converge to a single point at its tip.

physically. (Some contemporary geneticists might disagree, since, according to some, almost 90 percent of genes in the human genome are still dormant, that is, have never been turned on.)

The next great advance in evolutionary transformation, according to Teilhard, will be found in the gradual socialization of mankind. Because of the thrust of the divine milieu, this process will not cause humanity to devolve into a herd, but will rather produce a convergence of humanity toward a single society. Teilhard saw such evolution already in progress, happening through technology, urbanization, multinational corporations, and modern communications. Every day, Teilhard saw, more and more links were being established between different peoples' politics, economics, and habits of thought in an apparently upward spiraling progression. We can see this progression happening even more so in our day with computer technology, satellites, space stations, the Internet, and cell phones, none of which Teilhard lived long enough to experience.

Theologically, Teilhard saw the ultimate convergence point of evolution *(Omega)* as marking the full divinization of the Cosmic Christ. When humanity and the material world have reached their final state of evolution and exhausted all potential for further development *(pleroma)*, a new convergence between them and the supernatural order would be initiated by the Second Coming of Christ *(Parousia)*.

Perhaps, the *Parousia* indicated a totally new kind of sacred existence that would begin "in heaven" after the Omega Point. But for Teilhard our best way of preparing for the *Parousia* was to help bring about the *pleroma*, so that we could reach the *Omega Point*. He would prefer that we let life in paradise after the *Parousia* take care of itself.

Evil as an Inevitable Byproduct of Evolution

Teilhard believed that the work of Christ and the Christ Body is primarily to lead the material world to this cosmic redemption, while the conquest of evil is only secondary to the divine purpose. While many theologians, thinking morally, would label sin and evil as absolutely negative, Teilhard, thinking in terms of long-range evolution, represents evil primarily as a kind of "growing pains" — or passivities of diminishment — within the cosmic process. Such was Teilhard's optimism and hope in the Cosmic Christ! For Teilhard, one might say that "evil" is a suitable label for the present *disorder* on our planet that will eventually be resolved by a final synthesis into *order*, a synthesis still in process of realization.

This is a point where the church authorities had much difficulty with Teilhard. For church doctrine painted a very different picture of evil and sin — much more than a disorder that would eventually be put aright by the evolutionary process. However, please remember that in *The Divine Milieu* Teilhard consistently claimed to be describing the disorder he saw from the perspective of humanity's eons-long psychological-sociological evolutionary process. In contrast, a theologian might prefer to consider each single "disordered" event throughout history as an individual moral act for which some person is responsible before God. These are two radically different perspectives.

In this regard, it may be an interesting personal reflective exercise to look at some "sins" of your past from a psychological-sociological perspective, and ask if in your maturation (or evolution) some *order* has come into your life by resolving the *disorder* those "sins" caused.

I recall some of the people in my high school class, including me, who in our teen years deserved many of the following labels — selfish, cocky, thoughtless, greedy, cruel, lustful, jealous, and lazy. Some tried all of the vices available. Years later, most of those fellow students I've kept contact with have grown up and, as the saying goes, have "put their lives in order." Even though they may remember moments of their disordered youth with some fondness, today they are for the most part compassionate, caring, faithful, generous, and hardworking men and women.

A theologian might choose to isolate many of their specific teenage acts and label them as sinful and morally reprehensible. From his moral standpoint, the theologian is correct. However, looking at the same people, Teilhard would prefer to take an evolutionary perspective, or at least a long-range one. Instead of isolating their teen years and the specific acts they performed during that time, he would look at their whole life — how they turned out in the long run. If you take this very different perspective, you can begin to understand how Teilhard might describe their lives as growing through disorder into order. Growing through disorder into order is a very basic and common evolutionary process. We all recognize it taking place in ourselves and others.

Spiritual Exercise _____

Ω Teilhard is very optimistic about the "gradual socialization of mankind." It is quite easy for us, especially as we grow older, to feel that our world, far from evolving in an upward trajectory, is in a tailspin due to sin and evil.

See if you can note any signs of an upward spiral — of international cooperation and development in government, business, economics, science, religion, literature, the arts, philanthropy, etc.

_____

Parousia

The Parousia, in Teilhard's words, "will be the consummation of the divine milieu."

In *The Divine Milieu* so far, we have come to understand, thanks to Teilhard, that beneath all the ordinary events of life, through all our efforts salvaged for us by Christ, and through all our diminishments, "a new earth is being slowly engendered."

Expectation: The Key Word

The Gospel's advice, Teilhard tells us, is not to speculate about the time or the manner of this eschatological event. What we must do is *expect* the *Parousia*. And, of course, *prepare* for it and live in readiness for it.

One day the end will come. The apostles often asked Jesus about the Final Coming. In response, Jesus offered only vague images of lightning flashing, conflagrations sweeping over the planet, floods like thousands of tsunami that could carry away everything and everyone in their path. But he would immediately add that we should not be deceived by any of these signs, since they might not really be the true signs of the end.

In his text, Teilhard presents similar images for this final event. The "presence of Christ," he says "which has been silently accruing in things, will suddenly be revealed — like a flash of light from pole to pole." A *parousia* is always tangible and visible. At that moment,

Parousia

In Christianity, *Parousia* is the Greek word the early Christians used to denote *the Second Coming of Christ at the end of time.*

In Greek, *parousia* literally means "an appearance and subsequent presence with." A *parousia* appearance was always visible and tangible. In the ancient Greco-Roman world, a *parousia* might refer to an official visit by royalty to a group of people. It was also used to describe the appearance of a god who had come to help or save those under his protection.

The Greek word *parousia* was appropriated by Christians as a specialized term for Jesus' glorious appearance and subsequent visible presence on earth — primarily at his final return at the end of the world.

The Gospels contain several predictions made by Jesus regarding his return at the end of the world. These include Matthew 16:27, 24:26 –28, and 24:37– 41; Luke 17:22–37; John 14:3.

Jesus says that he will "come in the glory of his Father with his angels, and then he will reward each one according to his behavior" (Matt. 16:27) and that this will occur suddenly, "like a lightning strike in the east and flashing far into the west" (Matt. 24:27).

Catholic Christians have always believed that Jesus Christ would come back to close the period of human history on earth. The time when Jesus will return is given many names: the Day of the Lord, the *Parousia*, the end time, the Second Coming of Christ, and the Final Judgment. In theology, the Parousia is a major topic in the field of eschatology.

all the creatures of the world, whether they are inside the Christ Body or outside it (but always under the influence of Christ) will find themselves in a place of happiness or a place of pain as "designated for them by the living structure of the *Pleroma*" (Torchbook, 151).

If this last statement sounds unclear, in terms of what you have been reading of Teilhard's thinking so far, it is certainly ambiguous and confusing. As you have seen earlier, Teilhard has a lot of difficulty with the church's doctrine about hell. Many Christian see hell as quite densely populated; few cartoons ever show hell with just a handful of people in it. If Teilhard must believe there is such a state as hell, he hopes that, in fact, no one has or will ever reside there.

However, he acknowledges that if someone freely and in fullest consciousness chooses to cut himself off completely and irrevocably from God's love, then for Teilhard such a person refuses to participate in the building up of the Body of Christ and cuts himself off from that Body and refuses to live within it. However, according to Teilhard's understanding of the divine milieu, such a person cannot escape from Christ's divine milieu, no more than a human being walking on this planet can escape from the physical atmosphere we all breathe and the human milieu in which we all live. No matter how fervently a person wants to refuse to belong to Christ, such a person must remain "always under the influence of Christ."

Therefore, what would produce eternal pain and suffering for such a person is that person's own state of mind and heart, because he must maintain his strong resistance to loving or being loved, while living forever in a milieu saturated with divine love and happiness. The state of hell — for it is a state of consciousness rather than some physical location in the universe — would be like a person who hates jazz music and is forced to live in a place where he is surrounded by jazz twenty-four hours a day, every day for the rest of his life.

Teilhard claims he is saying no more than what divine revelation tells us to expect. He is just using different concepts. And he holds strongly to a limitless concept of God's mercy and forgiveness and a limitless belief in what the divine milieu can accomplish in any human soul.

Teilhard on Catholic Doctrine and the Parousia

In his treatment of the Parousia, Teilhard concurs with all the essential elements of the Catholic doctrine. Teilhard covers all of the following:

- ◆ Jesus' Parousia can be adequately described only in apocalyptic images. See Mark 13:26–27; Matt. 16:27; Acts 1:11; 1 Thess. 4:16–18.

- ◆ The Parousia will be unmistakable because it will be accompanied by unprecedented signs. See Matt. 24:27.

- ◆ Some signs refer to general events concerning the evangelization of the world. See Matt. 24:14.

- ◆ Other unmistakable signs will be more proximate and apocalyptic. See Mark 13; Matt. 24; and Luke 21. See also 2 Tim. 4:1–2; 3:1–5.

- ◆ No one knows exactly when the Parousia will occur. See Mark 13:32; 1 Thess. 5:2; 2 Pet. 3:10.

- ◆ We should avoid pointless speculations about the time, the details of the signs, and the nature of the Parousia. See Mark 13:33, 35–37.

- ◆ We should focus instead on the need for living the gospel so as to be prepared for the Parousia whenever it happens. See 1 Pet. 1:13–16.

An Issue for the World

However, even though his thought fits into Christian doctrine, Teilhard has a few things to add about our traditional understanding of the Parousia.

1. First, the Parousia, he says, is "an issue for the world."

At one level, for Christians this means *waiting for the Parousia with great expectation is our supreme function.* Perhaps this fervent longing for heaven is the defining feature of our Christian religious beliefs. From the earliest days of the Christian community, believers have been taught to fix their gaze on the future — to wait in eager expectation for the return of the Savior. Many of the stories of Jesus emphasize the importance of waiting and watching, being alert and on guard for the arrival of, variously, the master, the bridegroom, the lord of the manor, the thief, or the Son of Man. Invariably, in these stories, the important person appears at a time others don't expect, and they are often caught off guard.

At another level, the word "issue" is also a word used to describe the birth of a child, as in "a child issued forth from the womb." Perhaps in the back of Teilhard's mind the divine milieu is like a mother's womb, and the moment of the Parousia will be that moment when the Body of Christ emerges from that womb fully formed and fully conscious.

2. For those who have been longing for the fulfillment of the Body of Christ, this *expectation of the Parousia should not generate a frightening attitude or one of foreboding, but, rather an eager longing.* As Teilhard, says, "The Lord Jesus will come soon only if we ardently expect him." In other words, the accumulation of our burning desires is what is most likely to "cause the Pleroma to burst upon us." This is the flame we want to keep alive in the world, says Teilhard.

We know from stories about the early Christians who, through a childlike eagerness and an error in perspective, expected the Parousia to happen within their lifetimes. When it didn't happen as they expected, it left some of them disillusioned. Maybe, like them, says Teilhard, we too have become disillusioned and "have allowed the flame to die down in our sleeping hearts." After all, most of us will probably die before that awesome day dawns.

3. What we can do in the meantime, says Teilhard, is *keep spreading the dream of the New Jerusalem by keeping the flame of expectation alive*. To truly prepare for the *Parousia*, we must seek to create a more intimate connection between our work and the *pleroma* of Christ. There is still much work to do before we humans become "one with Christ" *in full consciousness*.

We must constantly remember that until the day of the *Parousia*, the Body of Christ on earth is "a ferment, a soul, and not a complete and finished organism."

Much Work Yet to be Done

The purpose for each of us in the Cosmic Body — my role in Christ — is to transform that small piece of the world immersed in matter provided especially for me. Teilhard utters these paradoxical words: "The expectation of heaven cannot remain alive unless it is incarnate" (Torchbook, p. 153). Heaven will always be immersed in the world. Christ's work is to transform the world, not to leave it behind.

What part of the Christ Body will you and I be, shaping out of the matter of life given to us today?

When Teilhard poses this question, he is giving us a different perspective on the *Parousia*. Instead of just helplessly or patiently waiting for the Final Day, we can be shaping some small part of the *pleroma* today. That's what we should be actively concerned about.

Spiritual Exercise _____

Ω Look at your calendar, and ask yourself: "What part of the Christ Body will I be shaping out of the matter of life given to me today and tomorrow?" First of all, you will be shaping *yourself*. But how will you do it?

Second, your words and actions—or failure to act—will have an effect on *others*, perhaps for years to come. Think carefully how you want to spend your energy today and tomorrow.

Third, your words and actions may help contribute to some small growth of knowledge, understanding, complexity and consciousness *in the larger world*. Can you consciously choose some of your words and actions that will help make that contribution happen?

Thank God for your ability to make a contribution.

When Jesus performed miracles of healing and curing, he was not merely using them as a means of advertising himself to build up a bigger and bigger audience for his sermons. Those healings and exorcisms were building the Body of Christ. Jesus was already at work on the big *Omega* project. And he was transforming, each day and with each personal encounter, that small piece of the world immersed in matter provided especially for him. He refused to helplessly accept diminishments, whether in himself or in others, but would do everything he could to make people healthy so they could be productive and contribute to the building up of society. For Teilhard, that's why he healed people. Jesus as a human felt the urgings of the divine milieu in himself and wanted everyone to be able to live and contribute to making people whole. Just as he could clearly see the shortcomings of mankind, he could see its potential. He loved the not-yet of the human race. At the same time he could see the entire universe growing luminous from within — and even more so up ahead in the not-yet. Jesus knew how to live with eager *expectation*.

What We Can Learn from "Worldly" People

Instead of being fearful of the world, the divine milieu urges us to harness its forces, "which need us, and which we need." Worldly people, who do not even know about Christ and the Omega project, embarrass us by their noble aspirations regarding the immense potential of the world, the greatness of the human mind and imagination, and the sacred value of every new truth that can be discovered. We Christians, Teilhard says, can learn a lot from these worldly men and women about *expecting* the future *and preparing* for it.

Progress in the human universe does not take place in competition with God. Nor does human progress squander the energies and devotion we rightly owe to God.

The more complex and the more conscious human beings become, the more united they will be in their desire to master the possibilities of the earth and to shape a Cosmic Body worthy of resurrection. That was Teilhard's vision.

Spiritual Exercise

Ω Think of someone you know who is not a person of religious faith and yet is dedicated to the improvement of humanity or scientific progress.

What can you learn from that person about expecting and preparing for Christ's Parousia?

Only One Center

Humanity cannot have two points of perfection, a human one and a divine one, no more than a circle can have more than one center.

To desire the *Parousia*, says Teilhard, "all we have to do is to let the very heart of the earth, as we Christianize it, beat within us."

Teilhard cries out, "Men of little faith, why then do you fear or repudiate the progress of the world?" He says there is no need to multiply warnings about worldliness or enact prohibitions about becoming involved in progress.

To divinize does not mean to destroy, but to sur-animate and sur-create. Christ is still in the Incarnation process. Christmas is not a day merely to be remembered as an important event in far off history, but an event happening all around the planet every day.

"We must try everything for Christ," Teilhard exhorts us. "We must hope everything for Christ."

Teilhard looks at the immense crowds of those who build the earth and those who seek what is best for it, working in laboratories, in studios, in deserts, in factories, and "in the vast social crucible." He asks us to join them consciously and intentionally. Anyone can participate — can join the Omega project — no matter who they are.

Teilhard's Final Prayer

In his final prayer he addresses, not God, but "Jerusalem!" God's favorite city, which represents the deepest religious longings of humanity. Speaking to this special locus of divine blessing about those who are building the earth, Teilhard says, "The ferment that is taking place by their instrumentality in art and science and thought is happening for your sake."

Once you understand the divine milieu, says Teilhard, what used to be called the temptations and seductions of the world no longer exist. He wants to be embraced by the earth. He doesn't care whether the earth fills him with life or beats him back into dust. When he looks at the earth, all he cares about is the expectation of the Great Being that "is maturing in her breast."

For Teilhard, the earth has become for him, "over and above herself, the body of him who is and of him who is coming. The divine milieu":

The Same Fundamental Vision

At the very end of the text, the French editor of *The Divine Milieu* found a statement written by Teilhard in the last month of his life, March 1955, in which he reaffirms the power of his vision of the divine milieu.

> Today, after forty years of constant reflection, it is still exactly the same fundamental vision which I feel the need to set forth and to share, in its mature form, for the last time. With less exuberance and freshness of expression, perhaps, than at my first encounter with it, but still with the same wonder and the same passion.

If There Were Only One Hundred People

Most of us know about life from our own nation. Most of us in the United States own homes, cars, television sets, computers, and telephones. Most of us have jobs, a decent education, and plenty of food to eat. But demographers, especially global ones, like to burst our bubble, and remind us that Omega probably is a long way off. Instead of giving us pie charts and percentages, they suggest we shrink today's world population to 100 people.

If that were the case, demographically,

- 57 of these would be living in Asia
- 21 would reside in Europe
- 14 would be in North and South America
- 8 would be in Africa

Of those 100 people, religiously,

- 30 would be Christian
- 70 would be non-Christian

Of those 100 people, financially,

- 6 would possess 59 percent of the entire world's wealth
- 80 would live in substandard housing
- 50 would suffer from malnutrition or dehydration

Of those hundred, educationally,

- 60–70 would be unable to read or write
- 1 would have a college education
- 1 would own a computer

Much work remains for us in the Body of Christ to bring enough complexity, consciousness, justice and equality to our world, before the Cosmic Christ can begin to reach fulfillment and completion (*pleroma*).

A Final Word

Teilhard is truly a prophetic voice for our new century. Like many of the other religious prophets of the twentieth century — think, for example, of Gandhi, Thomas Merton, Dorothy Day, Martin Luther King Jr. — Teilhard was dismissed and rejected by most during his lifetime. The visions of these prophetic ones did not fit well with the then current conventions of society. In some cases, however, their messages seemed much less intimidating a few generations later. However, while they lived, what they proclaimed seemed to threaten the establishment.

The Franciscan Richard Rohr once observed that most people assume that Jesus, because of his prophetic message, was killed by evil men. However, said Rohr, those responsible for Jesus' death were not evil. They were the people of the establishment, protecting what they had established. They would have considered themselves good people, doing what was best for society. They were merely conventional people, like you and me. Most conventional people resist accepting anything new and different from what makes them feel safe and comfortable.

Happily, the church that rejected Teilhard's ideas on evolution now accepts those ideas, at least most of them. Also some of his insights on love, marriage, social justice, ecumenism, ecology, human freedom, peace, the potential holiness of matter, the value of science, the importance of systems thinking, and many other matters have seeped into the thoughts of theologians, philosophers, scientists, and psychologists. Flowing from his insights about the divine milieu, his theological understanding of Creation, Incarnation, Resurrection, Eucharist, the Person of Jesus, the Cosmic Body of Christ have also influenced contemporary theologians, not only Catholic ones.

What remains is for Christians to put these ideas into practice, which is the domain of spirituality. In these pages I have tried to sketch some simple spiritual practices to give everyday meaning to Teilhard's ideas. Until we begin to practice these — and thousands of other ways of promoting the law of attraction-connection-complexity-consciousness that have yet to be discovered and designed — the work of building the Body of Christ will move forward far more slowly than it could be going.

If Teilhard's insights about the Cosmic Christ are coming from our benevolent and merciful God, they will penetrate like yeast to help the human race rise to its fullest potential. The future — the not-yet — provides the testing ground for all prophetic messages.

If nothing else, Teilhard at least released an inexhaustible flow of possible responses to the age-old spirituality question "What can I still do for Christ?"

References

Books by Teilhard de Chardin

Activation of Energy. Trans. René Hague. New York: Harcourt Brace Jovanovich, 1970.

Christianity and Evolution. Trans. René Hague. New York: Harcourt Brace Jovanovich, 1971.

The Divine Milieu. New York: Harper & Row, 1960.

The Future of Man. Trans. Norman Denny. New York: Harper & Row, 1964.

The Heart of Matter. Trans. René Hague. New York: Harcourt Brace Jovanovich, 1978.

Human Energy. Trans. J. M. Cohen. London: Collins, 1969.

Hymn of the Universe. Trans. Simon Bartholomew. New York: Harper & Row, 1965.

On Love and Happiness. San Francisco: Harper & Row, 1984.

The Phenomenon of Man. Trans. Bernard Wall. New York: Harper & Row, 1959.

Unfortunately, most of these titles are currently out of print, but you may find them through your local library or by using an Internet search engine.

Compilations of Teilhard's Essays

There are a number of compilations of essays written by Teilhard at various periods of his life and assembled after his death. Notable essays that deal with his spirituality are "The Mystical Milieu" (1917); "The Soul of the World" (1918); "The Spiritual Power of Matter" (1919);

"Pantheism and Christianity" (1923); "The Mass on the World" (1923); "The Divine Milieu" (1927); "The Road of the West: To a New Mysticism" (1932); "The Evolution of Chastity" (1934); "The Phenomenon of Spirituality" (1937); "The Spiritual Contribution of the Far East" (1947); "The Spiritual Energy of Suffering" (1950); "Some Notes on the Mystical Sense" (1951); "Research, Work and Worship" (1955).

Patristic Writers Cited in this Volume

Quotations from the patristic writers in my book were taken from the works of Emile Mersch, S.J., both of which are masterly tomes, but currently out of print:

Mersch, Emile, S.J. *The Theology of the Mystical Body.* Trans. Cyril Vollert, S.J. St. Louis: Herder Book Company, 1952.
Mersch, Emile, S.J. *The Whole Christ.* Trans. John R. Kelly, S.J. Milwaukee: Bruce Publishing Co., 1938.

Index

261